D0116428

From Yard to Garden

Center Books on American Places
George. F. Thompson, series founder and director

From Yard to Garden

The Domestication of America's Home Grounds

Christopher Grampp

The Center for American Places
at Columbia College Chicago

Published 2008. First edition.
Printed in Singapore on acid-free paper.

The Center for American Places at Columbia College Chicago
600 South Michigan Avenue
Chicago, Illinois 60605-1996, U.S.A.
www.americanplaces.org

Distributed by the University of Chicago Press
www.press.uchicago.edu

16 15 14 13 12 11 10 09 08 1 2 3 4 5

Library of Congress Cataloging-in-Publication Data
Grampp, Christopher.
From yard to garden: the domestication of Amercia's home grounds/Christopher Grampp. –1st ed. p. cm.
Includes index.
ISBN 978-1-930066-74-8
1. Gardening–United States. 2. Gardens, Amercian. 3. Gardens–Design. 4. Landscape Architecture. I. Title. II. Series.

SV451.3.G73 2008
712.60973—dc22

2008003903

ISBN-10: 1-930066-74-0
ISBN-13: 978-1-930066-74-8

Frontispiece: Berkeley, California, 1981. Photograph by the author.

For Nina Feldman

Contents

Prologue

To the best of my recollection, I was eight years old when I first considered gardens in any detail. In 1959, my family had just moved from Chicago to Berkeley, California, and the difference between our old house and the new one was dramatic. Our apartment in Hyde Park, two blocks from the University of Chicago, sat on a busy corner across from a drugstore and grocery. Some needly bushes grew against the building, and a low boxwood hedge surrounded the front lawn. There were rarely any flowers. The back yard was a gravel-covered lot surrounded by a chain-link fence where tenants hung their laundry. Gloomy, soot-covered stairs climbed the back of the building. For much of the year it was either too cold or too humid to spend much time in the yard, and the only things I recall doing there were playing marbles and tag and bouncing a tennis ball against the building next door. By no stretch would anyone call the grounds on which our apartment sat a garden.

Our new home in Berkeley, though, was surrounded by grass and flowering bushes, and it had an apple tree in which I promptly built a fort. My mother sat in the back yard and read while my sister tanned on the chaise lounge and I climbed the tree or played catch with friends. The camellias flowered all year, and the lawn was always green, even if we forgot to water it. The tree had apples that we actually got to eat (I cannot remember ever seeing fruit on a tree in Chicago). We grew some basil and lettuce, and I planted my first packet of Burpee seeds—petunias—next to the front door. A small ravine separated our back yard from a parking lot. The ravine was full of wild blackberries and pungent-smelling anise, and in the fall giant orb-weaving spiders hung suspended in their webs, shimmering in the sun. We spent lots of time outdoors year-round. We always called our yard the "garden," and, compared to what we had in Chicago, that designation seemed correct.

I continued to be interested in gardens as I got older, mowing the lawns and watering the flowers of neighbors who had gone on vacation, digging a fish pond when we moved to a new house in the Berkeley Hills, and spending hours in the pittosporum tree which formed a ladder to our roof, playing with its hard green fruit and taking in the sweet fragrance of the leaves and flowers. I'm not sure if it was "gardens" that interested me so much as the pleasant sensation of being outdoors.

My interest in gardens increased dramatically in 1974, after I graduated from the University of California, Santa Cruz, with a degree in political theory. After working in a retail nursery for several months, I helped a friend start a gardening business and spent the next four years designing, installing, and maintaining yards in the Berkeley and Oakland hills. I pruned trees and roses, clipped hedges, built compost bins, laid paths and patios, and bought lots of plants from retail nurseries for my clients. I also arranged patio furniture, swept decks, stacked firewood, cleaned drains, and hauled trash. Though I never quite questioned the matter, I felt vaguely uncertain about what to call the work I was doing or what to call the places in which I worked. They seemed to be gardens in the popular sense of the word, and yet less and less of my work seemed to address the care of plants for its own sake. Something else was going on that had yet to reveal itself to me, and I did not know what questions to ask to unravel the mystery.

Four years later, I entered graduate school in landscape architecture at the University of California at Berkeley, with the expectation of raising the level of the work I was already doing. I quickly learned that few of my professors had much interest in home grounds. Garden design had come to be regarded by professionals and academics alike as elitist and socially irresponsible, as catering to people with too much disposable income and nothing better to spend it on than leisure and decoration. My teachers and their colleagues in the private sector were busy preserving coastlines, planning inner-city parks, rating the visual qualities of parklands, and theorizing about the "urban fabric." Nothing rankled them more than being asked for advice about garden plants.

In one respect I understood their feelings: landscape architecture had the potential to move societies in much bigger ways than improving the quality of household lots. Yet I continued to be curious about the elusive "other dimension" of residential gardens that I had encountered earlier. I turned to the library and to my satisfaction found dozens of garden design books tucked into the stacks, mostly published before 1960 and rarely checked out. Some astute librarian had been clever enough to buy the books our professors did not want us wasting our time reading!

But now something else was wrong. I stared at yard after yard of paving: broad terraces of flagstone, brick, and concrete imbedded with little pebbles; stairs and paths lined with masonry walls; redwood decks in every shape and angle known to Pythagoras; and enough outdoor furniture to fill a showroom. People, if the photographer had included them (often they did not lest clothing and hair styles date the photos), nibbled on cheese and wine while reclining on canvas deck chairs, their well-behaved children playing in the background. There were plants, but seldom did they serve as objects of interest in their own right; rather they defined spaces, or provided textural backdrops, or screened unpleasant views, or defined entries and exits. I found plenty of technical information about plants in horticulture magazines: black roses, apple trees with five grafts, 700-pound pumpkins, square tomatoes, and other botanical curiosities. Landscape architects, however, would have little of this stuff. They used plants to create line and form, to generate visual rhythm, to sculpt space. Cultivation was best left for farmers.

I perused books by Thomas Church, James Rose, and Garrett Eckbo, three of the most famous modern garden designers of the twentieth century. Church, until his death in 1978, designed more than 2,000 gardens, many for clients with little interest in horticulture. "It's just as wrong to give an owner who is not an ambitious gardener a combination of natural plantings requiring expert knowledge and care as it is to give a real 'green thumb' gardener a garden with no soil to dig in," Church said in his revealingly titled book, *Gardens Are for People.*[1] I read *Sunset, House Beautiful,* and *Better Homes and Gardens.* I leafed through garden history books by Christopher Tunnard and Elizabeth Kassler. In each case I was confronted with more paving. Some gardens were beautiful, with modern sculpture and cubist-informed swimming pools; others had enough concrete to fill a bus station. Had the cement contractors of America conspired to monopolize garden design?

My quest to understand the American garden was going nowhere, and I turned my attention to the parks, malls, and civic plazas we were designing in class. In the back of my mind, though, the clock was ticking: either I was looking in the wrong place for the American garden or I had been looking in the right place for the wrong thing.

Then the alarm went off. Most of our designs in school had one common goal: making places *habitable.* Aesthetics, style, and materials were important. But most critiques eventually came around to one question: was this a space in which people (we called them "users") would want to spend time? When habitability was considered, the picture changed. No longer was a design judged solely on its appearance or its contents. What finally mattered was whether or not users wanted to spend time in them in the first place. Could not this critique apply to a garden?

While perusing a book by Garrett Eckbo, I noticed how much one of his designs resembled the room of a house. It had a floor, walls, and even a ceiling composed of acrylic panels popular during the 1950s. Toys lay about, tables and chairs were plentiful, shish kebabs sat poised for the grill, and decorations abounded: hanging baskets, pots of annuals, wind chimes, weather vanes, and bird baths carved out of rock. It looked as if someone had tipped the house on end and dumped the contents into the back yard. I had witnessed this scene hundreds of times as a gardener, but at a time when all I noticed were the plants for which I had been assigned to care. For the owners, though, these material contents transformed the garden into habitable space, as important as any room of the house.

I decided to investigate the garden as habitable space for my master's thesis, and during my final year of school I interviewed fifty people in the San Francisco Bay Area to learn what their yards meant to them. I spoke to a nurse from Fiji who planted her property in "islands" separated by seas of dirt, a veterinarian who regarded plants as pets, and an Israeli shop owner who loved to water most of all. I met a married couple who wanted to install a flush toilet in the yard for their dog, and a man who replaced his gardener with a goat. I met a militant extremist who loaded his rifle if the newsboy lingered too long on the front lawn. I met a retired machinist who invited me into his house to see evidence that the CIA had conspired with his children to steal his lawn ornaments. I spoke with several homeowners whose gardens violated every canon of bad taste: green-painted concrete lawns, bushes pruned into rabbits and corkscrews, bathtub Madonnas, Christmas displays left up through Valentine's Day, and the enduring symbol of questionable garden taste: the pink flamingo. Historian Fred Schroeder calls such displays "outlaw aesthetics,"[2] and I quickly learned not to dismiss them, as the closer I looked the more I saw how they revealed the owners' attitudes on community beauty, neighborliness, pride of homeownership, and creative spirit. I also spoke to many homeowners whose gardens—if they appeared plain and undistinguished—provided a valuable place to enjoy a few moments of sunshine while reading the newspaper or drinking a cup of tea or coffee, to enjoy a dinner with friends on a warm summer evening, to grow a few herbs and spices for the kitchen, to let their kids play free from the traffic in the street, to let the dog loose, and to simply enjoy some fresh air.

Most of all, I learned that basic habitability was far more important to people than was the pursuit of gardening. This is not to say that people considered gardening objectionable or a waste of time, but rather that it was neither their first concern nor the purpose for their yard. One of the women with whom I spoke, Rosemary, was a product designer who had moved to Berkeley from New York City in the 1970s. French doors along the back of her house opened onto a beautiful paved terrace furnished with canvas chairs and a table made from an overturned wine barrel. Dappled light poured through the branches of a tall elm. Wind chimes jingled in the breeze. "We use this every day, if the weather permits," Rosemary told me. "It's a very important part of our house, because our house gets quite dark. It's like an additional room. I think that's why I wanted it smooth enough for furniture." Small potted plants sat along the edge of the terrace, surrounded by Rosemary's ceramic sculptures. Camellias formed a green backdrop against the grape stake fence. Despite the numerous plantings, though, Rosemary had little interest in gardening. "I love to sit out on the porch and look into the trees. I'm not a serious digging gardener. I'm not involved in the whole growing cycle and nurturing. I love the visual aspect and the fragrance."[3] Rosemary's feelings for her garden underscored the sentiment of most of the people I interviewed.

In 1983, the University of California accepted my thesis, "Social Meanings of Residential Gardens." A few years later I turned the thesis into two articles for Bonnie Loyd at *Landscape* magazine titled "Gardens For California Living" and "The Well Tempered Garden."[4] Though the former discussed middle-class yards and the latter working-class yards, both articles emphasized the garden as a social space, where the day-to-day needs of people took precedence over plants, where gardening was an activity related more to household management than a love of horticulture, and where homes and their grounds in a particular neighborhood played an important role in community identity. The *Landscape* articles—which addressed contemporary people and events—fueled my curiosity about how the home grounds have gotten to where they are today.

This book constitutes my investigation into that history, a subject that turned out to be far more complex and wide-reaching than I had ever before imagined. While researching and writing the manuscript I have taught landscape design at Merritt

College in Oakland, California, and designed hundreds of private gardens. I have also traveled to cities across the United States to examine the way people have laid out and used their grounds, whenever possible speaking personally to the individuals who did the work to learn where they put their priorities. This combination of research, teaching, travel, and design has, I hope, allowed me to approach my subject from many angles and to account for the numerous social, economic, aesthetic, technical, and creative factors that have led Americans to turn their home grounds into habitable spaces.

Introduction: America's Home Grounds: Yard or Garden?

The home grounds—the space that surrounds the average American house—is at once one of the most familiar places in the landscape and one of the most narrowly construed. In its least glamorous incarnation it is bland, weedy, and neglected, a dreary way station for trashcans, firewood, a quick home repair, or to chain up a dog. At its best it is an enchanting garden, with scented roses blooming against white picket fences, colorful perennials swaying in the breeze, cooling waterfalls and ponds, comfortable benches set under vine-laden arbors, and hammocks stretched between sheltering trees. The home grounds, at its worst, commands little of our attention, and at its best is so well documented that, in the words of John Brinckerhoff Jackson, there is "*too* much garden literature available."[1]

Somewhere between the home grounds as wasteland and the home grounds as Eden lie millions of middle-class yards filled with trees, grass, patios, play equipment, small herb plots, and numerous other accouterments of outdoor living. Even if they might aspire to do so, few of the owners of these yards have retained the services of professional gardeners, and even fewer have hired landscape architects or designers to help them lay out their lots. Middle-class home grounds are so common we hardly look twice at them, and yet upon closer examination they reveal the numerous ways that the owners have worked individually and collectively to transform their properties into habitable space. It is here that the focus of this book lies.

The home grounds are what cultural geographers refer to as an "ordinary landscape." Ordinary or "common" landscapes—such as the small farm, the town square, the thirty-five mile-per-hour commercial strip, the miniature golf course, and the front and back yard—reveal the day-to-day lives of average people. What they lack in grandeur, style, and beauty they more than make up for in what they contribute to those who daily use them. In the words of Peirce Lewis, such places are "our unwitting autobiography, reflecting our tastes, our values, our aspirations, and even our fears, in tangible, visible form."[2] There is a small but concerted group of historians, geographers, landscape architects, and architects who have studied common landscapes, the most prominent of whom is the late J. B. Jackson.[3] Outside these efforts, though, ordinary landscapes—the home grounds included—have received too little scholarly attention, and as a result it is hard to find much written about them.

It is easy to understand the work of enormously influential designers such as Thomas Church and Fredrick Law Olmsted, who published often, freely admitted the influences and principles upon which they based their work, won many prizes, and designed numerous important projects. Common gardens, however, have evolved under circumstances at best tenuously related to professional design standards. At the turn of the twentieth century, for example, back yards often contained privies, cisterns, trash, and laundry lines rather than the flowering plants and picturesque scenery we typically associate with such yards at their finest. When looked at through the lens of professional design, such yards were disreputable, notorious, and defying all standards of good taste. When understood as responses to the meager level of public services typical of their era, such yards were arguably of great benefit to the functioning and comfort of the household, supplying utilities that no city dweller could live without. Unfortunately our preconceptions concerning garden taste have often kept us from appreciating these other purposes.

One indication of our undeveloped view of the home ground is that no one can quite agree on what to call it. I have heard people refer to the space around the house as a lot, plot, yard, yardscape, land, landscape, property, estate, tract, garden, site, lawn, field, grounds, home grounds, dooryard, south forty, patio, patch, courtyard, and even yarden. Then there are distinctions such as service yard, drying yard, utility yard, intimate garden, pleasure garden, private Eden, and outdoor living room.[4] One of the few people to scrutinize the terminology is Paul Groth, who has suggested that the space around a house undergoes an evolution that dictates its correct name at any given stage.[5] The first stage, according to Groth, is a lot, simply the land set aside to build a house. A lot is no more or less than a legal description of property, as designated by geometric coordinates, and shown on a plat map. Stage two is a yard, literally the space left over on the lot after the house is built. In most cases yards are utilitarian, "an area for special work, business, or storage." Ultimately, a yard is no more than the exterior setting for the house. The third stage is a garden, a place set aside for a special purpose such as growing flowers or vegetables. The trees, shrubs, and lawn around a house do not qualify as a garden, Groth argues, since they are "not special in their own right . . . . not even the foundation plantings and fence flowers around most ordinary houses, let alone the grass lawns, truly qualify as gardens. Rather, they are adornments of the yard. Americans have relatively few gardens—planted or decorated places to be appreciated in their own right—but many millions of adorned yards."[6]

Without question, Groth is correct that most yards lack the special qualities he reserves for "gardens." One can visit homes in metropolitan Atlanta, Boston, Chicago, Dallas, Denver, Kansas City, New York, Philadelphia, Phoenix, and Seattle and find yards full of picnic tables, basketball hoops, jungle gyms, trash cans, broken down cars, inflatable pools, stacks of firewood, and great swaths of concrete and asphalt. When asked about their garden, most homeowners will lead their guests to some vegetables set well away from the destructive swath of dogs and tricycles or to the living room to look at coffee-table books about English, French, and Italian estates, the places which Groth calls "special in their own right." Beautiful gardens are at once easy to spot and understand, and clearly most American yards fall short of this standard.

If we are willing to look beyond standards of horticultural excellence and beauty, however, and regard the home grounds as an exterior manifestation of the house, a much wider range of interpretations come into play. The home grounds reveal the real estate practices and zoning standards that led to the division of lots into front and back segments, each serving distinct household purposes. They reveal a timeline for the advent of municipal waterworks, sewerage, gas, electricity, and trash collection, since before cities introduced these services homeowners had to provide for their equivalents in their own back yards. The home grounds reveal the power of early twentieth-century civic beautification movements, which led to the ubiquitous front lawns and foundation plantings that have adorned American homes for more than a century. The home grounds reveal the ways populations have adapted to a region, particularly in California, where the mild climate has permitted residents to develop habitable gardens to extraordinary limits. Most of all, the home grounds reveal America's allegiance to the single-family house and the domestic lifestyle that accompanies it, both inside and outside the walls of the dwelling. Habitability is the quality that makes a place fit to be lived in, and—other than the house itself—few places more closely reveal how people live than the land on which the dwelling sits.

This study centers on the period from the early- to mid-1800s to the present. During this time the grounds have enjoyed three basic incarnations: first as an agricultural space related to family livelihood, then as an urban utility yard supporting the basic workings and comfort of the house, and finally as an outdoor family room for child rearing, entertaining, leisure, and day-to-day household activities. In none of these incarnations—with one important exception—do ornamental plants or the activity of gardening bear necessarily on the type of yard under discussion. Even the exception to this rule—the lawn and foundation planting style prevalent in front yards nationwide for the past century—reinforces the rule, as its popularity is related more to civic decoration than to an intrinsic love of plants.

In this respect readers might find this study different than what they had expected. Suburban and exurban neighborhoods are indeed alive with the sound of power mowers and hedge clippers on spring and summer weekends, vegetable gardens are a thriving back yard industry according to many studies, retail nursery sales keep pace with the nation's economy, American tourists flock to visit the Alhambra, Sissinghurst, Tivoli, and Versailles, and every year, garden club memberships continue to grow, and every spring season is replete with newspaper and magazine articles showing homeowners how to fill their yards with grass and flowers.[7]

Despite this horticultural enthusiasm, I have found that the home grounds are far more intimately connected to the broader needs of the household than to the activity of gardening. This is not at all to dismiss or devalue gardening, for gardening is a beloved avocation for millions of Americans, an endeavor well supported by the "green industry" in practically every state, one that generates numerous publications, that supports hundreds of college-level horticultural programs, that generates county-funded master gardener programs and cooperative education classes, and that supports arboretums, botanical gardens, and historical estates throughout the nation. It is a curious phenomenon, however, that home grounds have become popularly linked in the public mind to horticulture and gardening because, when one looks closely, this association usually does not bear out. Wilbur Zelinsky has called Americans idealists, and, however high they hold gardens in esteem and however much they promise to surround their homes with beautiful gardens, remarkably few people have gotten around to doing much about it.[8] This behavior does not reveal a problem so much as a preference, for, as I will suggest repeatedly, the habitable yard has proven itself a capable alternative to the botanical version.

My geographic orientation is twofold: the United States (which, for simplicity, I refer to as America), in general, and coastal California, in detail. Numerous factors—from climate and terrain to community history, from industrialization and transportation to building technology, from governmental programs and legislation to city planning and zoning practices, from individual expression to shared expectations of habitability—have produced common patterns in American home grounds regardless of location. These patterns are the focus of the first part of this book. The second part addresses coastal California, not because yards there differ from the mainstream, but because they have carried the underlying premise of habitability further than in most other regions of the nation. The same factors that have shaped American home grounds nationwide have shaped middle-class yards along the Pacific Coast, and as a result yards there share similarities with those in every major metropolitan area of the country. However, a unique set of circumstances—including the mild climate, the relative newness of the population, smaller lot sizes, and the proliferation of the so-called "green industry"—have allowed many Californians to transform their yards into outdoor rooms often as comfortable as the homes themselves. In this respect California home grounds come close to epitomizing the theme of domestic habitability that underlies typical American yards, and thus they warrant special focus.

In order to accommodate the vast amount of material that this study must include, I have sometimes found it necessary to generalize about region, climate, population patterns, and popular taste. Readers should in no way assume that such generalizations override regional variations of the particular subject under discussion.[9] The home grounds are the product of many influences, from climate and terrain to community history and ethnic origins, and from individual preferences all the way up to forces that have shaped us nationally, such as industrialization, transportation, building technology, planning and zoning practices, and governmental programs and legislation. A full accounting of this subject would require volumes, and there is much exciting work to be done in this area. This study, however, steps back from the topic to encompass a wide view of the forces that have shaped the home landscape. It is my hope that such broad notions will not only reveal underlying continuity with the wealth of regional variations that American home grounds exhibit, but also help to establish directions for future investigations.

Part One
American Yard

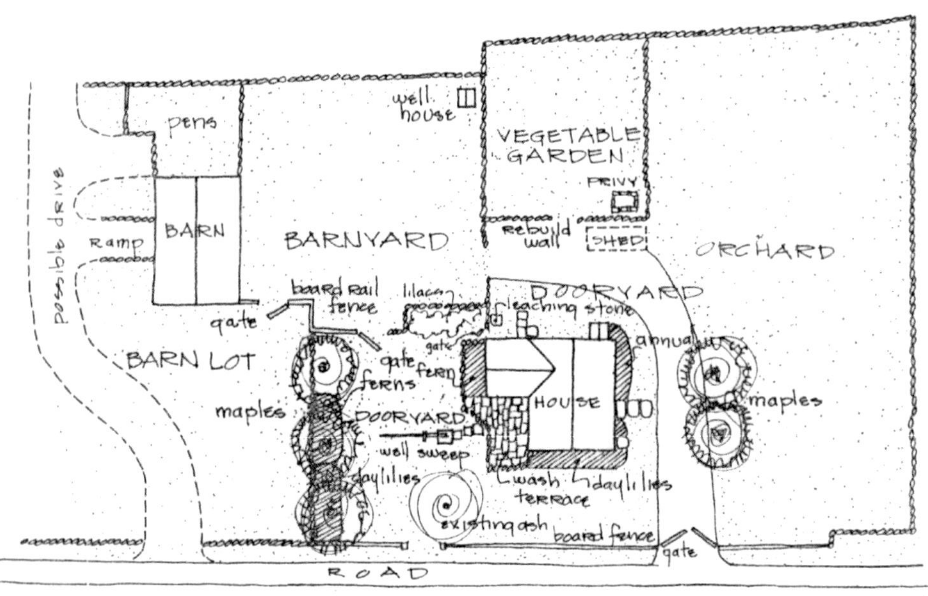

Figure 1.1. A colonial farmhouse in Hampton, Connecticut, with a barnyard, dooryard, and vegetable garden. Like most rural properties, the grounds were arranged to support the livelihood of the household. The drawing appears as Figure 8 in Rudy J. Favretti and Joy Putman Favretti, *Landscapes and Gardens for Historic Buildings: A handbook for reproducing and creating authentic landscape settings* (Nashville: American Association for State and Local History, 1978), 17. Reproduced by permission of Altamira Press.

Chapter One: From Dooryard to Urban Yard

The American home grounds as we know them today have their origins in rural communities dating back to the seventeenth century and, according to J. B Jackson, much earlier than that. The association of house and grounds, Jackson observes, is intrinsic to nearly all dwellings and ages, and, in order to understand one, you need to look at the other. "Garden comes from an Indo-European word, *gher*, which appears in many Latin and Greek and Slavic and Germanic words for apparently such disparate things as farmyard, pasture, sown field, hedge, house, fence, enclosure, stable, girder, fortified place—and garden." Each of these terms, says Jackson, suggests an enclosed space either related to the house or to activities necessary to secure the livelihood of the family:

> . . . the concept of the garden was, in early days, closely involved with the concepts of family or household, of property, of defense, and even community layout, and though the word becomes more closely identified in the course of centuries with the growing of plants, we can never entirely divorce the garden from its social meaning.[1]

Early American home grounds matched Jackson's description. The vast majority of the population was rural, and up until the Civil War the nation's economy was primarily agricultural. Most rural properties contained three distinct parts—a barnyard, a dooryard, and a garden—and each had an agricultural purpose. The largest allocation of space went to the barnyard, a place to house cows, pigs, fowl, and horses, to park plows, hay rakes, and other equipment, and to store feed. The barnyard was fenced to keep the livestock out of the crops and to provide protection from wolves and other predators. The barnyard was (and remains) synonymous with farm life, and it was closely associated with animals. Of the three yards it is the one least evident in contemporary American properties, owing to the steady separation of agricultural and residential land in the past 150 years.

The dooryard mirrored many of the activities taking place inside the house, and in many ways it functioned as a household extension. It was a dirt-covered space between the dwelling and various outbuildings—the cowshed, woodshed, hay barn, well house, granary, and animal pens. The dooryard was alive with activity. Families used it to butcher hogs, fix wheelbarrows, chop wood, press cider, and perform household chores and repairs. Pigs, roosters, chickens, rabbits, and goats scuttled about hunting for food. A few flowers—marigolds, hollyhocks, lavender cottons, and tulips—poked up at random, but the space was mostly free of plants. Apart from idle moments or breaks from work, the dooryard was hardly a place for leisure. Work rarely stopped on the farm, and, when it did, the family was more likely to rest inside the house or on the front porch or to ride the buggy to church or into town.

The third yard in rural American properties was the garden, a plot specifically set apart for growing vegetables, herbs, and fruits. The garden had little to do with the flowers, grass, and ornamentation popularly associated with the term. It occupied the sunniest spot of the property, usually well away from the shade of the dwelling and tall trees. The family fenced it to shield the plants from the wind and to keep out cows, pigs, sheep, wild rabbits, and deer. Free-roaming animals were common before the Civil War, and each household was responsible for protecting its own crops. The three-foot-high picket fence that adorns many American yards today had its origins in the rural yard. The slats were spaced slightly closer than the width of a chicken's body, and the ends were cut just sharp enough to deter a hungry pig from climbing over the top and devouring the produce growing inside.

Families often laid out their garden plantings in rows mimicking the larger fields or divided them into rectangular sections

Figure 1.2. A dooryard in Colorado Springs, Colorado, ca. 1870-1880, seen from the cupola of a nearby schoolhouse. Typical of its rural surroundings, the yard contained a privy, a well, animal pens, various outbuildings, and plenty of bare earth and weeds. B. H. Gurnsey, photographer. Photograph used by permission of the Denver Public Library, Western History Collection, call number X-14229.

separated by gravel and dirt paths. Smaller gardens were usually less geometrical, instead taking their form from the orientation to the sun and the lay of the land. The wife, often the unofficial family doctor, complimented the vegetable plantings with a "physick" garden of herbs, such as pennyroyal, marjoram, sorrel, liverwort, and fennel. Wives also made trips into the surrounding countryside to collect flowers to dry for fragrance, to grind up to make dyes, or to decorate the garden. For the most part, however, colonial home grounds contained few ornamental plants.[2]

When the United States government began keeping a census in 1790, ninety-five percent of the nation's population was rural.[3] Although farmers represented the bulk of the population, most small towns also included storekeepers, a doctor, a clergyman, a teacher, an innkeeper, a tailor, a baker, a shoemaker, a carpenter, a wheelwright, a blacksmith, a dressmaker, and other entrepreneurs. These residents usually lived near the main street in cottages built on small rectangular lots. Until the Civil War, few standards governed the position of dwellings on their lots, and builders simply placed homes where they deemed fit, generally away from the street to minimize the ill effects of dust, noise, and horse manure and to provide the family with privacy. Front yards often contained rough, grassy meadows with paths leading to the front doors, some flowers near the entries, and picket fences to mark the properties and to keep out wandering animals. The space that remained—particularly that in the back and out of view of the road—resembled the farmhouse dooryard, where families could store firewood, build horse and buggy barns, dig wells, dry laundry, and grow some vegetables. While not directly related to livelihood, the small-town home and grounds still served households in direct, useful ways.

After the Civil War, substantial changes occurred to the American home and its grounds, leading to the birth of front and back yards as we know them today. Underlying this change was a shift in the nation's economy from agriculture to industry and a parallel shift in the way business was conducted in town. Prior to the Civil War, the majority of Americans farmed for a living, and most towns were mercantile-based, depending on trade and services among the population. By the mid-1800s, however, the industrial revolution had reached formidable proportions and was creating an economic base rooted in manufacturing and mechanization. Technological innovations, such as the thresher, the cotton gin, and the steam engine, allowed one farmer to do the work of many hired hands and animals and decreased the need for manual labor. The expansion of the railroad, along with the development of refrigeration technology and artificial dehydration, allowed successful farmers to increase the size of their fields and expand the geographic range of their markets. At the same time, many small farmers were pushed to the wayside or forced to find other means of support altogether.[4]

Once a predominantly rural nation, the United States was now witnessing the growth of densely packed cities. As the number of farms decreased, industrial growth created an enormous demand for urban laborers. Country residents began selling their land and migrating to cities to join the vast number of newly arriving foreign immigrants looking for jobs in factories and mills. This migration represented a dramatic demographic shift. By 1860, twenty percent of Americans lived in urban areas, up from five percent in 1790; by 1880, the number of urban residents had climbed to twenty-five percent; by 1900, the number reached forty percent; and, by 1920, it was at fifty percent and still growing.[5]

Living conditions in nineteenth-century cities bore little resemblance to those of the countryside, where densities averaged less than one person per square mile. Cities typically took their form according to how long it took a person to walk to work or to market and how fast a messenger could get a letter

Figure 1.3. Mrs. Powers feeds her chickens in her dooryard at home in Kearney, Nebraska, 1907. The grounds contained a well, washtub, ash barrel, laundry line, ax and other tools, incubators, fruit trees, and wood-planked walkways atop the patchy ground surface. Solomon Butcher, photographer. Photograph used by permission of the Nebraska State Historical Society Photograph Collections, 1907, reproduction number RG2608.PH:000000-002608.

across town. Because transportation was slow, workers' homes, factories, offices, and stores were generally spaced no more than a mile or two from one another. This arrangement worked as population sizes stayed reasonable, but industrial cities were growing at a rate much higher than anyone could have predicted. By the latter nineteenth century, New York City, Philadelphia, and Boston had neighborhoods with densities of 80,000 to 100,000 people per square mile; in comparison, the largest American cities today have populations of 15,000 per square mile and their suburbs about 1,000 per square mile.[6]

The prototypical dwellings during this period were European style, brick row houses sitting on twenty-five-foot-wide lots. Row houses typically sat shoulder to shoulder, with facades abutting the sidewalk and little or no side yard or back yard space. Landlords often built second units on properties fortunate

Figure 1.4. At the turn of the twentieth century, American cities such as Cambridgeport, in Boston, pictured here (ca. 1902), were densely packed, with tightly spaced homes and small utilitarian yards. A. A. Shurtleff, photographer. Photograph used by permission of the Frances Loeb Library, Harvard University Graduate School of Design, reproduction number 119405.

to have back yards, in order to profit from the tremendous infusion of newcomers. Rear units not only raised densities, they blocked access to light and fresh air, increased the risk of fire, and heightened health risks from the buildup of uncollected trash and sewage. "These houses, hidden by the structures in front, are uncontrolled by ordinary police inspection and unaffected by public observation and criticism," wrote Charles Mulford Robinson in 1911. "They become such breeding places of disease and vice that at last, in city after city, it becomes necessary to forbid their erection."[7]

If an urban family was lucky enough to have a yard, it bore little resemblance to rural home grounds. There was often a privy or cesspool behind the house, and, when it filled, the family dumped the excess into the street, where it was eaten by droves of swine that ran at large. Most homes had poor or no indoor plumbing, and residents either got water from polluted wells, hydrants, and rivers or collected roof runoff in back yard cisterns. Lumber and firewood rested against dilapidated fences, ash barrels sat by the back porches, trash lay uncollected in alleys and yards, and laundry lines ran from yard to yard.[8] Wood planking provided pathways through the mud, garbage, and sewage that covered the ground. In the 1870s, there were more than 100,000 horses in New York City and Brooklyn, many of which lived in back yards, alleys, or on the street. Horse manure lay everywhere, and, when the animals ailed or died, their owners often left them to rot.[9] In the event their property had space to grow vegetables, families probably had little time to tend them in the face of seventy-hour or longer work weeks.[10] "I have worked in that hell hole for 36 straight hours, at a machine, and I was only a child," said Jack London of the Oakland cannery that employed him in 1890. "I knew no horse in the City of Oakland that worked the hours I worked."[11] If people used any outdoor area on their properties for leisure, it was the front porch where they chatted with their neighbors, read the paper, and watched the masses stream by.

In 1976, Robert Schuyler excavated an 1840s Brooklyn Heights brownstone yard to investigate the living conditions of the factory workers who once resided there. Armed with shovels and trowels, Schuyler and his archeological assistants uncovered a privy several feet from the back door of the now up-scale property, a discovery suggesting that the residents had limited or no indoor plumbing. Upon digging further, they found a thick layer of sand covering the entire yard, probably laid to neutralize the sewage and garbage that had collected there. Mixed into the sand and dirt were the bones of rats that had eaten the garbage the family tossed through the back door. Schuyler's team also found a cistern buried six feet deep near the back door, originally fed from a roof drainpipe by summer thundershowers. When the city of Brooklyn began supplying public water in 1860, the family abandoned the cistern and for the next decade filled it with pieces of ironstone china (a hard white earthenware), porcelain dolls, a child's tea set, high button shoes, cotton fabric, and dozens of rat-chewed bones. Schuyler conjectured that there was little reason for the occupants to venture into the yard unless absolutely necessary. "There was no evidence of a grassy retreat or garden refuge," he remarked.[12]

Properties in Oakland, California, have yielded similar contents. During the rebuilding of Interstate 880 after the 1989 Loma Prieta earthquake, the California State Department of Transportation funded a historical investigation of the proposed route in order to comply with the National Historic Preservation Act of 1966. As part of this work, archaeologists from the Anthropological Studies Center at Sonoma State University excavated the backyards of about 240 homes—many of which dated back to the 1860s—that sat near the proposed freeway route. The excavators, whose work the center meticulously documented in its report, "Putting the 'There' There: Historical Archaeologies of West Oakland," uncovered a richly detailed view of working-class and middle-class home life. The teams found evidence of privies on three quarters of the properties, most located in the far corners of the yards where their odors were less prominent. The diggers also found wells located perilously close to the privies, and the center speculates that, due to lime deposits in the wells (families commonly treated their privies with lime), sewage had likely leaked into the groundwater and contributed to several epidemics during the era.

Figure 1.5. A backyard in Chicago, in 1908, with a boardwalk cutting across barren soil to the rear of the lot. Lumber was stacked along the fence, and a laundry line was hitched to the porch. Photographer unknown. Photograph used by permission of the Chicago Historical Society, Chicago *Daily News* negatives collection, 1908, number DN-0052620.

Once cities began providing sewerage, families filled their privies with household items, such as crockery, bottles, and old silverware, but also with the bones of cows, sheep, chickens, and rabbits. The privy diggers also found piles of buried garbage, rat-chewed artifacts, clothespins, broken flowerpots (probably from indoor plants or ones placed on the back porch), seeds from flowers, vegetables, and weeds, and even a human skeleton. Privies and wells were not the only back yard features. Sanborn Insurance Company maps of the era revealed that many residences had stables and animal sheds and that families often built back porches onto their homes, probably to create additional work space. Though the teams turned up little evidence of recreational yard use, researchers found that some Greek families roasted meat over spits in the clearings between their privies, wood piles, and laundry lines.[13]

Worst off were the throngs of newly arriving European immigrants. Most of these residents had little money, education, or job skills, and they lived in enormously crowded tenements that exemplified the worst of urban housing. Few cities had laws regulating density or living conditions, and landlords rarely abided by the controls that did exist. Tenements had dark interiors, small rooms, poor air circulation, and little heat or running water. In 1908, social reformer Margaret Byington described the dismal houses and grounds occupied by Slav workers in the Pittsburgh, Pennsylvania, mill town of Homestead:

> From the cinder path beside one of the railroads that crosses the level part of the homestead, you enter an alley, bordered on one side by stables and on the other by a row of shabby two-story frame houses. The doors of the houses are closed, but dishpans and old clothes decorating their exterior mark them as inhabited.

Figure 1.6. A backyard in Boston's Cambridgeport, in 1902. The fenced property contained a wooden walkway, bare dirt, laundry line, few or no plantings, and little indication of social uses. Clotheslines were an integral part of the American back yard until the invention of the automatic washer and dryer in the late 1940s. As a result of these appliances, laundry lines disappeared, leaving middle-class homeowners more space in their back yards for family activities. A. A. Shurtleff, photographer. Photograph used by permission of the Frances Loeb Library, Harvard University Graduate School of Design, reproduction number 119407.

> Turning from the alley through a narrow passageway you find yourself in a small court, on three sides of which are smoke-grimed houses, and on the fourth, low stables. The open space teems with life and movement. Children, dogs and hens make it lively under foot; overhead long lines of flapping clothes must be dodged. A group of women stand gossiping in one corner, awaiting their turn at the pump—which is one of the two sources of water supply for the 20 families who live there. Another woman dumps the contents of her washtubs upon the paved ground, and the greasy, soapy water runs into an open drain a few feet from the pump. In the center a circular wooden building with ten compartments opening into one vault, flushed only by this waste water, constitutes the toilet accommodations for over 100 people. Twenty-seven children find in this crowded brick-paved space their only playground . . . . This court is one of many such in Homestead; one of hundreds of similar courts in the mill towns of the Ohio valley.[14]

While the Homestead yards Byington visited were especially notorious, the nineteenth-century urban yard was only meagerly habitable. It was a neglected, utilitarian space with little or no value for gathering or socializing. It was a prime agent in the spreading of disease. It housed sick and dying animals and was often strewn with garbage and filled with rats. It contributed to air pollution, fires, and second-unit crowding. In short, it was an inhospitable spot best kept hidden from public view and was avoided at nearly all costs.

Of all of the causes of urban crowding and its associated ills, poor transportation stood near the top of the list. The crushing density of American cities was paradoxical given the vast amounts of open space that surrounded their perimeters, much more space than could be found in comparable European cities. Moreover, American cities were ripe for expansion in numerous ways. The terrain and climate were largely friendly to settlement, as Kenneth Jackson points out, unlike that of equally spacious nations, such as Russia, Australia, and Canada, whose territories consisted of millions of square miles of desert or frozen tundra.[15] Raw building materials were abundant and lay reasonably close to major population centers. The invention in the 1830s of the balloon-framed house—an efficient building technique using

Figure 1.7. A 1902 urban back yard in Boston. Clothes and rags hung on a broken trellis. Wooden planking sat atop the bare earth, and a laundry line hung just over the fence. A. A. Shurtleff, photographer. Photograph used by permission of the Frances Loeb Library, Harvard University Graduate School of Design, reproduction number 119392.

small, milled members rather than mortise and tenon beams—offered average Americans the promise of owning their own homes.[16] Steam engines improved the productivity of companies mining clays for brick, ores for iron and steel, and gravel for macadamizing residential streets. The expansion of the railroads allowed developers to transport building materials throughout the nation.

Factories and businesses, however, usually lay in the urban core, and workers, because they lacked efficient means of transportation, had little choice but to live close to their jobs. Most mid-nineteenth-century city roads had not yet been macadamized, and they became heavily rutted and impassable in rain and snow. Street traffic typically consisted of horse-drawn carts, vans, and busses. Several animals were needed to pull a heavy vehicle, and drivers had to replace tired horses with teams of fresh ones at frequent intervals. Runaway horses were a common danger, and manure filled the streets. Fire trucks and ambulances stalled easily in the congested lanes. On average, travel on city roads was less than five miles per hour.[17]

Many of the problems associated with crowding stood to be alleviated if Americans could find a way to expand into the undeveloped land surrounding their cities. Electric streetcars—also called trolleys—helped to provide such a solution and, in doing so, helped to lay the ground for a new version of the house and yard. Electric streetcars, invented in the 1880s, traveled more than twice as fast as horse-drawn vehicles and were much easier to service and maintain. Because they rode on metal tracks, they were not slowed by poor paving. Electricity was cheap, fares were low (an average cross-town ride cost a nickel), and the cars could run in almost any weather. Within a decade, every major and nearly every minor American city had installed trolleys. Boston, Chicago, New York City, Philadelphia, and other industrial cities laid hundreds of miles of tracks throughout their downtowns, but it was Los Angeles, ironically, that had the biggest system in the nation, with more than 1,000 miles of track (almost none of which still exists). Hilly San Francisco and Berkeley both installed streetcars, and the Chamber of Commerce of Oakland, California, boasted that its city had the best trolleys in America, allowing residents to "leave the center of business activities at Fourteenth Street and Broadway and within a few minutes go by the best streetcar transportation service in the country to the midst of the residence districts of Piedmont and Claremont . . . . They found themselves as far removed from the dirt and turmoil of the work-a-day world as though they had traveled fifty miles into the mountains."[18]

Like spokes on a giant wheel, trolley lines extended as many as ten or more miles from city hubs into rural or otherwise undeveloped land. Seeing a major business opportunity, real-estate developers purchased acres of land along the tracks and placed hotels, amusement parks, monuments, and other attractions at the ends of the lines to lure riders past developing neighborhoods. As passengers traveled the routes, they looked out from the cars onto block after block of newly built, single-family homes with private yards. Many of the neighborhoods revealed the beginnings of a new landscape style composed of tree-lined streets, flowering bushes up against the homes, and lawns flowing out to the street. The buyers were part of an emerging urban middle class—shopkeepers, teachers, contractors, small-business owners, lawyers, and entrepreneurs—drawn to the promise of better homes and neighborhoods. "It was an environment no one could fail to relish: green, remote, and well isolated from the city," J. B. Jackson said of the new suburbs.[19]

The neighborhoods that sprung up along the trolley lines, sometimes called "street-car suburbs," were significantly different from urban and rural communities. Gone were the dark, narrow streets, as suburban avenues were broad and lined with trees and grass parkways. Gone were the zero lot lines and minimal set-backs of the city row house, as trolley line homes were often set ten or more feet back from the street and had their own side and back yards. Gone, also, were the noisy animals, rusty plows, dusty earthen floors, and unceasing toil of the rural yard. A new version of the home grounds was emerging, one that promised comfort, spaciousness, greenery, and a healthier life.

The streetcar suburb era ushered in the single-family house and yard as the preferred middle-class dwelling, a form that has become so pervasive that we hardly stop to contemplate upon it today. It is important to note, however, that there are many ways houses can sit on their lots. They can sit shoulder to shoulder and directly up against the sidewalk, as seen in the brick row houses of nineteenth-century cities. Homes may share walls on one side, leaving space on the opposite side for bigger side yards, such as the planned unit developments Tunnard and Pushkarev described in their book, *Man Made America: Chaos or Control?*[20] Homes can be grouped around common open space, as found in the "cluster housing" projects of the 1960s and 1970s, with private space relegated to small, fenced courtyards off the dining rooms and kitchens.[21] Homes along all four sides of a rectangular block can open up to a central commons—such as those found in Spain—where families dry laundry, grow vegetables and flowers, watch their children play, and simply enjoy the outdoors. Homes can sit randomly on their lots: one ten feet from the

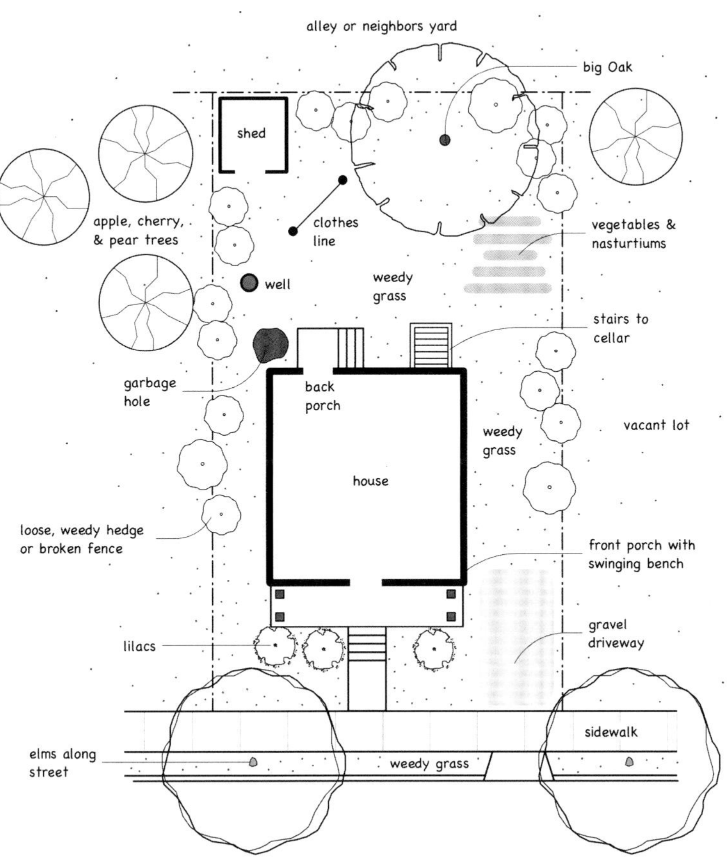

Figure 1.8. Home and garden magazines after the turn of the twentieth century promoted a romantic view of the home garden, usually based on an English cottage garden. Ordinary residences enjoyed no such luxuries, having plain yards given over to utility. In this diagram of Nora Shaw's Ohio home, circa 1925-1930, Nora recalls the yards around several homes in which she lived as a child. Drawing by the author, 2007.

street, another thirty feet back, another cocked at an odd angle, and another against the rear property line, an arrangement Roger Barnett calls the "libertarian suburb."[22]

The viability of these alternatives notwithstanding, the emergence of the single-family home as the dwelling of choice was consistent ideologically, practically, and aesthetically with larger strains of American thought. Since the publication of the Federalist Papers in 1787 (and informally for many years before that), Americans had espoused an ethic of individualism—a desire to define themselves singly or as families rather than by community ties—that was pivotal to their worldview.[23] American individualism emerged out of the doctrines of English political philosopher John Locke, who believed that people could only secure equal rights through the ownership of private property.[24] Locke deplored the arbitrary privilege the English upper class had conferred to itself and its denial of those same rights to people of lesser lineage. Class privilege went against the "laws of nature," but, in a land where class distinctions had existed for centuries, such privilege was hard to uproot. America was different. Free of England's political control and largely unbound by continental traditions and customs, the nation had the opportunity to extend rights to a greater portion of its citizenry. Individual rights were central to the philosophies of Americans James Madison and Alexander Hamilton, whose arguments in favor of private property ownership in the Federalist Papers formed the foundation for our constitution.[25] Thomas Jefferson, whose notions of liberty stemmed most directly from Locke, believed that freedom equated to a nation of small farmers, equal in their ownership of land and in their right to vote. While the small farm would steadily disappear, Jefferson's notion translated quite well to the ownership of a private home and grounds.[26]

Jefferson premised his theories on individual rights in part on an anti-urban bias that would find widespread acceptance

Figure 1.9. The single-family house has long been the preferred dwelling for Americans, and the home grounds have played a significant role in the appeal. This is a model of a single-family house for Greendale, Wisconsin, near Milwaukee, in 1936, one of three new towns developed under the New Deal. Marriemont, outside Cincinnati, and Greenbelt, between Baltimore and Washington, D.C., were the other two. Photograph courtesy of the Library of Congress, Prints & Photographs Division, FSA-OWI Collection, reproduction number LC-USF344-003389-ZB DLC.

among American intellectuals, politicians, and social reformers. During the seventeenth century, most Americans had viewed cities as prestigious. The Puritans believed a family's status increased the closer it lived to the village center. It was a disgrace to separate oneself or family from the community, and villages commonly punished lawbreakers and malcontents by banishing them from town. The vigor of commercial life itself was a strong social magnet. The division of trade labor required merchants to supervise personally their workers and thus to live close to their shops. Street life and pageantry made cities lively and festive. Main avenues were packed with farmers selling their produce, merchants, horse-drawn delivery carts, and messengers. The quintessential man of affairs was Benjamin Franklin, who found much in city life to engage his interests: church vestries, militia troops, celebrations, and parades.

Jefferson, though, believed that cities also had a dark side. To him, they represented centralized power at its most concentrated level and as such were a breeding ground for abuses of natural rights. Jefferson was no stranger to the city. He championed continental architecture and city planning, and his personal library of European architectural works was at the time considered the greatest collection of its kind in America.[27] At the same time, he viewed cities as aristocratic strongholds that were "pestilential to the morals, the health and the liberties of man."[28] Natural rights were at risk in cities, where crowded conditions made it easy for a ruler to control the citizenry. Rural land, on the other hand, was much harder to police and thus was more conducive to democracy.

Ralph Waldo Emerson, Henry David Thoreau, William Jennings Bryant, and other nineteenth-century intellectuals transformed Jefferson's agrarian ideal into an outright idealization of nature. Emerson's transcendental philosophy was at once individualistic and anti-urban: a person communes with God only through contact with pristine nature. "Whilst we want cities as the centers where the best things are to be found," he wrote, "cities degrade us by magnifying trifles."[29] Thoreau, who isolated himself for one year at Walden Pond, remarked that the best thing about Boston were the washrooms in the train stations. Reformer and editor Horace Greeley spent much of his life trying to persuade urban Americans to move to the country. For Greeley, city life equated to madness, and he advocated that the "sickly thousands" clustered there be "called forth into the green fields and the stout forests."[30] Repelled by what he termed the "poisoned tissue" of city life, Frank Lloyd Wright remarked, "to look at the cross-section of any plan of a big city is to look at something like the section of a fibrous tumor."[31]

Even city life at its best threatened to relegate citizens to a forced anonymity, to swallow up their individuality and render them rats in a maze. A family with a suburban home, on the other hand, could live as it chose, without sharing the building with the neighbors, listening to their conversations through the walls, or smelling other peoples' dinners through the windows. "You may find streets lined with walls of brick, displaying in dreary monotony, tower after tower, bay window after bay window," wrote *House Beautiful* columnist Alma Lutz in a 1919 article imploring readers to abandon their city apartments for the suburbs. "Sometimes these streets become acres. Here is a sense of prison walls, even a suggestion of striped uniforms, a loss of individuality, a herding of people together like cattle in so many stalls."[32]

Single-family dwellings promised to solve many problems associated with urban living, and the home grounds were an essential part of the equation. The development of such neighborhoods typically began with the city, through the services of either an in-house engineer or a private development company, partitioning land into rectangular blocks. The rectangular block was an outgrowth of a long urban tradition and of a land division system called the rural grid that the nation had used since the Land Ordinance of 1785.[33] Real estate developers found uniform or regular grids of streets and houses attractive for several reasons. Grids accommodated evenly graded streets, simplified the installation of utilities, and helped to unify neighborhoods by encouraging stylistically consistent facades. Street grids also represented a quick and profitable way to divide up land, facilitating the "buying, selling and improving of real estate," as a chief surveyor of New York City put it.[34] The urban grid was not without its critics, who argued that the system often ignored topography, drainage, and solar orientation; that it failed to take advantage of views; and, most of all, that is was utilitarian and boring. For all its shortcomings, supporters responded: the grid's expediency helped to make it possible for middle-class citizens to afford their own homes on a wide scale.

Once developers had laid out a new neighborhood's streets, they typically sold parcels of one to six blocks to speculators. The speculators in turn sold smaller portions to builders, carpenters, real estate developers, and private individuals, who then built homes on the lots.[35] These parties usually positioned the houses on the property according to commonly agreed-upon standards that were steadily coming into practice. Cities and suburbs were growing both rapidly and chaotically, and forward-looking developers and public officials were concerned not to duplicate the problems found in the dense urban core. In 1872, a Philadelphia engineer named P. Gerard published a scheme for regulating the placement of urban street plantings, setbacks, and utilities. Gerard was one of a newly emerging group of "municipal engineers," a position predating the profession of city planning and, like that endeavor, seeking to

Figure 1.10. Workers laying a concrete sidewalk along a residential street in a Nebraska town, 1908. Cities installed planting strips between sidewalks and streets to locate utilities and road signs, pile snow in winter, widen roads, and plant trees and grass to beautify residential neighborhoods. Solomon Butcher, photographer. Photograph used by permission of the Nebraska State Historical Society Photograph Collections, 1908, reproduction number RG2608.PH:000000-002952.

organize urban growth in a rational manner. According to John Reps, Gerard developed his ideas from "twelve years of travel and observation . . . especially in New York [City], Philadelphia, Washington, Paris, London, Liverpool, Vienna, Rome, Florence, Milan, St. Petersburg, Berlin, Hague, and Brussels." One of his reports, sounding quite familiar by today's standards, recommended that ". . . every house should have fronting the street a garden 40 feet in depth, in which a tree of the largest species should be planted, at 10 feet from the sidewalks, and in the centre line of the grounds. Between a sidewalk of 20 feet and the street should be a belt of ground in which should be planted another line of trees."[36] Gerard further advised that residential development be coordinated with the installation of sewer lines, warned of the deleterious effects of dumping ashes and trash in back yards (the "venom which inoculates itself into the system and produces terrible ravages"), and advocated higher standards of cleanliness throughout the city, beginning with private residences.

Setbacks and the practices related to them promised to address many problems of streetcar suburb design, from large neighborhoods all the way down to individual properties. With respect to public benefits, front set backs provided space along sidewalks to place utility boxes and electric and light poles, to locate fire hydrants, water meters, manholes, and trashcans, and to set hitching posts. Setbacks allowed for future street widening and made it easier for municipal workers to install and service utilities without disrupting buildings. Back and side yard setbacks allowed cities and developers to run sewer lines to properties that were otherwise difficult to reach from the street. They also helped to slow the spread of fires (many of which were caused by back yard cooking and incineration) and provided fire fighters access to all sides of a property.[37] With respect to public health, setbacks facilitated drainage, thereby reducing ponding and the dangerous mosquito-borne diseases that accompanied it.[38] With respect to civic beautification, setbacks created space for cities to plant great numbers of trees in the planting strips along roadways and created front yards which suburban homeowners filled with grass and flowering shrubbery. Such plantings helped to create a park-like feeling in trolley suburbs that extended from the homes all the way out to the roads and from block to block in every direction.

Setbacks provided at least as many private benefits as public ones. From the start, detached homes were easier to build than urban row houses. Because the latter shared walls with its neighbor, access to the sides and rear of the structure was limited, and builders often had to seek the permission of the neighbors before making major repairs. Builders had access to all sides of a detached dwelling, however, and could conduct their operations more efficiently. Again due to their shared walls, row houses often had fewer windows and less access to light and fresh air, amenities that urban reformers promoted as indispensable to personal health. Moreover, the tall structures often cast deep shade onto the street and yard below. Due to its separation from adjacent dwellings, however, a detached house potentially let more light and air into the structure and onto the grounds themselves. The detached house also helped keep neighbors at bay. "In a private residence section a uniform set-back from the street increases the attractiveness of the section and adds to the health and comfort of the inhabitants," wrote a contributor to *American City*. "It improves light and air conditions; makes possible the front lawn with trees and shade; removes the dwelling further from noise, fumes and dust of the street . . . without the establishment of a legally binding set-back line, each owner is at the mercy of his neighbors."[39]

Though years away from emerging as family recreation spots, the yard space behind detached dwellings served the family in numerous, practical ways. The public services that Americans would take for granted by the late 1920s were sporadic and uneven in the decades following the advent of the trolley. Cities and private utility companies were supplying more and more citizens with water, sewerage, electricity, trash collection, and street cleaning, but for numerous reasons the process was a slow one. In the meantime, many residents staged these utilities privately in their back yards. Privies, cisterns, ash barrels, firewood, trash piles, and small kitchen gardens were often as indispensable to a city household as the dooryard was to the small country dwelling.

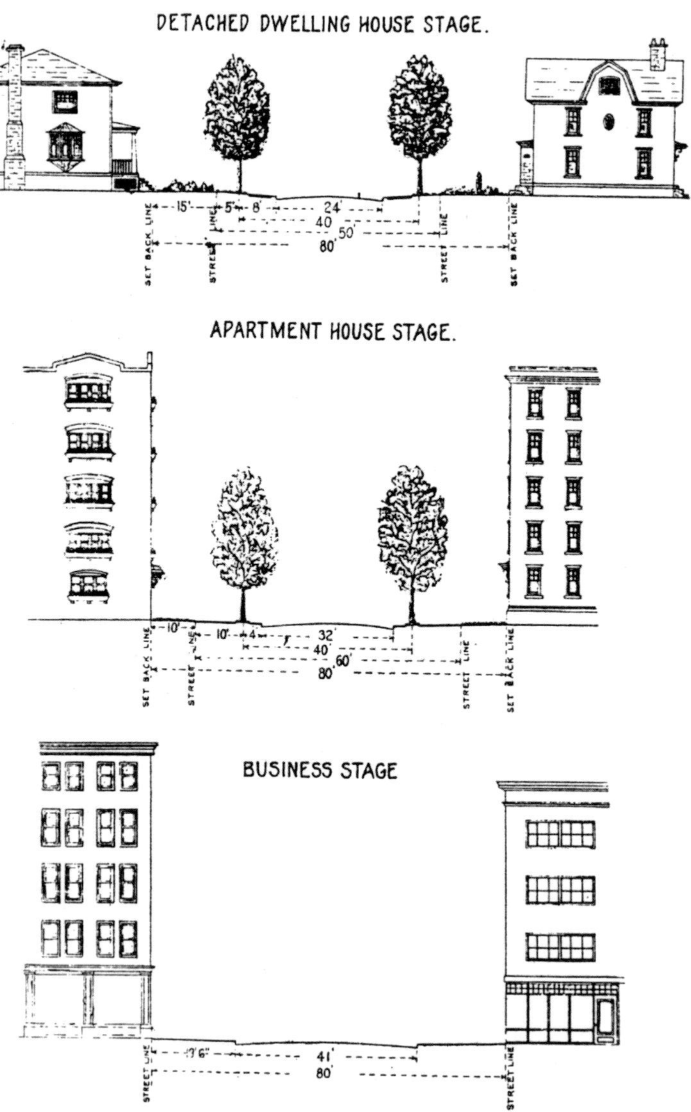

Figure 1.11. Standard and equal setbacks were a powerful tool during the early twentieth century, effectively insuring yard space around millions of new detached homes. From the *American City,* Vol. 16, No. 2 (February 1917): 146. Republished with permission of Copyright Clearance Center, Inc.

While no place for entertaining guests or spending leisure time, the city yard helped to keep the family clean, warm, bathed, and even fed.

The detached dwelling also fit well with the automobile. When Henry Ford introduced the Model T in 1908, middle-class Americans could finally afford to own their own cars. Most owners either parked their autos in the driveway next to the front yard to show them off to the neighbors or stabled them in the back yard alongside a horse. Initially a novelty item, the automobile soon began to create problems. In 1890, about sixty percent of vehicle traffic consisted of horse-drawn carriages riding on gravel, earth, or cobbled roads. The speed of transit was slow, less than ten miles per hour.[40] When Springfield, Massachusetts, resident Frank Duryea purportedly had the first recorded automobile accident in 1896, there were too few cars on the road to generate concern for public safety.[41] The rapid increase in faster-moving motorized traffic, however, not only caused more accidents, but also generated huge dust clouds that hung over heavily traveled routes. By 1910, the levels had gotten so high that the U.S. Department of Labor warned residents about the perils of lung ailments and cautioned cities to macadamize their roads as quickly as possible:

> If, as doctors say, dust means dirt, dirt means disease and disease means death, dusty roads have no place in our national economics. In the report of the Board of Health at Boston, where streets have been more or less oiled since 1906, the statistics show a steady decrease of tuberculosis and pneumonia, although the population was increased at the rate of over seven thousand per annum.[42]

The problem was understandable. In 1900, there were just 8,000 cars in America, but by 1920 the number had risen to 8,000,000.[43] By 1930, the number had tripled to more than 26,000,000.[44] Cities responded by paving their roads but often held off until they could first install underground gas, water, and sewer lines. In the meantime, grass and flowers in the front yard provided a zone to trap flying rocks, block engine noise, and collect dust before it filtered into home and lung.

Increases in traffic also contributed to the proliferation of sidewalk planting strips, places cities already used to locate utility poles, traffic signs, and fire hydrants. As more drivers took to the road, sidewalks became riskier. At the least a car might splash a pedestrian or frighten a horse. Worse, a vehicle could veer onto the sidewalk or strike someone who wandered too close to the curb; especially vulnerable were children, who, owing to the utilitarian nature of most home grounds, had few places to play but on the sidewalk. The planting strip, sitting between the sidewalk and road and oft times called a parkway, addressed all of these problems and more. It separated the street from the sidewalk, provided a transition zone for driveways to drop down to road level, and in colder climates provided a place for tractors to pile snow cleared from the street. One of the biggest effects, however, was visual: it provided earth for cities to plant millions of trees along residential streets. The resulting combination of street trees and grassy front yards would contribute significantly to the visual character of American neighborhoods nationwide by the 1920s.

Setbacks and the practices related to them were slow to emerge in residential neighborhoods. A walk today through urban and suburban neighborhoods built before the 1920s will usually reveal significant variations in house types and lot placement. Paul Groth and Marta Gutman investigated the 1890s blue-collar area of West Oakland, California, and found some homes within five feet of the street, others set well back on the lot, and some sitting nearly shoulder to shoulder, with little evidence of uniform standards.[45] Most cities initially left setback decisions up to private developers, but gradually they began to assume responsibility for them through the vehicles of municipal codes and ordinances. In response to the maladies accompanying nineteenth-century urban growth, new professions dedicated to the public welfare began to emerge, including sanitarians, municipal lawyers, landscape architects, and municipal engineers.[46] Each profession addressed various aspects of city development, such as transportation and communications, water quality, sewage disposal, trash collection, park design, street tree plantings, easements and rights of way, civic beautification, and other issues affecting public welfare.

One of the new professions was city planning. The job of planner appeared around the City Beautiful movement in the late 1890s, a campaign dedicated to bringing order, beauty, and rational growth to American cities. Spurred by the deteriorating condition of many cities, the United States Congress authorized investigations into the causes of urban poverty. American architects studied European solutions to city layout, such as the English comprehensive plan and German concepts of land planning. At professional gatherings, such as the First National Conference on City Planning in 1909, participants examined methods for alleviating crowding by distributing the rising middle class to the fringes of cities.[47] Urban reformers such as Frederick Law Olmsted, Daniel Burnham, and Harvard professor Charles Mulford Robinson promoted good-quality homes and neighborhoods as the foundation for urban fitness. "The most important features of city planning are not the public buildings, not the railroad approaches, not even the parks and playgrounds," wrote Mulford. "They are the locations of the streets, the establishments of block lines, the subdivision of property into lots, the regulations of buildings, and the housing of the people."[48] The American Institute of Planners, formed in 1918 to promote a higher quality of life, advocated the formation of standards guaranteeing the orderly expansion of American cities.[49]

One of the tools cities used to enforce setbacks and the development guidelines related to it was the practice of zoning. Though employed on a voluntary basis for years by private developers, one of the first examples of public zoning appeared in Los Angeles in 1908. City officials, alarmed at the spread of Chinese laundries, passed laws banishing such businesses to industrial areas. Los Angeles (like most American cities) was growing rapidly, and soon it expanded the laundry laws to govern the development of nearly all spheres of city life, including housing, commerce, recreation, and transportation. During the years 1908 to 1925, Los Angeles established many of the legal precedents for single-family home zoning, citywide land use zoning, and subdivision regulations.[50] Zoning laws not only separated the city into residential, commercial, public and industrial areas, but also helped to regulate the width of streets, the locations of trolley lines, and the flow of traffic. With respect to residential development, they codified into law a system of setbacks and easements similar to those proposed by P. Gerard and his colleagues a generation earlier. As has often been the case in American history, cities throughout the nation followed the Los Angeles example closely, and, by 1930, more than three-fifths of America's population lived in regions subject to some sort of zoning ordinances.

By the turn of the twentieth century, architects, engineers, landscape architects, developers, and city planners were well on their way to hammering out the general outlines of the modern American yard, and habitability was at the forefront of nearly all the measures they proposed. Yard space helped to reduce densities, provided space for public utilities and street trees, helped to slow the spread of fires, facilitated home construction and repair, helped to provide access to fresh air and sunshine, and afforded space for the day-to-day needs of the household. The onset of a powerful civic improvement campaign would shape the home grounds—particularly the front yard—even further, transforming it from a passive byproduct of house siting practices to a highly regarded object of public beauty.

Chapter Two: The Front Yard Beautiful

Just as there are many ways developers can site houses on their lots, there are many ways homeowners can design their front yards. They can enclose them behind walls, fences, or hedges and use the space for outdoor living, as residents of southern Italy, Spain, Greece, and coastal California have done. They can plant trees, shrubs, herbs, and flowers in the style of English cottage gardens, with small lawns weaving between curvaceous, overgrown planting beds, and hedges along the sidewalk. They can plant corn, tomatoes, lettuce, and string beans, if not for the public outcry and possible violation of public statutes. They can pour concrete from house to sidewalk, in the style of urban row homes and working-class neighborhoods in Albany and San Leandro, California. Each of these solutions and others can be found among the aggregate of American front yards. Yet, one style, in which residents cover the front facades of their homes with flowering bushes and let grass flow out to the sidewalk, has taken hold so firmly that it is difficult to find alternatives. When J. B. Jackson remarked in 1951 that, "all front yards in America are much the same. . . ," one could travel to almost any American town or suburb and see house after house set neatly back from the street, with flowering bushes climbing the front walls between the window, stately evergreens framing the entries, and lawns flowing unobstructed out to the street.[1] This style—called lawn and foundation planting—took hold during the civic beautification era at the turn of the twentieth century, and, in combination with street trees and grass that cities often planted along roadways, it created a green, park-like environment that unified new American suburbs. Due to its street-side orientation, the style also helped to solidify the growing division of the American home grounds into a publicly decorated front yard and privately oriented back yard. As a solution to front yard design it was simple and straightforward, but the reasons behind it were complex.

Large-scale forces, such as real estate practices, public health, urban crowding, municipal services, zoning, and transportation, had all shaped the rough skeleton of middle-class home grounds. In the public mind, however, front yards provided a way to fill cities with natural beauty, and that quickly became their popularly embraced purpose. The notion of Americans welcoming nature into their cities was paradoxical. Though eulogized in the writings of Emerson and Thoreau, nature had not always been benevolent. Since the New World landing of the Virginians in Jamestown in 1607, vast numbers of settlers had been killed off by severe winters and strange viruses, had suffered rough terrain and poor farmlands, were attacked by wolves, bears, and indigenous tribes, and had seen their animals perish from exposure or the inability to digest native feeds. Many newcomers from Europe died within a few years of reaching New World shores, and most of those who survived led difficult lives. The ideals of the Transcendentalists notwithstanding, the early American experience of nature was not always uplifting.

As Americans settled into their new surroundings, they steadily domesticated the land, clearing fields to create farmland, felling trees to build houses, barns, and fences, damming creeks and rivers to build mills, and laying roads between communities. The once primitive farm home slowly evolved into a romantic dwelling, protected from the wind and warmed by the hearth, grazed by gentle cattle and sheep, and welcoming friends and neighbors who passed by. While by no means without teeth, nature was no longer the fierce beast that greeted early immigrants. This idyllic vision, however, was nowhere to be found in cities, where meadows, trees, and brooks gave way to brick, stone, gravel, and macadam. As urban conditions deteriorated, reformers and sanitarians campaigned for more parks, greenbelts, clean rivers, street trees, and beautiful private gardens. Urban greenery promised to clean the air and slow the spread of germs. It provided parks for workers to rest and relax on Sundays and created spots of beauty amid the bleak, urban landscape. The call was not limited to big industrial cities. In what historians term the "Village Improvement Movement," nineteenth-century American townsfolk marshaled efforts to cleanse their surroundings of the filth wreaked by unrestrained industrial growth. Citizen groups united to clean mill and factory grounds, tear down dilapidated barns and fences, and haul off piles of abandoned farm equipment—the traces of a declining agricultural era—that lay along roadsides. Too often when one arrived at a village, he or she witnessed "unpainted buildings, bumpy railroad crossings, barren debris-strewn vacant lots . . . rusting tools under an apple tree. . . ." Worst of all were remnants of agricultural life—hog wallows, roadside manure piles, and "chickens scratching around their stilted legs."[2]

One of the earliest communities to lead the cause was Stockbridge, Massachusetts. In 1853, the town's newly formed Laurel Hill Association converted an abandoned hill into a public park and planted hundreds of trees along city streets. The association's efforts continued for twenty years and turned Stockbridge into a model New England community. In contrast to the wide boulevards, fountains, and monuments common to big city beautification efforts, the association focused on "coziness, neatness, simplicity."[3] By 1870, there were 200 village improvement societies in New England alone, and their numbers were growing. The goals were similar: the planting of trees and flowers around public buildings and factories, the installation of street lights, better public water supplies, well-maintained public walkways, and beautiful front yards. Arbor Day, proclaimed by Nebraskans in 1874, was a direct outgrowth of the Village Improvement Movement, and it launched thousands of tree plantings along residential and commercial streets nationwide for the next century.

The cause to beautify America embodied a widespread belief that urban problems might disappear if citizens could only make their cities more attractive. A principle force behind this movement was Chicago architect Daniel Burnham, the chief designer

Figure 2.1. Chicago schoolgirls planting a tree on school grounds on Arbor Day in 1915. Created in Nebraska in 1874, Arbor Day forged the way for millions of street tree plantings throughout the United States. Photographer unknown. Photograph used by permission of the Chicago Historical Society, Chicago *Daily News* negatives collection, 1915 number DN-0064349.

of the Colombian World's Fair of 1893. In collaboration with Frederick Law Olmsted and several local and East Coast architects, Burnham turned the dreary, swampy meadows of Chicago's South Side into a stunning fairground, with grand, neo-classical buildings, lagoons, and parks. Midway through construction, he decided to paint the entire exhibition white—in a quintessential expression of beautification—as a visual antidote to the dirt, smoke, and soot of the surrounding city.[4] In 1909, Burnham, in collaboration with his assistant Edward H. Bennett, produced *The Plan for Chicago*, one of the first examples of a comprehensive planning document to appear in America. Burnham and Bennett's plan included greenbelts to restrain growth and to add natural beauty in a city better known for its stockyards and tenements. Broad, tree-lined boulevards culminated in vistas of civic monuments and important buildings, and a chain of parks dotted the city.

The Columbian Exposition marked the beginning of the widely influential City Beautiful movement, sparking improvement campaigns nationwide for the next three decades and, in many respects, to this day.[5] In a similar fashion to village improvement societies, cities launched campaigns to clean and decorate their surroundings, and anything within the public view was fair game: road signs, flag and light poles, benches, vacant lots, river banks, back alleys, ravines, factories, sidewalk hot-dog stands, and millions of homes and yards. The National Cash Register Company was one of a number of businesses that sponsored garden contests for it employees. The company's president, John H. Patterson, hired Fredrick Law Olmsted's son John to beautify the company headquarters and to design a model yard around a small home after which company workers could pattern their own lots. Patterson offered cash rewards to workers who participated, and soon the neighborhood surrounding the factory (where many of the workers lived) began to look like a park.[6] Beautification was not for looks alone; it could also increase a company's profit margin. "When a passerby sees that an industry at least is trying to solve some of its problems he will automatically buy the product or tell what he saw to someone else," wrote Alexander Barker, a champion of beautification. "Would the average person eat pickles if he knew they were bottled near coalmines, steel mills or slaughter houses? If the pickle factory was located in a rural area and surrounded by beautiful landscaping, would not the pickle taste better?"[7] From an economic point of view, many business owners hailed beautification as good for a community's long-term growth. The railroad, trolley, and automobile were giving Americans unprecedented mobility, and it was in a city's interest to attract new residents of the highest possible repute. *House Beautiful* writer Russell told her readers:

> Each automobilist may be a potential citizen. If the things that meet his eye in the center of your town are uncared for commons, unattractive stores and untidy streets, be sure he will never chose to live there. If, on the other hand, he sees homes surrounded by green lawns, shrubs around a drinking fountain, avenues of well-cared for trees, and a general effect of 'Spotless Town,' he may be on your tax list before the year is out. It's a business proposition.[8]

Most civic cleanup campaigns relied heavily on voluntary compliance, as few cities were equipped to conduct such programs. In 1919, the Woodstock Improvement Society in New England funded its clean-up campaign through private subscriptions, at the rate of one dollar per year. The town used the funds to install a new sewer system and planted weedy, junk-filled vacant lots with grass and trees in hopes citizens would do the same in their own yards. "The Society hoped that these tiny public gardens, and other semi-public places which were treated in the same way, would stimulate residents to keep their own lawns and dooryards in better condition. This hope has been realized," remarked *House Beautiful* writer J. L. Dana.[9] The society placed rubbish cans—painted red and black in the town's colors—on street corners throughout the downtown. Next, they tackled the littered banks of the river. "Our little river was long the handy and natural receptacle for all kinds of rubbish and was anything but an object of pride," wrote the organizers. "Through the Society's efforts its banks have been cleared, in some cases by abutting property owners, and it is now almost as fresh and delightful as a mountain stream."[10] The organizers also used subscription money to buy land on the outskirts of town for a public dump, giving residents an alternative to dumping trash in their back yards.

Ladies' garden clubs emerged during this era as front-line warriors in the beautification effort. Garden clubs grew out of a long-established division of labor husbands and wives had worked out around the house, with men performing the heavier tasks, such as plowing the fields, felling trees, and building fences, barns, sheds, and even the dwelling itself, while the wives tended the home, raised the children, and planted the garden. In 1869, social and domestic activist Catherine Beecher clarified these roles in her book, *The American Woman's Home,* and designated garden care as the clear domain of the wife. "The family state, then, is the aptest earthly illustration of the heavenly kingdom, and in it woman is its chief minister." It was a man's destiny, she believed, "to till the earth, dig the mines, toil in the foundries . . . and all the heavy work which, most of the day, excludes him from the comforts of home."[11] Beecher believed

Figure 2.2. Boy Scouts cleaning up an alley in Chicago, in 1915, in a beautification campaign led by a city alderman. Civic leaders encouraged citizens to rid their back yards of combustible materials, haul away trash, tear down dilapidated fences, and plant trees and flowers. Photographer unknown. Photograph used by permission of the Chicago Historical Society, Chicago *Daily News* negatives collection, 1915, number DN-006452.

that industrialization was defining these responsibilities even more tightly. In agricultural societies, husbands and wives at least worked in close proximity to maintain the household. In industrial settings, however, husbands often worked long days in factories, offices, and markets, leaving the wives that much more in charge of households, including the grounds on which they sat.

In 1843, a young Delaware housewife named Kate—in what might have been one of the earliest garden club meetings—assembled a group of women at her home to discuss botany. "The ladies of Wilmington have formed a botanical society of which Lydia and I are members . . . . Our object is to make ourselves better acquainted with Botany, we have started meeting the first Saturday in every month . . ."[12] The ladies of Wilmington were likely the owners of expensive country estates, who had the leisure to study botany, who could afford expensive ornamental plants, and who had ample grounds in which to grow them. Though never formally constituted, the Wilmington Botanical Society was a precursor to the modern garden club, the first of which was purportedly founded by Cambridge, Massachusetts, housewife Mrs. John Hayes, who, on January 20, 1889, invited twenty women to drink tea and exchange advice on growing house plants.[13] Garden clubs often embraced ideals that combined gardens and civic improvement, and soon they emerged as warriors in the ongoing beautification war, the "Municipal Housekeepers," as Mrs. Edwin F. Moulton put it in 1913. "A first class housekeeper must be provident in those things that promote health, comfort and welfare of her family," wrote Moulton. "Every city, no matter as to size, should do as much."[14] Usually composed of the wives of affluent businessmen, the clubs eventually expanded their interests to include roadside wildflower plantings, horticultural therapy in hospitals, slum clean-ups, anti-billboard campaigns, and highway litter removal programs. With her husband busy at the office every day, it was a wife's duty to step forward and wipe out ugliness. Her purpose went beyond decoration; the very moral fiber of society was at stake, said Harlean James of the Baltimore Women's Civic League, and gardens offered redemption:

> Gardens, it has been found, will make juvenile offenders into responsible citizens, gardens will give saloon habitués something better to do; gardens will unite the family in at least one interest . . . social and civic workers are only beginning to realize that gardens will automatically prevent many of the evils they labor through an elaborate machinery of juvenile and police courts to correct.[15]

While most civic beautification campaigns initially addressed the public landscape, it was not long before the movement reached the home garden. In 1917, the city of Davenport, Iowa, earned the honor of "the city with the cleanest alleys," after four years of publicly sponsored garden contests. Residential alleys served a function closely related to that of back yards, channeling the flow of trash, water, coal, firewood, ice, and other deliveries in and out of the house. It made sense that if one should be beautified so should the other, and one out of five Davenport households entered garden contests that year. "Extraordinary steps were taken to keep the yards and alleys clean and to plant good vegetable gardens. Hundreds of homes which have not been able to lay special claim to beautiful surroundings have blossomed out each year in backgrounds which are making city life more attractive," wrote O. R. Geyer in *American City*, a journal dedicated to improving the nation's metropolitan areas.[16]

In the spring of 1915, the city of Boston proclaimed a cleanup week and singled out the home and yard for special attention. Monday was "Fire Prevention Day," with homeowners ridding their properties of oily rags, old newspapers, wood scraps, and other combustible materials. Tuesday was "Back-Yard Day," when homeowners tossed out junk and garbage piled behind their homes. Wednesday was "Front Yard Day," wherein homeowners mowed their lawns, trimmed the shrubbery, and tore down dilapidated fences. Thursday was "Paint Day," in which the house facade received a facelift. Friday was "Fly and Dandelion Day," in which residents wheeled their garbage cans out of view and weeded their lawns. Encouraging participation by the whole family, the city designated Saturday as "Children's Day." "Men and women will work better if they can look out at blooming flowers and green shrubs. In some factories the men spend part of their noon hour making garden plots, and keen rivalry is felt among them," remarked *House Beautiful* writer Elizabeth Russell of the campaign.[17]

Department stores in Columbus, Ohio, promoted home beautification by displaying window box models of neglected yards with broken down fences, piles of trash, and children playing with matches. One model was "a horrible example of a back yard, and typical of hundreds actually in existence all over the country," admonished the Columbus fire marshal.[18] The city of Pittsburgh, Pennsylvania, displayed scale models and before-and-after photos of newly beautified homes and gardens to inspire the public. "The lesson . . . is obvious," explained an *American City* writer. "One picture shows the house neglected and the grounds littered with all manner of rubbish. The other picture shows the same house and grounds after the owner had put them in order and given them an artistic touch."[19]

While clean and beautiful home grounds represented a pinnacle of beautification, many cities overlooked back yards,

Figure 2.3. A residential street in Loveland, Colorado, ca. 1900-1910. The city had not yet paved the street, possibly waiting first to install underground water and sewer lines. Grass covered the front yards, but foundation plantings would not become popular for another decade. L. C. McClure, photographer. Used by permission of the Denver Public Library, Western History/Genealogy Department, call number MCC-353.

spaces that were largely private and hidden from the street. The front yard, however, stood squarely in the public view, and as such emerged as a primary target for improvement. In 1909, a small suburb on the outskirts of Birmingham, Alabama, launched a sustained campaign to beautify front yards. The town's mayor, George B. Ward, believed that, if a few homeowners could be persuaded to plant their properties, the rest of the city might follow. Ward was an enthusiastic supporter of the City Beautiful movement, as *House and Garden* writer S. Mays Ball explained:

> Honorable George B. Ward, a gentleman of birth, breeding and culture, a lover of the beautiful has, among other good things, inaugurated during his most successful administration, what he tersely calls 'The City

> Beautiful' idea, which in his case really means particularly the 'Suburbs Beautiful, although he has extended his idea to include the residences, factories, mills, business houses, etc., through his endeavor to get business men to beautify as much as possible by use of evergreens, ivy, etc., all shops and buildings—in and out of the city proper.[20]

Claiming that residential sidewalks were the "index of the people inside," Ward urged residents to plant trees, flowers, and lawns right up to the street. Citizens should remove old trees, he advised, pull weeds, conceal their sheds behind rambling stands of sweet peas and hollyhocks, and fill their window boxes with geraniums. The town gave out forty-four prizes, including awards for the best-looking small lots, the best large lots, the best window boxes, and the best gardens of rented homes. When Ward advised homeowners to "pull down your fence. The city will haul it away and keep off the cows," he voiced a concern shared by many Americans about the appropriateness of fences in newly emerging suburbs.[21] Fences recalled a pre-Civil War era in which farmers allowed their animals to graze freely, and each property owner was responsible for fencing his or her land to keep the animals out.[22] While central to the welfare of earlier American villages, free grazing also created problems. Animals broke through fences to get to crops, left piles of manure everywhere, and when injured or dying were often abandoned by their owners in fields and along roadsides.[23] As early as the 1820s, towns began passing restrictions against free grazing, as Marion Nicholl Rawson recounted:

> [In 1824] a New York State village put its foot down and ordered that 'no neat cattle, horsers, shepps, swine, or geese' should longer run at large. Then came a noticeable shrinkage in the udders of the village bossies and the law was amended to allow milch cows to pasture on the village green and byways, from the first of May until November 15. Geese were abolished from the village streets by a fine of twelve and one-half cents an hour for their unguarded promenades. In time, the pound keeper with his open air stone jail attended to the wandring dobbins, and only dogs and cats and hens were given the freedom of the town.[24]

By the end of the Civil War, grazing was becoming a specialized activity less critical to the immediate needs of the community. As a result, most towns had banned free-roaming animals. Moreover, improvements in fence technology, especially the invention of barbed wire in 1874, enabled ranchers and farmers to enclose pastures and grazing land far more cheaply than with wood or stone. In response, many citizens began opening up their home grounds and promoting the belief that fences were old-fashioned and selfish. "Fences are often the most unsightly and offensive objects in our country seat," wrote Andrew Jackson Downing. "The close proximity of fences to the house gives the whole place a mean and confined character."[25] Part of the problem stemmed from appearance. A good fence, one with a solid frame and high quality boards, not only improved a property, but expressed the pride of land ownership. As they became less and less useful, however, most fences were simply left to decay, their frames overturning, their boards dropping out, their posts rotting, their paint peeling. Even worse was the anti-social message that fences conveyed. By the turn of the twentieth century, America had firmly revealed itself as an individualistic nation, from the affirmation of natural rights in the Constitution down to the ever-increasing prominence of the single-family home and nuclear family. When it came to front yard space, however, Americans were taking a more collective view. Most newly developing suburbs were spacious enough to keep neighbors a reasonable distance from one another, lessening the need for fences in all but the densest areas. Moreover, modern zoning and development practices were dividing the American yard in half, providing back yards for private purposes and front yards that served or supported public needs. Given these factors, combined with the population shift away from rural areas and the zeal with which Americans were beautifying their cities, the ground was fertile for anti-fence sentiment to develop. In 1913, J. H. Prost, Chicago Superintendent of Parks and City Forester, contended that fences selfishly privatized space and weakened the public spirit of beautification. "Unsightly and vine-covered fences or clipped hedges planted on the property line to divide the neighbor's yard are an expression of poor and selfish taste," Prost wrote.

"Such planting destroys the continuous street effect, looks unneighborly and makes one think the owners feared their yard would be stolen."[26] German city planner Werner Hegemann, in his master plan recommendations to the city of Berkeley, California, asserted that open, unfenced lots unified the street and promoted public interests over private ones. "Much can be said in favor of the American way of having the front gardens of small lots without fences and practically forming part of the street," he wrote. "This is a rather fine expression of community spirit."[27] Landscape architect Frank Waugh agreed. "I am glad that it is neither necessary nor fashionable for all my neighbors to shut themselves and their gardens up in high brick walls," he wrote in 1930. "This is nothing more or less than a fine, free, physical expression of democracy."[28]

Unbounded by fences, homeowners were free to design their front yards according to the prevailing prescription of the time, the lawn and foundation planting style. Precedents for both the style and the sentiments behind it could be found in the romantic suburbs (also called railroad suburbs) of the mid-nineteenth century. These affluent communities, which had

Figure 2.4. A residential street in Chicago, in 1905. The houses had small lawns and revealed the beginnings of the foundation planting style that would soon sweep the nation. The dirt street was adequate for the horse-drawn cart in the photo but was unsuitable for the faster moving cars that were becoming popular. Photographer unknown. Photograph used by permission of the Chicago Historical Society, Chicago *Daily News* negatives collection, 1905, number DN-0003053.

sprung up along the rail lines in the 1820s, were generally about an hour's commute from town, far enough away to avoid the ugliness of the city but close enough to allow wealthy merchants, doctors, and lawyers to conduct business. Railroad suburbs such as Rosedale (near Toronto), Lake Forest and Riverside (near Chicago), Dearman, New York, and Llewellyn Park, New Jersey resembled neither the city nor the farm. Spacious homes sat twenty or more feet back from tree-lined roads and were surrounded by lush plantings against the house walls, drifts of flowers, and oceans of grass. Traffic was light, wildlife abounded, and picturesque scenery flowed right up to the front doors. Though these communities differed significantly from the trolley suburbs in size, cost, and street layout (many used curved roads), they contained important elements that later generations of designers and developers would apply to smaller residences. These elements included a consistent pattern of setbacks, front yards full of greenery, and open street vistas shared by all the neighbors.

One of the first and most influential romantic suburbs was Llewellyn Park in New Jersey, a 400-acre community designed in 1853 by real estate developer Llewellyn Haskell and landscape designer Alexander Jackson Davis. Llewellyn Park contained numerous innovations in suburban layout that illustrated the country's infatuation with naturalism. Haskell's and Davis's first goal was to preserve the remote site's scenery, retaining ravines, hillocks, rock outcroppings, and native trees, rather than pursuing the usual practice of clearing and leveling the land. To protect the natural surroundings, they set aside nearly sixty acres of land through which all the residents could stroll. Llewellyn Park was one of the first gated communities in the nation, freeing homeowners from the intrusion of cross traffic, noise, and parades of curious strangers. In vivid contrast to gridded communities, the roads gently wound through the hills, ravines, and stands of trees, opening up onto dramatic views of the countryside and nearby towns.

Llewellyn Park's lots were three to ten acres each, assuring low density and spacious grounds for each homeowner. Homes sat well back from the street, surrounded by trees, flowering shrubbery, and large lawns. Unlike Llewellyn Park, most American neighborhoods had emerged on a lot-by-lot basis or in small clusters, with builders positioning houses (excepting row houses) on the property any way they wanted. Davis and Haskell, however, formed the entire neighborhood in one sweep, employing a formula of setbacks and spacious yards that created an unbroken river of greenery. To insure that all residents could enjoy this scenery, Haskell and Davis forbid the erection of front yard fences. Llewellyn Park introduced perhaps the first codified open front yard—and the picturesque standards of community beauty that accompanied it—on a mass scale.[29]

Even more famous was Riverside, Illinois, a 1,600-acre community built near Chicago in 1868. Riverside enjoyed greater visibility than Llewellyn Park for several reasons: it was four times bigger, its home prices were lower and thus affordable to a broader range of residents, and it was open to through traffic. Moreover, Riverside's designer, Frederick Law Olmsted, was the nation's most celebrated landscape architect, the designer (along with architect and colleague, Calvert Vaux) of New York City's Central Park, the United States Capitol grounds, Brooklyn's Prospect Park, and communities, parks, cemeteries, and university campuses across the nation. Olmsted's first concern in Riverside was to retain the town's "charm of refined sylvan beauty and grateful umbrageousness."[30] In marked contrast to the gridded streets of nearby Chicago, Olmsted laid out Riverside's roads in broad curves echoing the Des Plaines River that flowed through the development. Olmsted favored curved roads not only for their beauty, but also because they encouraged leisurely travel, a key benefit of suburban life:

> In the highways, celerity will be of less importance than comfort and convenience of movement, and as the ordinary directness of line in town-streets, with its resultant regularity of plan would suggest eagerness to press forward, without looking to the right hand or the left, we should recommend the general adoption, in the design of your roads, or gracefully-curved lines, generous spaces, and the absence of sharp corners, the idea being to suggest and imply leisure, contemplativeness and happy tranquility." [31]

Unlike tiny Chicago properties, Riverside's lots were a half-acre or bigger (typically 100 feet x 200 feet). Like Llewellyn Park, the homes were set twenty or more feet back from the street, and residents were encouraged to plant lawns and two trees in their front yards. As planners Michael Southworth and Erin Ben-Joseph point out, Riverside's front yards were more than ornaments. They helped to shield houses from street noise, they filtered dust kicked up by carriages, and they provided a safeguard against an architect who might design an ugly home and then feature it too prominently. "We cannot judiciously attempt to control the form of the houses which men shall build," Olmsted wrote. "We can only, at most, take care that if they build very ugly and inappropriate houses, they shall not be allowed to force them disagreeably upon our attention when we desire to pass along the road upon which they stand."[32]

Riverside's streets were carefully engineered, with cobble gutters along the edges to collect runoff. In addition, the residents received sewers, running water, gas, and streetlights. Olmsted placed planting strips between the public walks and the streets to place trees and grass, to compliment front yard plantings, to separate pedestrians from carriage traffic, and to unify the landscape. Riverside may have been the first community to

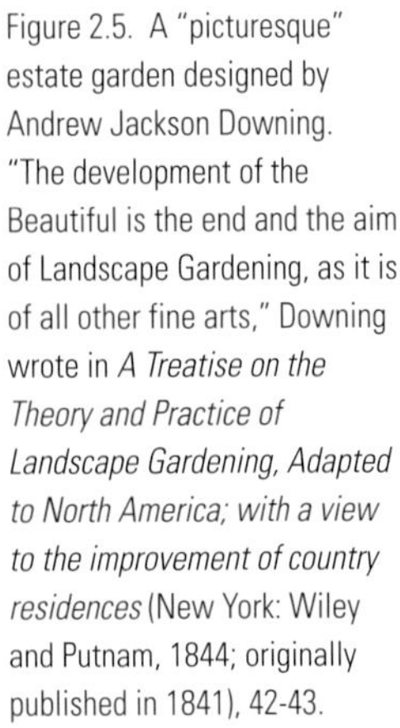

Figure 2.5. A "picturesque" estate garden designed by Andrew Jackson Downing. "The development of the Beautiful is the end and the aim of Landscape Gardening, as it is of all other fine arts," Downing wrote in *A Treatise on the Theory and Practice of Landscape Gardening, Adapted to North America; with a view to the improvement of country residences* (New York: Wiley and Putnam, 1844; originally published in 1841), 42-43.

use curbside planting strips on a large scale, setting a precedent that numerous middle-class suburbs would follow.[33] The generously sized front yards, fence restrictions, trees, and continuous flow of grass and shrubbery from house to house became key visual elements of the community. The overall effect, according to Olmsted, was "positively picturesque . . . when contrasted with the constantly repeated right angles, straight lines, and flat surfaces which characterize our large modern towns."[34]

Riverside was more than just a beautiful place in which to live. The spacious lots, the broad river, and the abundance of vegetation promised relief from urban smoke and tainted water, rest for nervous disorders, and a physical barrier to slow the spread of germs. The private garden was an essential part of this therapeutic formula, according to Olmsted, providing "health and comfort, like the beds and the baths. Yet, the frequent action of free, sun-lighted air upon the lungs for a considerable space of time is unquestionably more important than the frequent washing of skin with water or the perfection of nightly repose . . ."[35]

Olmsted and Davis notwithstanding, the most influential residential garden designer of the era was Andrew Jackson Downing. Garden historians generally regard Downing as America's first landscape architect. His 1841 book, *A Treatise on the Theory and Practice of Landscape Gardening, Adapted to North America; with a view to the improvement of country residences*, had an enormous influence on the design of the romantic suburbs, the street car suburbs of the 1880s, and even the automobile suburbs that appeared after World War II.[36] It is not an exaggeration to suggest that Downing has had more effect on the home grounds, especially the front yard, than any other single designer.[37]

Downing's principal area of interest was the country property, but his designs contained few agricultural references. Like Olmsted, Davis, and a later landscape designer named Frank Jessup Scott, Downing often planned entire neighborhoods, from the street layouts, parks, and commons all the way to the positioning of homes on their lots and the plantings surrounding them. His vision was one of rustic lanes sheltered by oaks and willows, stylish estates emerging from a sea of grass, trees, and flowers, and genteel residents politely conversing, tending their flowers, and mowing their lawns. Dearman, New York, was one such community. The homes sat along broad streets on lots four times the width of typical New York City properties. Each house had a large private garden, and Downing placed a park at the middle of the town center for all residents to enjoy. He believed that neighborhoods such as Dearman elevated people to a higher level of civility. "So long as men are forced to dwell in log huts and follow the hunter's life, we must not be surprised at lynch laws and the use of the bowie knife," Downing remarked. "But, when smiling lawns and tasteful cottages begin to embellish a country, we know that order and culture are established."[38]

Downing embraced design formulas that borrowed heavily from the English landscape garden style he studied as a young man. The landscape garden, a product of the Romantic movement in the seventeenth and eighteenth centuries, typically included large grassy parklands, grazing animals, groves of trees, gooseneck streams, and lagoons with classical temples perched along the shores. English garden architect Capability Brown (1716–1783; so named because he advised his clients of the "capabilities" of their land) once engineered a river of such beauty that he declared, "Alas! The Thames will never forgive me!"[39] Landscape designer Humphrey Repton prepared "Redbooks" for his clients depicting before and after views of their properties, with hedge-row enclosed fields replaced by curvaceous meadows, lakes turned into serpentine rivers, and rows of trees replaced by informal groves.[40] American landscape architect Fletcher Steele aptly described the style's gentle pastoral qualities as "tamed scenery." [41]

Downing worked on few projects of such vast scale, but applied many British garden design principles to his designs. "In the orchard, we hope to gratify the palate; in the flower garden, the eye and the smell, but in the Landscape Garden we appeal to that sense of the Beautiful and the Perfect, which is one of the highest attributes of our nature," he wrote. The suburban garden was like a painting to be viewed from the house, or on strolls or rides, rather than a place to grow food, raise animals, hold social events, or engage in gardening for its own sake. Suburban homes offered refined country living with all the conveniences of the city, and should not be constrained by livelihood or other practicalities. "The development of the Beautiful is the end and the aim of Landscape Gardening, as it is of all other fine arts," Downing explained. "The ancients sought to attain this by a studied and elegant regularity of design in their gardens; the moderns, by the creation or improvement of grounds which, though of limited extent, exhibit a highly graceful or picturesque epitome of natural beauty."[42] Downing's words presupposed a distinction between the *activity* of flower gardening, in which the work itself is the source of satisfaction, and the *result* of flower gardening, which is pleasant scenery. This distinction would become pivotal to the middle-class yards that emerged in the 1880s and beyond, in which the owners found themselves choosing between growing plants for their beauty of for love of working the soil.

Downing would not live long enough to see most of his ideals take form. He died at age thirty-seven, at the peak of his career, in a steamboat accident. However, his books (*A Treatise on the Theory and Practice of Landscape Gardening* and *The Architecture Of Country Houses)* had a great influence on future generations. They were among the first (and few) publications of the era that systematically laid out the requirements for managing suburban estates. Perhaps more importantly, the ideas therein proved adaptable to the smaller suburban properties to emerge a generation later, especially with respect to front yards. Downing knew that average Americans would never dwell on the grand scale that he witnessed in England. At the same time, he believed that democracy would allow Americans to own homes and gardens in numbers greater than English citizens could ever match:

> In the United States, it is highly improbable that we shall ever witness such splendid examples of landscape gardens as those abroad, to which we have alluded. Here the rights of man are held to be equal; and if there are no enormous parks and no class of men whose wealth is hereditary, there is, at least . . . the almost entire absence of a very poor class in the country; while we have, on the other hand, a large class of independent landowners, who are able to assemble around them, not only the useful and convenient, but the agreeable and beautiful, in country life.[43]

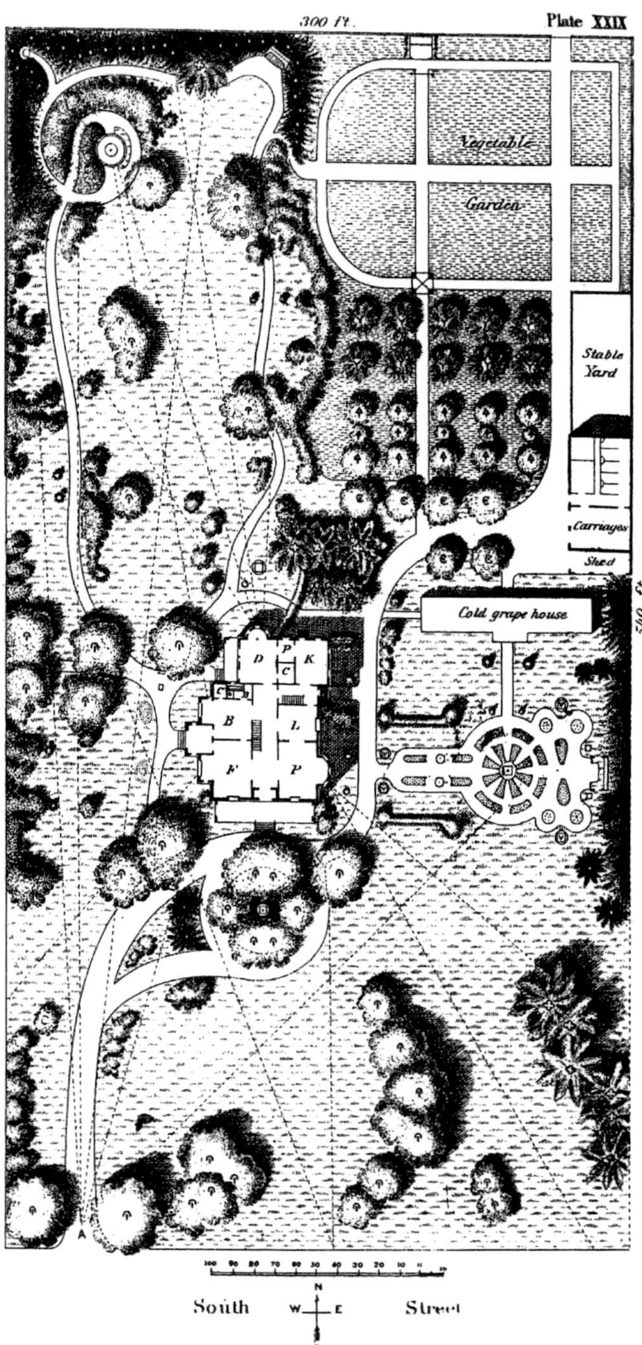

Figure 2.6. A large suburban property, ca. 1870, designed in the picturesque style by Frank Jessup Scott, a former apprentice of Andrew Jackson Downing. From Scott's *The Art Of Beautifying The Home Grounds* (New York: D. Appleton and Company, 1870), Plate 29.

If at first the romantic suburbs were only to be had by the wealthy, within seventy-five years, just as Downing had predicted, almost half of all Americans would own their own home and yard. The stage was thus set for Downing's ideas to emerge on a national scale, and lawns and foundation plantings were poised to do the job. While its roots went back for several decades, the style began to achieve popular recognition in the 1870s as a compliment to Victorian architecture. Victorian homes sat high off the ground to protect the dwelling from floods and to make room for a new household appliance, the central furnace.[44] A home built high above ground level might expose as much as six feet of stone or brick foundation that beckoned to be concealed behind a bevy of plants, as a young housewife might learn by reading the *Ladies Home Journal:*

> . . . [Elizabeth] found out about foundation planting. Simultaneously she found out about bridal wreath, Spiraea Van Houttei. Soon the house was set afloat in a billowing sea of bridal wreath. Not the slightest contact with the earth was visible . . .45

Flowering bushes not only adorned the house, but they helped to soften the sharp ground-to-wall angle that had long plagued garden designers. Restraint was nonetheless called for, warned landscape designer Frank Jessup Scott, for if bushes were too tall, the owner risked making the home "dark and damp enough to induce consumption and other diseases; and physicians have been obliged to protest against their injurious effects on the health of the inmates."[46] Scott continued:

> Because they sat prominently in the public view, foundation plantings and open lawns served the ends of civic improvement perfectly.
>
> A house that is nested in shrubs which seem to spring out of its nooks and corners with something of the freedom that characterizes similar vegetation springing naturally along stone walls and fences, seems to express the mutual recognition and dependence of nature and art . . .[47]

The Victorian style ran its course in a few decades, but by then America was awash in thousands of new middle-class suburbs

Figure 2.7. A subdivision in Dundalk, Maryland, ca. 1915-1920. The tracts, "bare as billiard balls" as garden journals sometimes put it, created a large market for grass and flowering plants. Photographer unknown. Photograph used by permission of the Frances Loeb Library, Harvard University Graduate School of Design, reproduction number 118341.

with barren front yards. Unlike Haskell and Davis at Llewellyn Park, economy-minded developers of trolley suburbs had cut down trees, leveled hillocks, filled in creeks and ravines, and dynamited rock outcroppings, effectively clearing the land of many traces of its past. The abundance of new homes sitting on block after block of gridded streets only heightened the bleakness. Owners who buried their new homes behind billowing seas of shrubbery, however, might not only beautify their properties, but lend them an air of permanence and history. "Who does not remember in childhood, certain houses that were extravagantly admired, and others that were cordially detested?" wrote *House and Garden* writer Grace Tabor. "Were not the former 'snugly' in the midst of flowers, with Missouri currant—oh! delectable scent of paradise and fairyland commingled—hovering near? And were the others—the hated places—not devoid of these things absolutely? Surely they were—as bare as a billiard ball of any kind of planting,"[48] Horticultural nurseries, which historically had offered few species other than fruit trees, raced to keep up with the demand for flowering plants. "One year a bare foundation—the next this charming effect. At the front steps are Hicks

Boxwood and Dwarf Japanese Cypress," advertised grower Isaac Hicks & Son, one of many nurserymen who offered foundation planting stock in house and garden magazines.[49]

At the turn of the twentieth century, America's nurseries offered little in the way of ornamentals. The industry had gotten its start selling fruit trees to farmers, many of whom were developing homesteads. In 1848, the C. M. Hovey nursery in Cambridge, Massachusetts, offered a wide assortment of fruiting species:

> . . . of pear trees, it shows 1,000 healthy and beautiful specimens growing in avenues, embracing about 400 varieties . . . . Of peaches, there are some 8,000 trees; of apples, 200 varieties, and some 30,000 trees for sale; of plums, nectarines, apricots, cherries, about equal number . . .[50]

In 1856, California nurseryman William Wolfskill's catalog listed 9,000 orange trees, 6,000 lemon and lime trees, and deciduous fruits such as quince, fig, and bananas.[51] Two pieces of federal legislation had helped to boost nursery sales. First was the Homestead Act of 1862, a law that awarded settlers 160 acres of free land, as long as the settlers lived on the land and fenced at least one quarter of it.[52] Homesteaders bought vast numbers of trees to plant windbreaks and orchards, create firewood, and generate lumber for building and fencing projects. Second was the Timber Culture Act of 1873, a law that required many homesteaders to plant forty or more acres in trees spaced no more than twelve feet apart. Congress passed the act out of fear that homesteaders would deplete the nation's supply of trees. Taken literally, the act translated to the astonishing requirement of about 7,500 trees per homestead. Congress was unable to enforce the bill and eventually overturned it. In the interim, however, nursery sellers traveled from county to county selling fruit, nut, and timber trees out of the backs of wagons. Pear trees sold for about thirty-five cents and apple trees for about twenty cents. Many of these trees and their offspring—especially black walnuts—still grow around rural dooryards.[53] Isaac Hicks was one of the sellers, offering fruit trees in the Long Island area for twenty-five to fifty cents each and hauling them for ten miles for as little as a penny.[54]

American nursery inventories also included popular ornamental plants, such as chrysanthemums, lilacs, and roses. Thomas Brown found more than 1,200 rose cultivars listed by nurseries nationwide between 1850 and 1900.[55] Most buyers of such plants, however, were affluent homeowners or collectors with large gardens and servants to care for them. Grower inventories reflected this specialized demand: in 1890, ornamental plants constituted only about ten percent of American nursery stock. As middle-class homeowners beautified their front yards with flowering plants, however, the market for ornamentals swelled. "There is a strong and growing demand in Southern California for ornamental trees

Figure 2.8. The Isaac Hicks & Son Nursery of Long Island, New York, was a major supplier of ornamental plants to new middle-class homeowners. "Once a bare foundation—the next this charming effect," Hicks promised buyers. From an advertisement in *House and Garden* (May 1912): 58.

Figure 2.9. Nursery workers planting field stock in the 1930s. The market for ornamental plants grew rapidly in the twentieth century, far surpassing edible species that had once dominated. Photograph undated and unsigned. Courtesy of Evergreen Nursery, Sturgeon Bay, Wisconsin.

and shrubs," the *Los Angeles Times* reported in 1904, as people from the East Coast and Midwest began relocating to the state in huge numbers. ". . . particularly is this true of palms . . . no one is starting any considerable stock, and yet all the nursery trade knows that the demand will always be greater than the supply."[56] By the early twentieth century, about fifty percent of the plants offered by retail nurseries were ornamentals; by 1925, the number had risen to seventy-five percent. [57]

While Andrew Jackson Downing focused principally on the country estate, one of the first professionals to address middle-class properties was Frank Jessup Scott. Like many other designers of the era, Scott was heavily influenced by Downing and had even apprenticed in the latter's office. In 1870, Scott published *The Art Of Beautifying Suburban Home Grounds,* a book laying out clear, straightforward rules for designing the smaller suburban properties that were springing up on the outskirts of cities.[58] While concerned with beauty, he also advised readers on practical matters, such as selecting vegetables, choosing foundation plantings, screening service yards, and allowing lawns to flow from house to house. Scott warned readers that the demands of city life did not leave much time for vegetable gardening, raising animals, or cultivating flowers. Moreover, as David Handlin has observed, Scott recognized that most Americans could not afford to hire servants and moved so often that it was unlikely they would pass their home onto their children.[59] For these reasons, he limited the size of kitchen gardens, recommended low maintenance trees and shrubs, and covered his gardens with plenty of grass, a surface that had become easier to groom due to the recent invention of the lawn mower.

Scott believed that it was selfish for homeowners to regard their front yards as private spaces. From a visual standpoint, the house facade and front yard were equally the domain of the owner and the street, and wherever possible the garden architect should treat all the homes on a block as part of a common landscape. In *The Art Of Beautifying Suburban Home Grounds,* he proposed a design for an entire block of middle-class Ohio homes. His first step was to keep the lots small, in order to reduce loneliness and encourage companionship among wives.[60] He set each house a good distance back from the street, placed foundation plantings against the fronts and sides of the house, and added

Figure 2.10. A small subdivision in Ohio proposed by Frank Jessup Scott in 1870, with uniform setbacks, plantings around the houses, and front lawns flowing from property to property. Scott's design portended the enormously popular lawn and foundation planting style that Americans embrace to this day. Frank Jessup Scott, *The Art Of Beautifying Suburban Home Grounds* (New York: Appleton and Company, 1870), Plate 22.

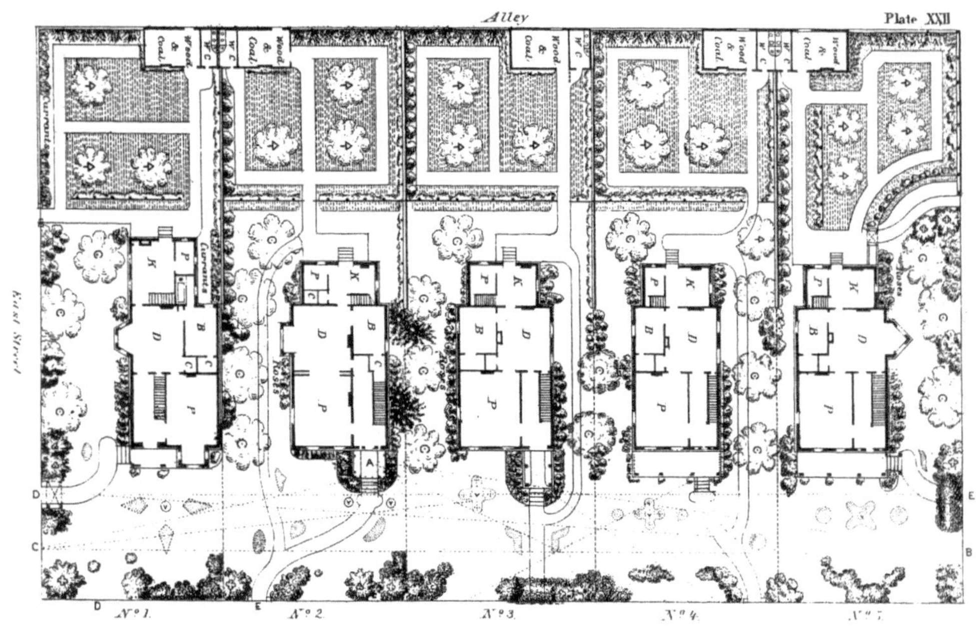

lawns that flowed from house to house and right out to the sidewalk, interrupted only by driveways, walks, and scattered shrubbery near the street. In order to keep the front yards open to view, Scott warned homeowners not to build fences. "It is unchristian to hedge from the sight of others the beauties of nature which it has been our good fortune to create or secure," he admonished.[61] This scheme, so familiar today that Americans hardly look twice at it, represented one of the earliest attempts to develop a unified middle-class neighborhood composed of detached dwellings. Fred Schroeder speculates that developers browsed copies of Scott's book, one of the only ones like it at the time, and copied the formulas for want of alternatives. Scott's father was, in fact, a prominent real estate broker in Ohio and likely provided his son with connections to developers and city building departments.[62]

Before long, most homeowners were putting lawns and foundation plantings in front of their homes. Here was a space not only perfectly suited for civic beautification, but originally conceived in large part to create spacious, healthful neighborhoods. Thus, it made sense that Americans would be willing to beautify their front yards and share them visually with their neighbors. The style became so popular that it was difficult to find a garden design book from the 1880s up until World War II (and to a large extent to this day) that did not encourage it tacitly or overtly. "We plant trees and shrubs on the front lawn, not entirely for their own sake, but primarily for the houses' sake," wrote Peter J. van Melle, in his introduction to Leonard Johnson's 1927 book, *Foundation Planting*. "There is no more perfect means of emphasizing the proportional beauty of our homes and grounds than that of architectural plant."[63] Van Melle's advice portended a growing shift in gardening books from horticulture to aesthetics. It spoke to homeowners more concerned with beautification than gardening, and nothing presented the house to the street better than stately evergreens framing the entry, flowering shrubs arching over the windows, and vines climbing the chimney.[64]

Once a family had planted shrubbery against the walls of the house, the next step was to put in a front lawn. If any one plant

Figure 2.11. Pennsylvania Avenue in Denver, Colorado, ca. 1900-1920. Tree-lined streets, foundation plantings, and lawns flowing from house to sidewalk suggested a middle-class version of Andrew Jackson Downing's "picturesque" landscape style. L. C. McClure, photographer. Photograph used by permission of the Denver Public Library, call number MCC-1933.

would come to dominate the home landscape, it was grass; no other plant even came close in popularity. Bluegrass (*Poa pratensis* or "Poa of the Meadow"), the most widely planted grass across America, originated by most accounts in ancient Greece. Meadows and pastures were an integral part of the Mediterranean economy and landscape and appeared frequently in the verses of Homer, Virgil, and other writers of antiquity. "Classical mythology unfolded in a pastoral landscape," writes Paul Shepard. "Grazing animals remove brush and lower limbs and mow the lawn beneath the trees, creating that penumbras grove in which lovers dance, the weary traveler pauses to drink, the shepherd rests and plays, the philosopher meditates, and the youths compete." The mythological figure Pan, half man, half goat, symbolized the "intimate relationship of shepherd, grazing animals, and environment."[65] The pastoral ideal in Greek mythology eventually informed the artists of the Italian Renaissance, whose masterpieces supplied the picturesque underpinnings of the English landscape schools of painting and gardening. Andrew Jackson Downing brought the landscape garden style to America largely through the influence of his English mentor, John Claudius Loudon. Grass—whether it was the grazed meadows of a Greek or Italian hillside, a bucolic pasture along the Thames River dotted with sheep and cows, or the lawns flowing from house to house in Dearman or Riverside—was an essential part of the domesticated landscape.[66] And, by the time Columbus sailed across the Atlantic Ocean in 1492, bluegrass had spread through much of northern Europe, intermixing with native American grasses, and following the path of nomadic tribes who cleared the land to farm, build dwellings, and distance themselves from the dangers of the forest. As J. B. Jackson observed:

> When a Canadian today cuts down trees in order to start a farm he says he is 'making land'. He might with equal accuracy say that he is 'making lawn', for the two words have the same origin and once had the same meaning. Our lawns are merely the civilized descendants of the Medieval pastures cleared among the trees. In the New England forest a 'lawn' is still an open space in the woods where cattle are fed.[67]

Figure 2.12. A grassy mountain meadow is a landscape type that many people believe was an ancestor to the modern lawn. For example, J. B. Jackson wrote: "Our lawns are merely the civilized descendants of the Medieval pastures cleared among the trees." From John B. Jackson, "'Ghosts' at the Front Door," *Landscape* (Autumn, 1951): 6. Photograph by the author.

Bluegrass came to North America inadvertently, probably mixed into the livestock feed early settlers brought with them. In 1620, just thirteen years after the first English settlers landed in Virginia, John Smith found grass everywhere: "James Towne is yet their chiefe seat, most of the wood destroyed, little corne there planted, but all converted into pasture and gardens; wherein doth grow all manner of herbs and roots we have in England in abundance and as good grasse can be." By 1640, Rhode Island merchants were selling twenty-three varieties of *poa*. French explorers and missionaries probably introduced *poa* to the Ohio Valley in the early 1700s. Wind carried the seeds into the surrounding land, often years before European settlers arrived there. When Daniel Boone got to Kentucky, he came upon shimmering fields of the grass, a bluish cast emanating from the blades. Boone's discovery prompted *poa*'s common name, Kentucky bluegrass.[68]

By the end of the nineteenth century, grasses of numerous varieties were to be found everywhere, and most had been brought to America from other countries. They grew wild in the fields of homesteaders. They had been long established as a cover for town commons. They flowed from house to house in the romantic suburbs, providing a simple but beautiful cover that suppressed mud and dust, unified the private lots, and created a pasture-like feel evoking the picturesque. They could be found in public parks and gardens, college campuses, cemeteries, boulevard strips, civic centers, and practically every public space set aside to grow plants. They contributed to the rising popularity of archery, badminton, tennis, bocce ball, lawn bowling, golf, polo, baseball, and football. When, in the 1930s, landscape architect Frank Waugh advised readers to plant lawns "as large and as little interrupted as circumstances will allow," it was hard to find an American gardening book that did not extol the virtues of a greensward.[69]

As a fixture in middle-class properties, however, the lawn was slower to take hold. Until the 1880s, most of the grass found around home grounds was thin, patchy, and weed-infested. Planting a lawn was difficult and maintaining it not much easier. Most lawns were more accurately mixtures of meadow grasses,

Figure 2.13 The lawn mower was invented in 1831 by Edwin Budding, an Englishman looking for a way to cut the pile off a carpet. Fifty years would pass before the invention gained widespread acceptance, but by 1994 Americans owned eighty-nine million mowers. From *House and Garden* (May 1914): 424.

Figure 2.14. Homeowner Harry F. Rhoads, of Denver, Colorado, mowing his lawn, ca. mid-1920s. Americans often faced extra yard work upon moving from small city dwellings into suburban properties. The development of the lawn mower, grass seeds, sod harvesting, and selective herbicides all amplified the task of lawn care. Harry M. Rhoads, photographer. Photograph used by permission of the Denver Public Library, call number Rh-1412.

wildflowers, and weeds. To keep lawns under control, homeowners trampled them, hacked them with hoes and scythes, and let goats and sheep chew on them. The invention of the lawn mower, however, made maintenance much easier and marked the beginning of a new attitude towards the plant. Probably as an adaptation to millenniums of grazing, grasses (unlike almost every other plant) grew from their root crowns rather than from their apical meristem (tip). Thus, their blades could be repeatedly grazed or mowed and continue to regenerate. Considering how similar turf is to a rug, the lawn mower's origins are ironic. In 1831, English inventor Edwin Budding designed a machine to cut the pile off of wool carpeting and inadvertently discovered that his invention was even better at cutting grass. Budding's machine was initially slow to take off, as its market was limited. As suburban home ownership increased, however, the mower steadily gained popularity and the mechanics improved. In 1870, Richmond, Indiana, inventor Elwood McGuire introduced a model accessible to the general population, and mowers that followed included blades mounted around cylindrical shafts, rollers to flatten the grass after cutting, and baskets to catch the clippings (features that are still found on mowers today). The rise in sales was dramatic. The 1880 census revealed nearly 300,000 Americans (one-half percent of the population) owned a mower; by 1885, the nation was building 50,000 mowers a year.[70] Advertisements assured buyers that the units were lightweight and easy to operate, and they often depicted children and housewives at the helm.[71]

If the lawn mower helped make grass accessible to the middle class, civic beautification sentiment persuaded homeowners to plant it in vast quantities. Spacious, picturesque neighborhoods were a primary goal of twentieth-century reformers, and front lawns played a key part in the formula. Owing to the widespread adoption of the lawn mower, grass could easily be kept to a height of three to four inches. Higher plants, on the other hand, could significantly clutter the street view. "This mode of planting implies visibility from the street," explained Peter J. Van Melle. "It makes for 'open lawns', which have come to characterize our suburban streets and give them a feeling of spaciousness . . . . We turn our dignified side towards the street and strive to display, on our front lawns, primarily, a fine sense of proportions."[72] Of all the amenities front yards had to offer, beauty and spaciousness spoke most directly to homeowners. Street widening, utility lines, light poles, and traffic lights were all factors in the initial rationale for front setbacks, but they were largely impersonal matters settled on long before families occupied their homes. Grass and foundation plantings, however, were a family's contribution to the unbroken funnel of green that stretched for block after block through many suburbs and cities. Fences, hedges, and tall shrubbery that broke this funnel selfishly diminished everyone's view and bespoke poorly of the owner. "A dense forest around a home," warned Frank Jessup Scott, "suggests the rudeness of pioneer life, not the refinement of culture."[73]

As civic beautification campaigns gained momentum, city governments, rotary clubs, house and garden magazines, garden clubs, and other civic-minded groups encouraged homeowners to plant grass. In 1912, Kansas City, Missouri, gave citizens generously wide street-side parcels that might otherwise have gone for median strips or road widening. The city did not require residents to plant the land with turf, but municipal planner Fred Gabelman had no doubt that residents would do so on their own:

> There is no ordinance or provision giving the city authority to sod and maintain the lawn spaces, nor requiring the property owners to sod and maintain same, but the property owners almost invariably sod and maintain these lawn spaces the same as the lawn on their own property. They do this cheerfully, willingly and as a matter of pride in keeping up their front lawns and premises.[74]

Figure 2.15 A suburb in Cincinnati, Ohio, in 1935. By the 1930s, lawns and foundation plantings were the prevailing front yard style across the nation. Carl Mydans, photographer. "Housing on Laconia Street in a suburb of Cincinnati, Ohio," December 1935. Photograph courtesy of Congress, Prints & Photographs Division, FSA-OWI Collection, reproduction number lc-usf34-000547-d.

With homes set twenty feet back from the street, with anti-fence sentiment sweeping the nation, and with families filling their front yards with grass and flowering bushes, Downing's romantic scenery had finally found a home in the small property. By the 1930s, lawns and foundation plantings had so firmly established themselves in American front yards that it was rare to see other styles. In a 1937 story about regional architecture,

Better Homes and Gardens unwittingly revealed just how pervasive the style had become. In the 1930s, houses—due to widely adopted construction practices, mass-produced materials, middle-class mobility, and nationally embraced zoning goals—were starting to look more and more alike. In order to illustrate a more creative approach to building, the author featured homes from six parts of the country, each of which was designed to reflect local climate, materials, and lifestyle. Here was the perfect opportunity to include front yards that responded to region; few things, after all, were more primary to local character than native vegetation. From the Southwest was an adobe-style house, with a paved courtyard shaded for outdoor living and relief from the heat; the front yard: lawn and foundation plantings. The Pacific Northwest house was built from wood logged from nearby forests; the front yard: lawn and foundation plantings. The Upper Midwest house was built of brick made from local clay pits; the front yard: lawn and foundation plantings. From Pennsylvania came a farmhouse made from native fieldstone; the front yard: lawn and foundation plantings. The New York state home resembled a colonial barn; the front yard: lawn and foundation plantings. The Deep South home revealed a Spanish "Monterey" style adapted to tropical heat and humidity; the front yard: lawn and foundation plantings.[75]

The *Better Homes and Gardens* article represented only six houses, but the sample was accurate. Nearly all garden design advice in books, newspapers, and magazines were now recommending shrubs against the facade of the house and lawns running to the street. The style's very pervasiveness had, according to Peter Van Melle, perhaps become its crowning achievement, standing forth as a unique American creation. "We are really developing something like a distinctly American school of suburban planting," wrote Van Melle, "which not only demonstrates love of plants and trees but emphasizing strongly their value as an adjunct to architecture."[76] The still-young nation had little in the way of a garden style it could legitimately call its own, having borrowed heavily from England and, to lesser but important extents, from Italy, Spain, and Japan, countries that had developed garden styles over centuries. Middle-class

Figure 2.16. The lawn and foundation style, as seen in this Berkeley, California, property in 2005, continues to thrive today. Photograph by the author.

Americans had yet to prove themselves to be astute horticulturists, but they had something their overseas counterparts did not: an opportunity to inhabit gardens on a mass scale unthinkable by European or Asian standards. Lawns and foundation plantings had become the exclamation mark on the public face of the home grounds, a botanical expression of American democracy and an enduring symbol of civic beautification.

Chapter Three: The Back Yard Sanctified

By 1920, almost half of all Americans lived in cities or nearby suburbs, a figure that had doubled since 1880.[1] Home ownership had risen at a correspondingly large rate; by 1925, nearly half of all Americans would own their own dwellings. While front yards had undergone several decades of beautification, back yards lagged behind, surrounded by the symbols of an older way of life. Earlier generations had filled their yards with privies, cisterns, ash barrels, and trash because they had no alternatives to these items. Now, due to the modernization of cities, public expectations were beginning to change. For years, *House Beautiful* writers commented on the situation. In 1912, M. Roberts Conover noted the irony of how Americans "adorn the frontage of our dwellings with spectacular floral arrangements, garden furniture and other formalities, while in the rear are clothesline poles, the scraggy end of a wood pile, and ill-kept next door lot or untidy line fence, and tolerated because the world does not see them!";[2] and, in 1915, Content York lamented the sorry view that middle-class Americans suffered out their kitchen windows, replete with the dreary artifacts of the past, "the ash barrel, the garbage bucket, and worse. Even when these things had been razed, the barren spot was dismal with associations."[3] In 1922, Esther Johnson repined how many back yards revealed little more than an "amply filled clothesline."[4]

Tarkington Barker, the author of *Yard and Garden: A Book of Practical Information for the Amateur Gardener in City, Town or Suburb,* deplored the "littered back yard" common to most cities, suggesting that citizens of good standing ". . . avail themselves of

Figure 3.1. An alley in Claymont, Delaware, ca. 1920s. Utilitarian back yards—with laundry lines, trash, dilapidated fences, and minimal plantings—abutted the unpaved roadway. Photographer unknown. Photograph used by permission of the Frances Loeb Library, Harvard University Graduate School of Design, reproduction number 117965.

the opportunity to add so much enjoyment for themselves and for others by improving the grounds at their disposal, instead of making it a place for the deposit of old barrels, boxes, tin cans, and other rubbish."[5] Ida D. Bennett decried the back yard as "a place to dump rubbish" and admonished that, should the owners attempt to put it to better uses, "the first thing which will be required will be to give it a thorough cleaning. . . ."[6] In his fittingly titled 1912 article, "Sanctifying the Backyard," *House Beautiful* writer Harry Martin Yeomans remarked, "Those of us who live in the city and have tried to satisfy the gardenlust have heretofore been content with a grass plot, or else abandoned the back yard as hopeless and fitting only for the storage of garbage pails and the drying of wash."[7]

If there was now pressure to sanctify the back yard, the City Beautiful movement certainly played a role. But another factor loomed much larger. As they expanded outwards, cities and private developers began offering residents services that steadily replaced back yard utilities. One of the first of these services was running water. Before the Civil War, the only places likely to receive running water were expensive hotels, prominent businesses, and the headquarters of important public officials. Average families instead took water either from wells, rivers, and lakes or from public hydrants fed by these sources. Many households supplemented their supply by collecting rainwater in buckets or in back yard cisterns fed by roof gutters. What waterworks did exist were often run by private companies and were highly polluted from sewage and industrial discharge. Cholera and yellow fever were rampant. One-third of all newborns in New York City died within a year of birth, and almost half died before reaching age six.[8] In response to these diseases and to demonstrate a commitment to the public welfare, many cities began developing their own water supply systems. Martin Melosi notes that, in 1870, there were only 244 public waterworks nationwide. Due to the improving fiscal status of cities, to growing cooperation between local and state governments, and to a broadening of municipal powers, however, the number began expanding faster than the urban population was growing. By 1890, the number of waterworks had increased seven fold to nearly 1,900 and, by 1925, to nearly 10,000.[9]

Figure 3.2. A utilitarian yard in Boston, ca..1902, with a small vegetable plot, storage shed, wooden walkways, patchy grass, and scattered ornamental plantings. A. A. Shurtlef, photographer. Photograph used by permission of the Frances Loeb Library, Harvard University Graduate School of Design, reproduction number 119406.

Figure 3.3. Workers laying sewer pipes in Kearney, Nebraska, in 1889. By the turn of the twentieth century, cities and private companies were extending waterworks, sewerage, and trash collection to more and more neighborhoods, allowing homeowners to free up their back yards for new uses. Solomon Butcher, photographer. Photograph used by permission of the Nebraska State Historical Society Photograph Collections, 1889, reproduction number RG2608.PH:000000-002504.

Running water represented a dramatic improvement over wells, hydrants, and cisterns. It was safer and better tasting due to newly developed filtration and purification techniques. It facilitated fire fighting and street cleaning and helped to suppress roadway dust. It attracted businesses and tourists to town. It helped to modernize private homes and their grounds by freeing owners from more tedious collection methods, reducing the risk of falling into wells, and eliminating buckets and cisterns, which freed up space to plant and irrigate grass, shrubbery, trees, and vegetables.

Running water also figured prominently in the emergence of another major utility: public sewerage. Prior to the spread of citywide sewage systems, households typically disposed of waste in a privy vault or cesspool. Neither method had much to commend it. Their contents often leached into the groundwater and pol-

luted nearby wells and waterways. They released foul odors, and, when they filled up, household members had to relocate them in a different part of the yard. They occupied plenty of space and rendered most of the area around them uninhabitable. Public sewers were slower to emerge than waterworks for a variety of reasons. Sewers required deeper trenches and bigger pipes than did water lines and the piping had to be pitched to exacting standards—especially in flat regions—to insure that the contents would flow to their outlet. The system required a suitable outlet, and the contents needed to be treated for cholera and a host of other diseases. Importantly, sewers needed regular flushing with clean water and thus required a waterworks system to function properly. Martin Melosi notes that, like waterworks, public sewerage was slow to take hold. In 1870, only 100 American communities had such systems; by 1920, however, public sewerage had spread to some 3,000 communities, serving eighty-seven percent of the population.[10] The combined advent of running water and sewerage allowed homeowners to remove or abandon their privies and cesspools, fixtures that were unequalled in the limitations they imposed on back yards. Considerable space was thus freed up for a variety of domestic activities that were previously unthinkable in city and suburban yards.

While public waterworks and sewerage helped to make yards more habitable, homeowners confronted still another issue affecting their home grounds: the disposal of trash. In rural America, the great majority of garbage was organic and easy to dispose of. In cities, however, a different sort of waste was generated. High urban densities were contributing to a tremendous accumulation of trash in alleys, vacant lots, riverbanks, street curbs, and back yards. Dumps, if any were to be found, were usually located a good distance away from urban centers, and private hauling was expensive. Moreover, prior to the 1880s, civic leaders commonly regarded refuse as a nuisance not yet worthy of public intervention, and public garbage collection was accordingly limited. In 1880, only twenty-five percent of American cities had refuse collection programs, and the services were limited in scope.[11] At the same time, Americans were beginning to witness the beginnings of what journalists would come to term the "disposable culture."

Figure 3.4. Workers' houses in Cincinnati, Ohio, in 1935, with small back yards, privies, and lean-to shacks. The property in the foreground contained a weed-covered orchard and woodpile. None of the yards appeared to offer opportunities for outdoor living. Carl Mydans, photographer, "Row of identical houses off Eastern Avenue, in Cincinnati Ohio, showing back-yard outhouses. Ohio River Valley is in the distance," December 1935. Photograph courtesy of the Library of Congress, Prints & Photographs Division, FSA-OWI Collection, reproduction number Lc-Usf34-000650-D.

The burgeoning industrial economy was producing a vast array of new household products—couches, chairs, bedsprings, kitchen utensils, lamps, bathroom products, bicycles, crockery, window shades, and the like—that needed disposal when they wore out. Many families discarded smaller items in their privies or cisterns, especially if they received running water and sewerage. Digger O'Dell, an artifact collector from Ohio, has dug up back yard privies for years to salvage and sell household items he has uncovered. O'Dell has found artifacts dating as recently as 1930, indicating that many Ohioans kept their privies open long after the cities had installed public sewer lines. He has unearthed a wide variety of nineteenth-century soap, perfume, and medicine bottles, stoneware crocks and jugs, pipes, coins, marbles, doll parts, china, Civil War projectile shells, Indian points, pot lids, locks, and numerous household objects. One excavation yielded "ten jelly jars, 2 vanilla bottles, a broken wide mouth kitchen crock and a number of wax seal fruit jars, several 1858 masons, one baby bottle, a Parlor Pride stove polish and a broken imported crockery gin bottle." O'Dell has traced these artifacts back to the nineteenth century, and he attributes their eventual decline to the advent of public garbage collection:

> Wholesale dumping of household trash, based on our archaeological evidence, began increasing around the 1840s–1850s commensurate with the rise in industrial capability. As people began to accumulate greater and greater quantities of refuse we find greater quantities of these artifacts in the outhouse. With the rise in the incidence of indoor plumbing, other places had to be found for dumping, hence the increase in the number of town and city dumps.[12]

Figure 3.5. A utilitarian yard in Chicago, in 1907. Lumber, possibly for firewood, was stacked against the fence in front of a dilapidated shed. Trash was piled in the rear, and bricks sat under a wooden bench against the house. Photographer unknown. Photograph used by permission of the Chicago Historical Society, Chicago *Daily News* negatives collection, 1907, number DN-0004985.

According to Susan Strasser, a third or more of urban garbage was organic, including vegetable matter, bones, animal carcasses, and manure. Many residents—even into the late 1800s—simply dumped this material into their yards or tossed it into the street where it was eaten by roaming animals.[13] The odors intensified in hot weather, and the health risk was high, as the rotting garbage attracted rats, flies, and maggots. Families often burned what items they could and either dumped non-combustibles—such as broken glass, crockery, and tins cans—in their privies and cisterns or buried them behind their homes. In 1960, jazz singer Barbara Dane planted a vegetable garden in her back yard in Brooklyn, New York. Once she started digging she unearthed piles of household items:

> We found all this junk that the Italian families who originally lived in the house had buried—a car bumper, a bicycle frame, a bed springs, even an entire icebox. Our neighbors found the same stuff in their yards. Apparently no one hauled anything away. There was so much stuff there that we just left it and planted the vegetables in raised boxes.[14]

Uncollected garbage was both a health risk and a target for the civic beautification campaigns sweeping the nation. As they had done with waterworks and sewerage, cities steadily began providing trash collection, some done in-house and some contracted to private companies. Planners and heath departments scrutinized various disposal methods and gradually phased out questionable practices, such as dumping in water and in the vacant lots of poor neighborhoods. Many cities began selling organic garbage to farmers, and New York City was one of several large cities that developed programs to sort and recycle waste. To contain diseases, many cities drained mosquito-infested swamplands and converted them to dumps. Sanitary engineers developed various types of incinerators to burn waste matter, though the technology required constant modification and adjustment to increase efficiency and reduce smoke pollution. By the 1920s, the number of cities offering trash collection was three times that of 1880 and rising quickly.[15] In addition, many municipalities

Are you ashamed of your back porch?

Garbage is not only an embarrassing nuisance, but a distinct menace to health.

Unwelcome—and yet no place to go. That is the plight of the garbage. How it heaps up!

Always accumulating and making you ashamed of the back porch. The clouds of flies, the bad odors, disease germs, yowling cats that come at night, all can be traced to the influence of the garbage pail.

The truth is that we have been putting up with make-shift methods of garbage disposal.

You can't throw it in the furnace lest the grates clog up and the house be filled with foul odors. Strangers must be permitted to prowl about the place if it is to be hauled away—a none too safe idea. How simple is the army method in comparison as embodied in the Ranz Garbage Destroyer!

A Ranz Garbage Destroyer slips into old or new buildings (or outdoors) as easily as a stove, and costs less than one.

Dump all wet or dry garbage, old papers, trash, tin cans, bottles—in fact everything—into it. A steady draft of air dries out the garbage and carries away all odor. Touch a match once a week and the job is done. Everything is reduced to ashes or sterilized. Every inch of your place is kept sanitary and clean when there is a Ranz around.

Ranz Garbage Destroyer

Fine homes, apartment, business blocks and picnic grounds find it indispensable.

A Ranz Incinerator will increase the value of your property. Ten years from now every building will have one, as surely as they have doorbells and bath tubs today. If you want to be proud of your place, you must have a Ranz.

For old or new buildings or outdoors

Write today for free booklet on sanitation. Read how the U. S. army keeps things clean. Your name and address in the coupon below brings it to you.

Snip this out with your scissors and mail today

Neenah Brass Works,
Dept. 27, Neenah, Wis.

Please mail me your booklet on garbage disposal for homes, apts., hospitals, picnic grounds (check).

Name................................

Address..............................

....

Figure 3.6. Prior to the advent and spread of municipal trash collection, many city residents suffered "the clouds of flies, the bad odors, disease germs, yowling cats that come at night" that resulted from the accumulation of back yard garbage. Advertisement in *House and Garden* (July 1922): 105.

enacted blight ordinances that banned not only the dumping of trash along roadsides, riverbanks, and vacant lots, but also letting it accumulate on private properties. No longer needing to dispose of garbage behind the house, a family could now put a considerable amount of yard space to new uses.

Electric refrigeration was another key invention that freed up yard space. Homeowners who had the time and opportunity to plant their back yards often included some fruit trees and a small kitchen garden. Kitchen gardens had long been part of the American home grounds. They were often the first improvement a homesteader made to the land, an integral part of the rural grounds and a prominent feature in country estates, where they often occupied thousands of square feet and were tended by servants. Improvements in farming and food distribution, however, were lessening a family's need to grow produce. The inventions of artificial dehydration (1870), the refrigerated boxcar (1880), and the quick freezing of vegetables (1912) all allowed farmers to ship fresh produce quickly and efficiently to distant markets, reducing the nation's reliance on small local farms.[16] Homegrown produce was not only less essential, landscape architect Frank Jessup Scott intuitively noted; it was fast becoming an indulgence:

> A wealthy citizen, who had been severely seized with some of these horticultural fervors, invited friends to dine with him at his country seat. The friends complimented his delicious green corn. 'It is capital, I'm glad you appreciate it,' said he; 'it is from my own grounds, and by a calculation made a few days since I find that the season's crop will cost me only ten dollars an ear.[17]

Prior to refrigeration, families stored perishables in root cellars, pantries, or iceboxes. Iceboxes needed periodic replenishing, and in 1910 there were more than 2,000 commercial icehouses serving the nation. The first refrigerators were costly, and in 1921 Americans only owned 5,000 of them. Following the path of other household appliances, however, the technology improved and costs fell. By 1931, more than 1,000,000 Americans owned refrigerators, and, by 1936, the number had risen to 3,000,000. Families could now keep store-bought produce fresh for days rather than grow it in their back yards. Nor did they have to suffer the intrusion of the iceman as he made deliveries through the back yard and into the house. As a result, homeowners reduced the size of their kitchen gardens or abandoned them altogether, opening up still more back yard space to new uses.[18]

As homeowners phased out their back yard utilities, they confronted an important question: to what uses might they put the newly opened up space? In 1910, *House and Garden* writer Russell Fisher laid out the problem quite clearly: the urban back yard, since its inception, was firmly inscribed in the public mind as little more than an outdoor basement. "The element of beauty did not enter into the matter to any appreciable extent," Fisher wrote. "The term 'back yard' became one of reproach, and the gardens consisted of a long suffering shrub or two and perhaps a bed of geraniums and coleus set in the middle of a moth-eaten lawn bounded by the high board fence."[19] Moreover, the simple elimination of utilities did not in itself solve the back yard problem; there needed to be a shift in public attitudes towards the space and a viable direction in which to take it.

Middle-class homeowners were not without choices in how to sanctify their back yards. An obvious option was to arrange the back to mimic the front, with bushes against the house, flowers near the back door, and a lawn flowing to the property line. Though a fair number of homeowners adopted such yards after the 1920s, the solution amounted to little more than picturesque scenery. It offered no privacy, its connection to the dwelling was tenuous, and it accounted for few of a household's day-to-day needs.

A second possibility was to copy the rural dooryard. Dooryards still thrived in rural America and in transitional communities near the urban fringe. Dooryards were suited to enterprising families who offered services such as horseshoeing, rabbit and chicken breeding, carriage repair, fruit canning, and firewood sales out of their homes. Though suburban living generated plenty of small projects best done in the yard, most homeowners were otherwise employed and thus had little reason or opportunity to work out of the house. Moreover, the divisions between rural and urban America were deepening. Zoning laws—directed to reducing noise, smoke, odors, dust, and trash—were steadily pushing agricultural enterprises to the outskirts of cities and suburbs. At the same time, small town and rural economies were beginning to shift away from the house. Due to the increased mobility afforded by truck and car ownership, small entrepreneurs could now conduct business across a much wider geographic area. With less dependence on their property for livelihood, John Jakle points out, many entrepreneurs eliminated the hen houses, barns, woodsheds, gardens, and orchards that once occupied their grounds.[20] In short, the suburban back yard was not destined to return to its roots on the farm.

There still remained a compelling model for the suburban back yard: an English cottage garden. Since its inception, America had revered many things English, and gardens were no exception. By the turn of the twentieth century, England had produced some of the most celebrated gardens in the world: Munstead Wood, Millmead, the Deanery garden, the Royal Horticultural Society's garden at Wisley, and many others just as magnificent. "Gardens, be they cottage, urban, suburban, the window box or the area, absorb the energies and much of the leisure of a large proportion of the British people," wrote English journalist Gillian Darley. ". . . we do not sing, or dance, we garden—and the repository of that art, in all it's extremes, is the small garden."[21] The effect on American garden design was smothering. Though there were a handful of landscape architects who looked elsewhere for inspiration, most designers produced gardens that were highly derivative, if not indistinguishable, from those coming out of England.[22] "An American's first day in England . . . is one of mingled rapture and despair. He is intoxicated with the architecture, the history, and the landscape," wrote Wilhelm Miller in his 1911 book, *What England Can Teach Us About Gardening.* ". . . And if he be honest, all his defiant patriotism melts and runs away. For in his guilty heart he knows that we have not 'found ourselves.' He understands now why people accuse us of having no 'American style' in architecture, in gardening, or in anything else."[23] Moreover, the civic beautification zeal of the past two decades had produced millions of small front yards that were deeply steeped in the British picturesque tradition. "The architectural evidence suggests," Peirce Lewis has remarked, ". . . the melting pot is largely myth—that from the beginnings we were an English people, culturally if not biologically . . . . Tudor houses cling to the hills in Pasadena, and English roses and English lawns perennially wilt under the blistering Kansas sun!"[24]

If the picturesque scenery of American front yards was inappropriate for the back, the cottage garden offered more promise. Taken literally, the term "cottage garden" referred to the kitchen gardens, flowers, orchards, and work areas found on the grounds of ordinary rural homes. Such gardens could be traced back for centuries in Europe and, though not without charm, were more notable for serving family livelihood than expressing romantic beauty. As an expression of beauty in its own right, the cottage garden sprung into prominence in England during the Victorian era of the latter 1800s. It was moderately sized—less than half an acre, advised garden architect J. C. Loudon—to leave time for other family concerns. ". . . The extent of the garden of the labourer ought never to be such as to interfere with his regular employment," Loudon wrote, echoing a concern that would later appear frequently in American gardening books.[25] The cottage garden served the household in straightforward, practical ways, almost all of which involved the use of plants: roses to fill the garden with scent, flowers to beautify the exterior and provide cut flowers for the house, fruit trees to put apples, pears, peaches, plums, and lemons on the dining table, herbs for the kitchen, vines to cover sheds and crumbling walls, and unusual species of plants everywhere to satisfy the curiosity of the homeowner. Plantings in Victorian gardens were exceptionally diverse compared to gardens in other countries. Worldwide trade and exploration had brought thousands of new species to England, such as Australian tree ferns, Siberian alpines, African and South American tropicals, Malaysian orchids, and Canary Islands succulents. English garden design entered an eclectic period, with a liberal mixing of styles from Italy, Asia, France, and other countries on the shipping routes. The cottage garden reflected this cross-cultural diversity, and what it lacked in size it more than made up for in variety and detail. "Potatoes and cabbages were planted at random among foxgloves, pansie and pinks," Englishman Laurie Lee said of his mother's charmingly overgrown cottage garden.[26] "One can hardly go into the smallest cottage garden without learning something new," wrote Gertrude Jekyll, the grand dame of twentieth-century English gardening. "It may be some two plants growing beautifully together by some happy chance, or some pretty mixed tangle of creepers, or something that one always thought must have a south wall doing better on an east one."[27]

The cottage garden was primarily a working person's affair. Its profusion of flowers, however, was so attractive to the English upper-middle-class that prominent garden designers

Figure 3.7. A perennial bed in the cottage garden style, Berkeley, California, 2005. Photograph by the author.

soon began making the style over in their own image. The most noted example was William Robinson's invention of the perennial border, a wildly popular form later carried to perfection by Jekyll. The border consisted of a long, narrow bed stuffed to the edges with penstemon, verbena, alyssum, foxglove, dianthus, jasmine,lilies, hosta, hollyhock, lavender, iris, phlox, aster, sunrose, and countless other flowers of every description. One of the most famous examples was Jekyll's border at Munstead Wood, a fifteen-acre estate in Surrey. The border consisted of eighteen species of shrubs and trees and more than seventy-five perennials that put on a dazzling color show lasting from early spring until late fall, when the last bloomers finally quit and died to the ground. Jekyll had been a painter before failing eyesight induced her to turn her creative energies to gardening. She believed that visual effects were a garden's primary purpose, and she put great emphasis on texture and color. "Grey foliage, white, pale blue and pink move toward stronger vivid blue and primrose yellow," she recommended for one section. In another, "feathery cream plumes link brighter yellows to orange, flame, and scarlet." In another, "dark red fades to warm yellow, white and cream with blocks of blue-green foliage." And in another, "foliage separates sulfur yellow, blue and pink ending in lavender, mauve and darker mauve, blue and white."[28] The perennial border was ideally suited to Victorian-era housewives who wished to decorate their homes with flowers. Its soft blend of colors and textures was the incarnation of Impressionism, the prevailing style of painting in Jekyll's time and, according to many surveys, the style of art preferred by most twentieth-century Americans. Importantly, the border's narrow width lent itself to a small lot. No other English garden element—the parterre, maze, topiary, knot garden, or tea garden—would achieve the enduring popularity of the perennial border, even to this day.

"Did it ever occur to you that there is a latent potentiality in even the most ordinary back yard?" wrote *House and Garden* writer William Draper Brinckle in his 1910 article, "Making a Garden of the City Backyard." "No, not any feeble insipidities—screening the garbage-cans by rows of sunflowers, veneering of back fences with morning glories—but the possibility of a well studied bit of garden design?"[29] Brinckle was one of numerous journalists of the era who promoted gardenesque designs in the English style for city and suburban yards. The conditions appeared right for such a transition. The small scale of middle-class American yards was much more suited to a cottage garden than to the country estate style. Gardening books of the era provided ample coverage of Gertrude Jekyll and the Loudon style. Moreover, local garden clubs, school districts, chambers of commerce, and other civic groups were outspoken about of the virtues of gardening. Espousing a stern moral tone, *American City* writer Edward T. Hartman admonished readers in 1910:

> The man without a garden generally has no avocation or, if he has, it may be as useless as postage stamps, brass buttons, clips; or if it is golf or any one of fifty often followed it keeps him away from his home, he is usually a poor man, and the barroom is his club where he wastes his money and his health, his family has stale vegetables or none, he loses time from his work and is often unemployed, he has no pride in his home or its appearance, he is a wanderer. Such men do not help to build villages, do not become useful citizens, are a tax on the community because they fill the hospitals, the courts, the jails, the wayfarers' lodge.[30]

In a 1910 campaign to improve the city's back yards, Northampton, Massachusetts, sponsored its tenth annual Flower Garden Competition. More than 900 homes competed for prize money. "Many garden competitors started in the competition with their lawns merely grassless yards, or a waste of sand and weeds," wrote Mr. H. D. Hemenway, secretary of the People's Institute. "Now in place of these unsightly yards we have beautiful, well-kept lawns and appropriately planted shrubbery. This was done not only by persons who were well-to-do, but by persons working in mills who are simply tenants of the places in which they live."[31] In 1914, the Spokane (Washington) Chamber of Commerce assisted local garden clubs in solving the "vacation problem" for boys and girls by encouraging them to transform "disorderly or unused back yards into flower and vegetable gardens." The committee in charge claimed that, in addition to beautifying the neighborhoods, they saved more than $6,000 from the use and sale of produce.[32] The Civic Improvement Committee of Kewanee, Illinois, launched a campaign in 1915 to encourage school children to improve their front and back yards. The club issued memberships cards and had children sign an oath vowing to plant flowers, bulbs, vines, and shrubbery, to make gardens and keep good lawns, and not to litter, spit, or deface buildings. The club's criteria for assigning prizes revealed the dismal nature of the yards and promoted plants and flowers as integral to the solution:

> Cleanliness of back yard with reference to rubbish of all sorts—cans, broken glass, ash piles, straw, chips, or litter of any kind, Unsightly fences or sheds covered with vines or screened with flowering plants, such as hollyhocks or caster beans, Ornamentation by means of flower beds, Sink holes or low, muddy places in yards to be surrounded with tall-growing flowering plants so as to be screened from view of passers-by, yards to be smooth or level, free from large stones, clods or unsightly hummocks.[33]

It was common for garden clubs and civic groups to make children the focus of their campaigns. In 1906, the Civic League of Salem, Massachusetts, launched a garden contest and awarded prizes for fence and wall improvement, for the best window boxes, and for home and school gardens built by children. The league even created a special category for contestants under ten years of age and distributed more than 25,000 packets of seeds to interested participants. One young contestant was so fond of his newly renovated back yard that he would not let his baby sibling eat cookies in it, "for fear the crumbs would spoil the smooth appearance of the lawn. The same lawn a year ago had been nothing more than a neglected can-strewn ash-heap." A barefoot Polish girl with no yard planted window boxes on the veranda of her fourth-story tenement, and the children of the Canizarrios family converted their burnt out, trash-filled yard into a pleasant sitting area. Even the very young got to participate, as *American City* writer Miriam Adelaide Tighe described:

> Far away from this school, in a narrow dirty street near the railroad track, from the door of a poor looking untidy house came forth an unattractive ill-kept woman. One would know at a glance at her slack, ragged garments and frowzled hair that she was an occupant of a dirty house. Not a spot on the back porch could be found which did not require the services of a scrubbing brush. But as one looked about, in back of the miserable dwelling could be seen a garden of exquisite beauty and neatness. It was that of her eight-year-old daughter. The faded eyes of the mother glowed as she looked over it and told its history. 'It all came,' she said, 'from ten cents worth of school seeds and lots of hard work.' As a result this poor tired woman had before her a little picture which in its refreshing neatness brought every day a ray of brightness and sunshine.[34]

The horticultural emphasis civic groups placed on back yard improvements stemmed from a popular notion that the home grounds were primarily a place for plants. Not only was this belief derivative of the English garden tradition, but it was vigorously promoted by Andrew Jackson Downing, Andrew Jackson Davis, Frank Jessup Scott, and numerous other landscape architects. It figured prominently as a solution for country estates and romantic suburbs, and up until the mid-1920s it had been the bailiwick of all the major house and garden magazines and books. Moreover, it was a primary driving force behind America's zeal to beautify front yards, an attitude millions of citizens embraced willingly and passionately.

Despite its attractions, the cottage garden harbored significant limitations as a solution for middle-class yards. For one thing, such gardens were historically rooted in a rural way of life. Garden-grown vegetables, fresh fruit from the orchard, tasty herbs, and scratching chickens recalled a time when most Americans lived off the land. While a colorful dooryard suggested a romantic picture of country life, in reality most Americans were in no position to adopt such a garden. The great majority of the urban and suburban population worked in factories, businesses, and enterprises away from their homes and thus regarded their properties as places for shelter and comfort rather than livelihood. While homegrown produce appealed to a portion of the population, most homeowners—with the notable exception of war-time Victory Gardeners—were choosing store-bought produce and refrigerators over growing food in their yards. Moreover, a cottage garden—even one planted in the Jekyll style with colorful flowers rather than edibles—took a tremendous amount of expertise and time to maintain. The owners of such a garden spent every free moment amending soil with bone meal and gypsum, pruning fruit trees, and dividing bulbs. They pulled out dandelions and crabgrass, warded off whiteflies and aphids, covered seedlings with netting to keep birds away, and hauled bags of debris to the trash can or compost pile. They pruned second-year wood on fruit trees (first learning to distinguish it from first-year wood), built scarecrows, and battled gophers and moles. Jekyll's perennial border was the most work of all, requiring the owner to deadhead the flower stalks, pull slugs and snails off the delicate leaves, separate plants that competed for space, replace spent species with budding ones, and keep the bed weeded and watered. Anything less and the border turned ugly, with limp, insect-chewed leaves, desiccated flowers, brown stalks flapping in the wind, and tangled masses of once-beautiful plants. The cottage garden was a place for people willing to spend the weekend pulling weeds in lieu of driving to the countryside or the beach. It was a place for people willing to assemble a small library of gardening books and subscriptions to horticultural magazines. It was perfectly suited to a population that preferred gardening to singing, dancing, or any number of other recreational activities. But was there any indication that average middle-class American homeowners were prepared to devote this level of time and dedication to raising plants?

The cottage garden, though Loudon and others advised that it be kept small, could also consume a sizeable portion of a middle-class property. By the time one added up the fruit trees, rose beds, kitchen garden, cutting garden, sinewy meadows, perennial borders, and thick hedges that wrapped the perimeter, little space was left over for other uses. The owners of country estates and large suburban homes could enjoy all those features and still have room for a drying yard, chicken coops, an orchard, a greensward, a stable, and a walled patio. Moreover, they could afford servants to care for the grounds, leaving them ample time to enjoy the garden. Middle-class Americans, however, had to make a hard choice about how to use the space around their house, and gardenesque solutions competed directly with child rearing, entertaining, travel, leisure, and numerous other domestic concerns.

If the cottage garden embodied too many limitations, homeowners quickly discovered that the house itself was a more useful design guide. The decline of back yard utilities had opened up a significant square footage of usable space behind the house, often as big or bigger than the kitchen, dining room, and parlor combined. Back yards were private, shielded from the street by the house and shrubbery and, in some parts of the nation, by fences. They sat close to kitchens and utility closets, rooms that were vital to the day-to-day working of households. Nothing prohibited families from planting a full garden in the back, nor was there a strong historical tradition for them to do so. English gardens notwithstanding, the exterior use of most ordinary properties historically mimicked the activities that took place inside the dwelling.

Figure 3.8. A house in Kearney, Nebraska, in 1911. The yard contained little more than some young shade trees and patchy grass, leaving the porch for outdoor socializing and relaxing. Solomon Butcher, photographer. Photograph used by permission of the Nebraska State Historical Society Photograph Collections, 1911, reproduction number RG2608.PH:000000-002616.

Figure 3.9. Their back yards often given over to utility, families conducted outdoor gatherings on their porches. An advertisement for Komi Green Painted Porch Curtains, in *House and Garden* (May 1912): 69.

Americans, in fact, had good reason to look to their back yards for living space. Until the 1920s, families generally relied on their front porches for outdoor gatherings. The front porch had originally come into favor, according to *House Beautiful* magazine, due to "the rise of two very conspicuous features of American life, the suburb and the summer vacation, both of which seem to have become more prominent during the ten years following the Civil War."[35] Porches were logical places for families to spend time. They sat comfortably against the house, shaded by from the sun by the eaves of the roof and open to cooling breezes in the evening. In the summer, they were often cooler than the interior rooms. Homeowners furnished them with wicker chairs, wooden tables, canvas awnings, flower baskets, and other household accouterments that magazines were advertising with increasing frequency. Porches were places to relax and watch the world go by, and, should a family invite guests inside, the parlor was conveniently located just inside the front door. In good weather, families spent hours on their porches sewing, ironing, preparing food, reading, and conversing.

Figure 3.10. After Henry Ford introduced the Model T in 1908, residential streets became increasingly crowded, dusty, and noisy. Owing to improvements to home grounds made possible by the spread of municipal services, families could shift activities from their front porches to their back yards. Photographer unknown, and no location is listed for this image. Photograph used by permission of the Frances Loeb Library, Harvard University Graduate School of Design, reproduction number 119062.

Front porches also formed important connections to the neighborhood. American street life was lively at the turn of the twentieth century, an attribute many planners and landscape architects regarded as indispensable to community welfare. Workers strolled home from the trolley stops, shopping, eating, and socializing as they made their way home. Children played on sidewalks and front lawns and out in the streets. Merchants with horse-drawn carts sold their wares to passersby and offered to haul away trash and perform minor household repairs. Because the front porch related to both the house and the street, it bridged the gap between private and public life.

By the 1920s, however, the street was losing its friendliness. Zoning ordinances were steadily separating commercial sectors from residential ones, a practice that created quieter neighborhoods but also diminished the opportunities for spontaneous social interaction. Due to rapid suburban growth, families often found it harder to get to know their neighbors or to develop a comfortable familiarity with their surroundings. Even more problematic was the increased commotion wrought by 8,000,000 new cars and trucks, the dust and gravel kicked up by tires, the noise and fumes of puttering engines, the clatter of bumpers and transmissions as vehicles rattled down the bumpy roads, and the endless procession of headlights at sunset when residents of nearby houses, weary from a day's work, might want to relax on their front porches. Homeowners were becoming plagued with solicitations from traveling salesmen or drivers who were lost, out of gas, or needed help fixing flat tires. Residents in especially congested neighborhoods responded by erecting front yard fences, a taboo practice in most parts of the nation, but understandable given the effects of increasing traffic levels. By 1925, businesses such as the Dubois Company, the Anchor Fence Company, and the Cyclone Fence Company were advertising fences to block out auto noise and headlights, stop children from running out into the street, and keep snooping strangers at bay. The automobile had also ushered in a new activity: the Sunday drive. Suburban families often found themselves besieged by curious drivers who putted into their neighborhoods and sometimes right onto their properties simply to have a look around.

During the 1930s, Anchor Fence ran ads depicting gypsies and hobos begging suburban residents for money, drivers gawking at homeowners working in their yards, and well-dressed families parking in the yards of strangers to enjoy leisurely picnics. "Motoring picnickers think that 'No Trespassing' and 'Keep Off' signs are to be read—then ignored: any and every open property is their camping ground," an ad warned. "An Anchor Fence eliminates this annoyance."[36]

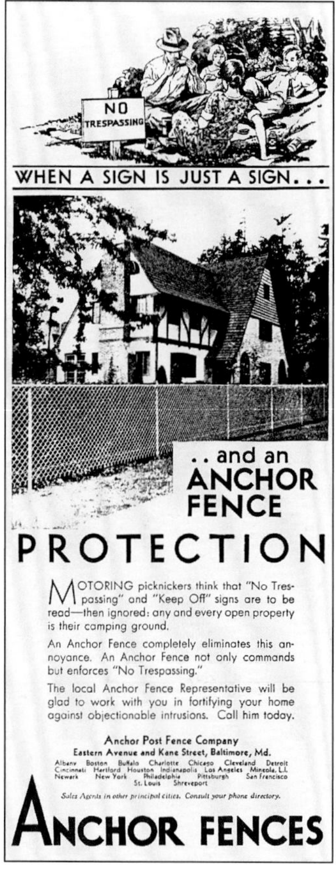

Figures 3.11 (left) and 3.12 (right). The rapid growth of early twentieth-century suburbs, combined with the enormous proliferation of the automobile, incited many homeowners to break with tradition and fence their front yards. Left: An Anchor Post Fence Company advertisement, "When a Sign is just a Sign . . ." in *House and Garden* (September 1930): 150. Right: A Cyclone Fence Company advertisement, "Their Own Yard," *House and Garden* (May 1925): 177; in *House and Garden* (June 1935): 74. Used by permission of the Cyclone Fence Company.

With streets losing their friendliness and properties shedding their utilities, families could now shift their activities to the back yard. "Porches are good enough for rainy days, but even then one prefers them turned away from the trivial drama of the street with its hucksters and milk wagons and gossip, to the serenity of trees and flowers in the back yard," wrote Esther Johnson in *House Beautiful* in 1922. "All through the West and the middle-West, where towns were built in the front-porch period, attention is turning to the garden in the back yard."[37] By the 1920s, house and garden magazines were beginning to expand their focus to include middle-class residences. In the late nineteenth and early twentieth centuries, most articles were written for the owners of country estates. But the readership was changing. The advent of the trolley suburbs and the emergence of an urban middle class had created a clientele with smaller properties, reduced budgets, and the desire to balance family needs with horticulture. This readership might well appreciate the beauty and scale of an estate garden, but readers were more interested in learning how to develop a yard requiring little more than lawn mowing and trimming foundation plants. The new readers were ones who preferred a weekend of walking through the woods, shopping at downtown department stores, or sitting at the beach rather than pruning or harvesting fruit trees; who appreciated the beauty of plants but had little time to care for them; who preferred to use back yard space for relaxing, entertaining, and child rearing rather than raising plants. These sentiments did not mean that middle-class Americans disliked traditional gardens; it was, in fact, the presence of plants that helped make the home grounds so pleasant to begin with. The sentiments revealed, rather, that living space was a more pressing need than horticulture.

Cleared of its utilitarian functions, the back yard was—during the warmer months of the year—prime real estate for raising children, eating and entertaining, engaging in small building projects, or simply being outdoors. This did not portend the end of the garden in the popular sense of the word but rather placed it, in the minds of most homeowners, behind household needs. In 1923, *House Beautiful* sponsored a contest in which contestants were given a wooden model of a house on an empty

WHEN YOU PLAN YOUR GARDEN

Let the Garden Fit the Site Rather than Force the Site to Fit the Garden

Figure 3.13. Until the mid-1920s, most house and garden magazines wrote for the owners of large estates such as the one shown above. As the number of middle-class homeowners increased, journals shifted their focus to smaller, middle-class properties. Philosophies of design, such as the one offered here, were also meaningful guides. "When You Plan Your Garden," *House and Garden* (November 1922): 78.

lot and instructed to design the grounds. One of the judges, well-known landscape architect Fletcher Steele, observed that each contestant had turned the house such that the most actively used rooms now faced the back yard. Likely a response to the increased noise, dust, and commotion of automobile traffic, to the decline of the service yard, and to the growing demise of the front porch, these schemes marked a significant departure from the traditional practice of facing the house proudly towards the street. ". . . the great majority of the exhibitors—including all the best designs—agreed that the living quarters of the house should face back on the lot, not towards the street as is the all too common custom," wrote Steele. "In most cases, the house was put near the street, thus leaving to the gardens behind the house the maximum space."[38] The contestants included vegetables, fruits, and flowers in their schemes, but, in contrast to the gardenesque orientation of country estates, they placed much more emphasis on recreation, family raising, and practical day-to-day household needs.

Steele himself was no stranger to domestically arranged back yards. In 1924, he published the concise, persuasively written book, *Design in the Little Garden,* showing readers how to renovate back yards and, importantly, make them extensions of the living room of the house.[39] While the home grounds of our ancestors served outmoded utilitarian purposes, he argued, neither had homeowners taken the trouble to modernize their yards. In a chapter entitled "Outdoor Living Rooms," Steele presented a hypothetical scenario in which a young, house-hunting couple deliberated between three adjacent residences, each with a seemingly promising floor plan and yard layout. Though initially attracted to the superficial qualities of the first two traditional yards, the couple soon realized the advantage of the third, atypically designed yard. The front was enclosed behind a hedge that screened off the bustling street, unlike the other properties in the neighborhood. The garage sat by the sidewalk rather than consuming yard space at the rear of the property. The formal, geometric bed layouts of the first two gardens gave way in the third garden to a softer, naturalistic layout that provided numerous pleasures and delights and required less stringent upkeep. The living room sat at the back of the house, flooded by sunlight through big windows that brought the garden into view. The living room opened up onto a spacious outdoor terrace where the family could eat dinner and entertain guests, while the back porches of the other houses only minimally adjoined the yards. "Dollar for dollar and foot for foot, there is little question which one is the best for the money or gets the most out of the land," wrote Steele.[40]

The combined themes of family living and horticultural simplicity spread rapidly as a new generation of Americans moved into detached homes. Free from the agricultural ties of their ancestors, the utilities that had once dictated yard uses, and the expectation that a property must resemble a page out of the Gertrude Jekyll workbook, middle-class families now had a chance to develop in the back what lawns and foundation plantings had contributed in the front: an indigenous garden style.

The integrating premise—outdoor habitability—was finding its way into more and more gardening publications. In his 1930 book, *Landscaping the Home Grounds,* Leonidas W. Ramsey called for homeowners to recognize that "the real function of attractive grounds is to make the grounds part of the home and provide a summer living space for all the family and friends."[41]

Ramsey believed the yard was an especially important place for children to play, since the soft surfaces were unlikely to cause injuries and the plantings engendered an appreciation for nature. In their 1932 book, *The Outdoor Room,* Ramsey and co-author Charles H. Lawrence argued that the grounds could be far more than just a "setting for the house" and that even the smallest properties could support outdoor living. "After all, we can use but a small portion of our grounds at a time, and the average home lot is large enough to satisfy the social and recreational needs of the family," the authors wrote in the chapter entitled "An American Ideal In Gardening."[42] In 1937, *Better Homes and Gardens* ran an article entitled "Gardening in the American Manner." Robert Franklin Ross, the author, argued that a national style should reflect the "American spirit" and particularly the quest for "freedom." Freedom, in this case, was no nebulous Jeffersonian construct concerning natural law, liberty, and equal rights; it meant selecting plants "requiring the least possible care" in order to release the homeowner from yard work. Native plants were particularly desirable, Ross argued, because—unlike the throngs of exotics introduced during the Victorian era—they were truly American. Moreover, natives required less maintenance because they were already adapted to local soils and climate. Garden maintenance was a linchpin in the design of the small suburban yard, and owners needed to take steps to minimize yard work. To this end, Ross's sample design contained few flowers, and, in place of what would ordinarily have been a vegetable garden, there lay nothing more than a large, grassy plot, labeled "abandoned field," in which the family could do anything it chose. This was a garden for people on the move, who could turn their attention to other things without fear of the consequences. ". . . when the urge comes, the owner can slip away, without too much worry of what will happen if the garden is without his tender care," Ross explained.[43]

The conversion of the back yard to an outdoor living room portended a growing privatization of twentieth-century American neighborhoods. As people gradually shifted their activities to the back of their homes, their front yards—already established as public decorations—became even more impersonal. Pedestrian activity along sidewalks was declining as car ownership increased, and many residents now entered and exited their homes through their garages rather than their front doors. Gone, or reduced to a decorative adjunct, was the front porch. The invention of the home radio brought even more people indoors, as it was difficult to listen to programs while sitting on the porch. In addition, communities across the nation were enacting fence prohibitions (particularly along quieter roads) in order to preserve picturesque street views. "In this country a young man would as soon meet his girl in front of the department store show window as in the garden," remarked landscape architect Frank Waugh of the fish-bowl character of the front.[44] Apparently, the loss of front yard living space did not significantly affect homeowners. A 1930 New Haven (Connecticut) City Plan Commission poll found that most people wanted large front yards, even if they could think of no use for them other than aesthetics.[45] Nor did most homeowners lament the decline in street life. With the shelter and security afforded by a detached dwelling, the private sociability of the radio, the mobility of a car, and the outdoor living space offered by the back yard, the street was fast becoming, like the front yard, a nice place to be when you were on your way somewhere else but hardly a destination in its own right.

Chapter Four: The Modern Yard Emerges

The transformation of the back yard from a service area to a family room, though well underway in the 1930s, slowed as the nation plunged into economic depression. After the economic crash of 1929, official unemployment rates soared to more than twenty percent, house construction stalled, and mortgage defaults reached an all-time high. People fortunate to keep their homes had little capital to improve them or the grounds on which they sat. As personal incomes declined, articles, such as *House and Garden*'s "The Recent Rise Of An Old Habit—Staying Home," appeared, describing the activities a family could do around the house, such as play board games, write letters, and listen to the radio.[1] The back yard, now freer from the limitations of utilities, offered yet another opportunity for families to stay home, enjoy the outdoors, and grow vegetables to save money.[2] In 1941, the United States entered World War II, and the nation's economy shifted to supporting the war effort. Housing starts plunged even further, falling to nearly half the Depression-era levels. Sales of consumer goods—cars, appliances, clothes, furniture, and yard items—declined steeply, as landscape-related businesses such as the Toro Lawn Mower Company and Anchor Post Fence Company converted their operations to war-time manufacturing. Then, as dramatically as the economy had slowed, it erupted again at a furious pace when peace was declared in 1945. The suburban home and grounds entered an extraordinary period of development, solidifying their position for the next generations as the primary symbol of the nuclear family. This change happened rapidly and on a vast scale never before seen in the nation's history.

In 1945, millions of servicemen returned from overseas to a newly prospering country. The combination of the war-revived economy, government-sponsored financial incentives, and a steep demand for houses created an enormous real estate boom. The housing shortage was so great after the armistice that the Army quartered more than 50,000 veterans in Quonset huts.[3] In June 1944, Congress had passed the G.I. Bill of Rights, allowing servicemen and women to secure federally guaranteed home loans with no down payment. An ex-soldier now needed no more than a steady job to enter the housing market. Millions of veterans bought homes, joining the huge numbers of Americans who were finally returning to work and signaling the start of a housing boom that lasted nearly twenty years. Between 1935 and 1945, housing starts had averaged just 375,000 per year; from 1945 to 1960, they were four times greater, averaging almost 1,400,000 starts per year.[4] American demographics were also shifting. From 1950 to 1980, eighty-three percent of the nation's growth took place in the suburbs. Three quarters of the nation's biggest cities lost population during that time, while the suburban population increased by 60,000,000.[5] Accompanying this shift was a dramatic rise in suburban jobs. By 1960, middle-class families had moved into 21,000,000 brand new homes, with front and back yards of bare earth awaiting inscription by their new owners. Never before had so many Americans had the chance to decide how the home ground should look, how it should be used, and what it should be called.

Two federal programs stimulated the national housing market. One was the law permitting homeowners to deduct mortgage interest from their income taxes (created at the inception of the income tax law in 1913), allowing private citizens to reap substantial dividends. A second factor, larger still in shaping the home grounds, was the creation of the U.S. Federal Housing Administration, or FHA. Congress created the FHA in 1934 during the Depression to support the faltering house-building industry. The agency's purpose was to provide homeowners and developers with federally insured home loans, thereby reducing the numerous Depression-era mortgage defaults and bankruptcies. FHA planners were avid promoters of the detached home and yard, and they encouraged developers to build dwellings of this type on a massive scale. One of the FHA's creations was the "Pre-Improved Subdivision," a policy that encouraged large-scale housing tracts. As outlined in the agency's *Technical Bulletin No. 7*, a pre-improved subdivision was one in which developers installed all the roads, utilities, homes, and even front yards before anyone occupied the land.[6] Such developments relied on highly standardized practices regarding grading, house size and orientation, yard shape, street layout, median strips, and street trees.

The FHA guidelines did not emerge out of a vacuum; rather, they stemmed from a compilation of proven methods and solutions that architects, landscape architects, planners, and developers had employed for the previous twenty-five years. A prominent example was Radburn, New Jersey, a two-square-mile subdivision designed by architects Clarence Stein and Henry Wright in 1927. Modeled after English garden cities that Stein and Wright had visited, Radburn revealed numerous innovations. Its overall organization was based on the superblock, a land division system that, in contrast to the grid, employed a hierarchy of road widths, cul de sacs, and shared open space. Radburn's streets were separated into heavily and lightly traveled routes, with the less-trafficked ones made narrower to give over more space to private yards. Most of the roads were tree-lined cul-de-sacs, a solution that eliminated through-traffic and encouraged pedestrian activity. The cul de sacs backed up onto common green spaces within a short walk of all the homes, for all the residents to enjoy.

Radburn's houses were not cheap. Still, the community's improved livability was obvious, and FHA policy bulletins recommended many of its elements, such as the cul-de-sac, the hierarchy of road widths, large lots with generous setbacks, curving streets lined with trees, and prohibitions against front yard fences in order to accentuate greenery. The FHA promoted these solutions for a number of reasons, but at the top of the list one purpose stood out: the agency believed that this sort of neighborhood represented the lowest risk investment.

Technical Bulletin No. 7, one of the most influential FHA publications, encouraged developers to adopt picturesque street lay-

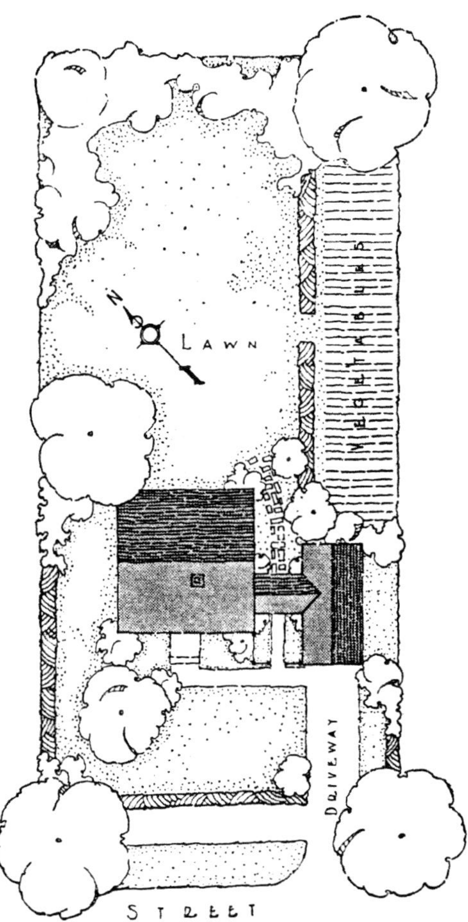

Figure 4.1. A suggested U.S. Federal Housing Administration plan for a suburban home grounds, emphasizing "economy, livability, and convenience." From "Principles of Planning Small Houses," *Technical Bulletin No. 4* (Washington, D.C.: U.S. Federal Housing Administration, 1940): 43.

outs rather than utilitarian ones. The bulletin included prescriptions such as "Preserve Natural Features of Site for Improved Appearance" and "Protect Residential Lots Against Major Street Traffic." Beautiful neighborhoods, the agency believed, allowed profitability and livability to go hand in hand. "As a rule the pleasing appearance of small community of houses of consistent character is directly reflected in its increased marketability," stated *Technical Bulletin No. 7*. Above all, commerce was deleterious to property values and had no place in residential neighborhoods. "Business encroachments have depreciated neighborhood property values through lack of restrictive covenants and zoning," the authors wrote.7 FHA *Minimum Requirements* booklets contained artistic sketches of homes set far back from the street, with charming yards afloat in seas of greenery. The booklets further encouraged that an ample—but not wasteful—amount of space be included on single-family lots for "gardening, landscaping, outdoor living or other uses considered essential to the type of dwelling under consideration."[8] To help accomplish these goals, agency planners often recommended that garages be placed adjacent to houses (rather than at the rear of lots) to free up back yard space and that front walks come off driveways rather than sidewalks to avoid cutting up front yards. The agency further encouraged the use of trees and shrubs to enhance a house's architecture and livability, and, echoing the advice of Frank Jessup Scott, it warned against using tall species that could "develop quickly into a miniature forest behind which the small house is hidden."[9]

When it came to laying out entire neighborhoods, the FHA advocated curved street layouts over gridded ones. Agency planners disliked the grid for several reasons. It often ignored topography, drainage, and other unique site features in favor of expedient subdivision practices. It made it harder for builders to orient homes and yards towards favorable views and a favorable orientation to the sun. It thwarted diagonal travel, and the long straight streets encouraged speeding. The grid was a real estate opportunist's solution to doing business, a way to squeeze plenty of lots onto a tract. Moreover, the grid was too urban-looking. Rectangular blocks were appropriate for business districts but lacked the special character that residential neighborhoods deserved.

As an alternative, FHA planners recommended curving roads and cul-de-sacs in the fashion of Radburn and other romantic suburbs, such as Riverside, Illinois, and Llewellyn Park, New Jersey. Curving roads served a number of purposes. They encouraged low density, as the non-rectangular lots that resulted from them were harder to subdivide into small, uniform parcels. A 1938 bulletin exhibited a "before" plan presumably submitted by a developer, with straight roads and 440 uniformly sized lots.

The "after" version, re-platted by the FHA to reduce density and to improve neighborhood character, contained gently winding streets, 147 lots of irregular shapes and sizes, and about one-fifth of the development set aside as park land.[10] Streets with curves not only were more attractive, but they helped to reduce speeding, as drivers were more wary of on-coming cars appearing around the bend. As John Archer puts it, curving streets even implied a leisurely lifestyle:

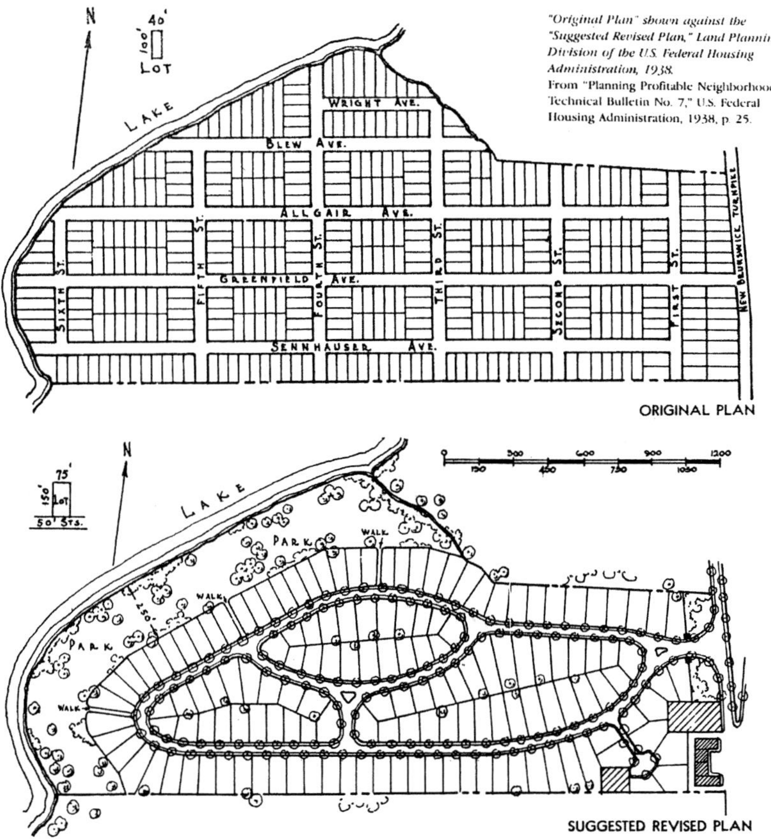

Figure 4.2. "'Original Plan' (top) shown against the 'Suggested Revised Plan' (below), Land Planning Division of the U.S. Federal Housing Administration." The revision (below) is a counterpoint to a "gridded" neighborhood plan (top). The agency reduced the top layout of 440 lots to 147 lots of greater size, curved the roads, and set aside ample space for greenways. From "Planning Profitable Neighborhoods," *Technical Bulletin No. 7* (Washington, D.C.: U.S. Federal Housing Administration, 1938): 25.

> Curving, winding streets are aimless and they are timeless. They presuppose that one really doesn't have to get anywhere and that one has all the time in the world to arrive. Both the commuter returning home and the family going to visit a neighbor participated daily in the luxury of such leisure, which is a manner of consuming surplus time and freedom with which they are privileged. In some respects, these curving, winding streets are even placeless. To this day, many romantic suburbs pride themselves on not having street numbers for houses. The implication is that the house and family define their own existence, without need of sanction or corroboration from the society at large.[11]

With respect to the home grounds, curving streets played a visual trick that accentuated front yard greenery. The urban grid, in its many variations, was most compelling when the views at the end of boulevards culminated at landmarks, monuments, or public squares, such as one might see in Washington, D.C. In residential neighborhoods, however, the grid produced a disappointing view at the end of each street, a "vista to nowhere," as Christopher Tunnard and Boris Pushkarev put it.[12] The rigorous monotony of most tract homes compounded the problem; nowhere, it seemed, was there a pleasing scene to capture the

Figure 4.3. Curving roads, in conjunction with street trees, speed limits, and fence restrictions, provide viewers with a continually unfolding view of front yard greenery in San Ramon, California, 2005. Photograph by the author.

eye. Curving streets never produced a terminal vista, instead presenting the onlooker with a continually unfolding landscape of grass, foundation plantings, and street trees.[13] With generous front setbacks, homes softened by billowing shrubs, and grass flowing nearly unbroken from property to property, curving streets had the potential to make a front yard's greenery the defining element of a neighborhood's character. Such a view was only possible if homeowners kept their yards unfenced or unhedged. To this end, FHA policies often discouraged or prohibited front yard enclosures.[14]

The FHA published its guidelines widely in construction and real estate trade journals. Developers were free to challenge the agency's requirements, but the paperwork took time, and there was no guarantee of getting a variance. Construction delays and unoccupied homes could cost developers a sizeable portion of their profits, so time was of the essence. As has often been the case with building regulations, most developers simply complied with the rules in order to get on with their work. From 1934 until 1960, the FHA underwrote twenty-five percent of all new home loans and financed improvements for nearly twice that number of existing homes. In 1939, for example, Peter Rowe reports that the FHA reviewed 2,625 residential subdivisions—more than fifty percent of the total housing starts (515,000) for that year.[15] Its influence proved to be greater still: many cities and banks voluntarily adopted FHA guidelines rather than take the time to write their own.[16] By 1959, the FHA claimed that three out of five families were living in homes for which it had underwritten the funding.[17]

The massive number of FHA pre-improved subdivisions revealed a significant change in the American housing market, in which real estate developers were transforming the business of home building from a small operation to one involving thousands of homes in a single sweep. One of the most influential individuals was William Levitt, a developer who launched an enormous building crusade after World War II that dwarfed all previous American housing projects. Levitt learned about modern building practices during World War II. Wars have been beneficial for technological advances; historians, for example, have remarked that aircraft design would have needed seventy peacetime years to evolve as far as it did from 1941 to 1945. House building procedures followed a similar crash course. When Congress declared war in December 1941, the United States needed to quarter a huge number of soldiers in short order. The U.S. Army hired building contractors who not only employed fast-paced assembly line and prefabrication techniques, but also used innovative materials, such as exterior plywood, latex glue, sheet rock, and composition board, to assemble living units as rapidly as possible. Levitt was one of the contractors, and he took careful note of the techniques he and his competitors used. After the war ended, Levitt applied many of the same assembly line methods to house soldiers once again—this time veterans who had returned home to start families.

Levitt's homes, along with the FHA's pre-improved developments, signaled the birth of the mass-produced "cookie-cutter" subdivision. In 1947, Levitt completed the first of three subdivisions that would bear his name. Levittown, New York, on Long Island, was a 17,000-unit development of single-family detached homes, parts of which were built at the unprecedented rate of 300 units per day. Levitt was careful to treat the grounds as an integral part of the property. To provide spacious surroundings, he made sure that his homes took up no more than twelve percent of their lots, and he located the kitchens in the rear so that mothers, while cooking, could keep an eye on their children playing in the back yard. Each property came with its own tree and sometimes a lawn. Setting an example for future communities, Levittown required residents to cut their grass once a week, prohibited fences, and forbade the hanging of laundry on Sunday. Levitt's houses varied only slightly from one another, prompting the infamous "cookie-cutter" label. What they lacked in individuality, however, they more than made up for in usefulness and affordability—each cost $7,990, with a $100 down payment. Buyers lined up at the doors of the sales office early each morning, and many of the homes sold out before the carpenters had finished nailing the numbers to the doors.[18]

Levitt went on to build developments bearing his name in New Jersey and Pennsylvania during the 1950s. Developers imi-

tated his work throughout the nation, especially in California where the population would nearly triple from 1930 to 1960. So many "cookie-cutter" subdivisions went up after 1947 that the small builder—who typically constructed fewer than five houses per year—was all but eclipsed from the housing market.[19] By 1949, only ten percent of all contractors were building nearly seventy percent of U.S. housing; by the mid-1950s, three-quarters of all new housing developments in metropolitan areas were in subdivisions.[20] It is one of the remarkable features of mid-twentieth-century suburbs that they looked so much alike, molded by fast-spreading, nationally embraced guidelines and building practices.[21] The American yard, once the domain of privies and garbage, was re-emerging on a genteel scale never before witnessed.

Figure 4.4. Levittown, Pennsylvania, in 1959, the third "cookie-cutter" suburb developed by William Levitt. (The other two were in New Jersey and on Long Island.) The middle-class home and its grounds emerged on a scale never before seen in history, with back yards firmly inscribed in the public mind as outdoor family rooms. Photographer unknown. Photograph obtained from *Images of American Political History*, on the Internet, http://teachpol.tcnj.edu/amer_pol_hist/fl/00001ad.htm (accessed 31 October, 2007).

Chapter Five: A Back Yard Family Room

During the late 1940s, as Gwendolyn Wright has observed, two new rooms appeared in middle-class American homes: the utility room and the family room.[1] The utility room sat just off the kitchen and housed two popular new appliances: the automatic washer and dryer. The family room, also called the "rec-room," the "multi-purpose room," and the "rumpus" room, was furnished with a television, record player, game tables, oversized pillows, and comfortable furniture. Wright could well have added a third room to her list: the back yard living room. The tract homes into which many families were moving, because they were affordable to a wide income-range of buyers, were often smaller than dwellings of the previous generation, especially in milder climates where slab-on-grade construction had eliminated basements. Moreover, the year 1946 marked the beginning of an eighteen-year baby boom, and child rearing had become a primary activity for many couples. The back yard was thus an opportunity to reclaim living space.

By the 1940s, back yards had opened up even further as a result of recent changes to houses. For one, domestic life was steadily migrating to the rear of dwellings, with fewer residents using their living rooms and front yards for family activities. For another, garages in suburban developments were now typically built into the front of the house, consuming less yard space.[2] Garages had gotten much bigger, and the unused stalls were good places to store trash cans, firewood, gardening tools, the lawn mower, ping pong tables, canoes, and other items that a family might otherwise leave in the yard. The automatic dryer permitted homeowners to dispense with clotheslines, signaling the demise of the drying yards that had long consumed space on the home grounds. With basic utilities, such as privies and cisterns, no longer in the way, families could play croquet and badminton, splash in wading pools, relax on outdoor furniture, and barbecue dinner. *House Beautiful* captured the steady civilizing of the middle-class back yard in the aptly titled article—designed to show homeowners how to convert their yards into genteel gathering spots—"Who Wants To Dine Among Cans and Clotheslines?"[3]

Many post-war suburbs were laid out around the mobility afforded by private automobiles, and the sheer number of cars was helping to reshape the home grounds in its own way. "The most notable factor in our 20th-century home-site usage is the effect of the automobile, since nearly every family has one," wrote *House Beautiful* in an article entitled, "How Our Cars Have Changed Our Gardens." Homeowners were reacting to the

Figure 5.1. By the end of World War II, house and garden magazines were running frequent articles on arranging back yards for domestic activities rather than gardening. "36 Ideas Show You How To: Use the Outdoors as Part Of Your House," *House and Garden* (July 1951): 34. Reproduced by permission of The Conde Naste Publications, Inc.

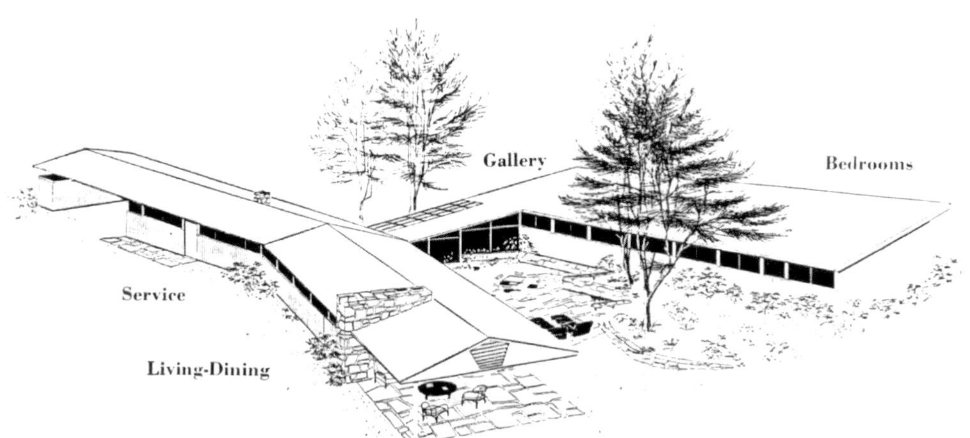

Figure 5.2. In the 1940s, the American back yard—which a generation earlier had been given over to privies, cisterns, ash barrels, trash, and bare earth—was joining the "rumpus room" as a family activity center. Arthur Rothstein, photographer, "Yonkers, New York. Mr. Garrity building a wading pool in the backyard for his children," August 1942. Photograph courtesy of the Library of Congress, Prints & Photographs Division, FSA-OWI Collection, reproduction number LC-USW3-005627-D.

automobile, the author explained, by choosing to spend leisure time at home rather than on crowded streets, by building fences and walls to block out engine noise and blaring horns, and by arranging their back yards to "have an air of serenity and produce a sense of peace and ease. For now more than ever we want the calming effect that the presence of nature has always had for mankind."[4] Furthermore, post-war suburbs were often located miles from parks and recreation areas, bus service was limited, and many tracts had no sidewalks—planners and developers often eliminated these due to the low number of pedestrians. A family thus had all the more incentive to stay at home and enjoy the yard.

With car ownership on the rise and garages filling with household items, where were people to park? Driveways and the street were an obvious solution but not a guaranteed one. Many communities, especially more affluent ones, began limiting curbside parking to one space two hours a day—partly to give drivers a better view of children playing near the street, but also to ward off "Manhattanization," a term planners coined to describe congested neighborhoods. In the 1956 article, "Planning With the Automobile," *Sunset* magazine showed readers how to scoop out a big section of lawn to create parking for eight cars.[5] In a similar story, *House Beautiful*'s article, "Let's Get Parked Cars Off The Street," showed how to remodel a suburban front lawn to accommodate up to twelve vehicles.[6] While directed to the owners of larger properties, such measures reflected the problems suburban homeowners suddenly faced in accommodating so many new vehicles. To this day, numerous communities enforce off-street parking ordinances and link parking regulations to the size of house additions, lot coverage percentages, and the number of occupants per dwelling.[7]

Of all the elements comprising the post-war suburban yard, the swimming pool most epitomized outdoor habitability. Here was a feature that was warm and sensuous, provided relief from summer heat, and symbolized recreation and leisure at their best. Residential pools first appeared in the 1920s and were well beyond typical middle-class budgets. Most early pool builders came from other industries. One of the first, Pascal Paddock, had previously built retaining walls and tennis courts and designed municipal waterworks and sewage systems. Building a pool was an arduous, costly procedure, as Paddock soon learned. The contractor began work by digging a deep, wide pit, a task in which off-loading the soil could be as arduous as excavating it in the first place. If a property was inaccessible by backhoe, the excavation had to be done by hand, and the work could take months. Next, the workers lined the edges of the pool with wooden form-boards to contain the concrete while it cured. The forms needed to be thick and unbendable to keep from bulging, and, as a result, most pools were rectangular in shape. Prior to the pour, the contractor lined the forms with reinforcing steel and placed expansion joints within the structure to accommodate shifting soils and temperature changes. Once the concrete had cured, the masons waterproofed and plastered the shell and set tiles along the waterline.

Finally, the pool water needed filtering and purification, and, in cooler climates, the owners needed a cover and had to drain the shell in winter. Swimming pools were expensive, costing from $5,000 to $10,000 in the 1920s, a sum greater than the value of most middle-class homes. As a result, pools were limited to public venues and the estates of wealthy businessmen and celebrities. From 1920 to 1930, pool contractors in Southern California built only about twenty pools a year.[8]

Middle-class Americans first started buying pools on a noticeable scale after World War II. By now, pools had become more affordable due to a recent invention called gunite, a process in which workers sprayed wet concrete against an earthen excavation. The U.S. Army Corps of Engineers utilized gunite in the 1930s to line drainage channels, and the technology suited pool building perfectly. No longer limited by stiff form-boards or concrete block walls, a contractor simply used the earth to shape the walls of the pool. As a result, an owner could choose from a wide range of shapes, including the popular "free-form" and "kidney-bean" styles that landscape architects were popularizing in house and garden magazines at the time. After inscribing the outline of the pool on the ground, the contractor could now dig the pit, a task that was becoming much easier due to the introduction of compact excavators.[9] Next, the builder lined the earthen sides of the excavation with a web of thin, bendable steel bars and sprayed it with the gunite, a slurry of cement, sand, and water shot out of a hose under extremely high pressure. The mixture compacted into a dense shell as it rammed into the sides of the excavation. Once the gunite cured, the contractor plastered the sides, tiled the waterline, edged the coping with stone or brick, and sometimes added boulders near the edge to serve as seats or diving boards.

Gunite pools, because they were smaller and malleable, fit comfortably into middle-class back yards. Most importantly, they were significantly cheaper than pre-war pools. A small gunite pool cost about one-fifth to one-half of a poured-in-place model, making it affordable to a greater proportion of homeowners. The gunite process was slow to take off, because few builders were skilled in its techniques or had the proper equipment.

Figure 5.3. A "kidney-bean" shaped pool in Santa Barbara, California, 2004. The invention of gunite—a mixture of sand, cement, and water sprayed at high velocity against an earthen excavation—made pools more affordable to a wider range of homeowners. Photograph by the author.

Despite these limitations, Southern California pool builder Philip Isley's contracts jumped from forty pools a year to 226 when he switched to gunite in 1940; by the 1950s, residential pool builders were working in every area of the nation.[10] And if homeowners could not afford an in-ground pool, they could order an above-ground kit from Macy's, Bloomingdales, Montgomery Ward, Sears, and other retail outlets. The cost was about ten to twenty percent the cost of a gunite version, and the family could be splashing around in the water within a day or two of delivery.[11]

A back yard living room provided a family with many benefits, but it also represented a responsibility: just like any other room of the house, it had to be kept clean, orderly, and functional. Housework was a major concern in post-war suburbs. Surveys revealed that American women were spending anywhere from thirty-two to fifty hours a week shopping, cooking, cleaning the house and yard, and running their children to and from school.[12] In 1947, *House and Garden* ran an article entitled, "Ten men in your life, They design appliances that help to take the work out of housework."[13] The author profiled the inventors of the G. E. Stratoliner range, the Tru-Heat iron, the Hoover vacuum cleaner, pre-fab cabinets, the Juice-King juicer, the Cory coffee brewer, the Hamilton dryer, and the Westinghouse toaster, each of which had modernized the house and, according to the author, promised to save a housewife's time.[14]

The *House and Garden* editors could easily have extended their list to include inventions that simplified the care of the back yard. Owing to the domestic uses to which a homeowner typically put it, back yard management was not unlike cleaning and straightening the interior of the house: clearing off tables and chairs, sweeping patios, covering the portable pool, picking up toys, washing dishes and utensils after a barbeque, and bringing jackets, books, games, and newspapers back inside at the end of the weekend.

In order to serve growing suburban markets, a group of businessmen called the National Landscape Association sponsored a design contest in 1945 for a drive-in garden center. The rules stipulated that, along with plants, the outlet was to sell hardware and accessories, provide thirty parking spaces, and have excellent visibility from the road. Winning an honorable mention and a twenty-five dollar prize was Thomas Church, one

Figure 5.4. Evergreen Garden Center in Sturgeon Bay, Wisconsin, during the 1960s. The first drive-in garden center opened in Detroit in 1946, and others spread quickly to serve millions of new suburban homeowners moving into tract homes with undeveloped yards. No photographer is noted by the nursery. Photograph used by permission of Evergreen Nursery, Sturgeon Bay, Wisconsin.

of the twentieth century's leading garden designers.[15] The association displayed the winning entries from coast to coast, and, based on these models, the nation's first drive-in garden center, Frank's Nurseries, opened in Detroit in 1946. For the first time, homeowners could fill their autos with gardening and household items, all bought under a single roof and all to make the home grounds more habitable. Garden centers spread quickly, especially across Florida and California, where the warm weather permitted residents to use their yards year-round.[16] Spurred by the success of this contest, the National Landscape Association began an annual residential design competition and established rules that affirmed the home grounds as a family recreation area rather than a horticultural one. Over the next twenty-five years, designers were encouraged to enter projects in four areas: single-family, front entrance, active-use, and passive-use areas. The criteria the judges used to evaluate the plans included plant selection, but, significantly, equal emphasis was put on tennis courts, children's play areas, patios, swimming pools, and other uses unrelated to gardening.[17]

Even the most botanically simple yards, however, required some gardening expertise on the part of the owners. To enjoy flowering bushes against the house, a homeowner needed to choose an appropriate species, plant the specimens without damaging the roots or burying the crown, keep them fertilized and watered, and clip them back on a regular basis. Lawns needed periodic weeding and weed control, fertilizing, raking, mowing, and edging. When newly planted or during hot dry spells, the yard also needed sprinkling. In response to these concerns, house and garden centers began to stock numerous maintenance products, such as electric hedge clippers, rotary tillers, edgers, pole pruners, insecticides, fungicides, weed killers, fertilizers, aerators, sprayers, and more. Of all the products and techniques that emerged, however, three stood out for their ability to help the general public manage it yards: containerized nursery stock, PVC (polyvinyl chloride) irrigation, and the development of lawn grasses and sod.

One of a family's first steps in improving its yard was to visit a local nursery to buy some plants. This endeavor, however, was

Figure 5.5. Prior to the large-scale adoption of containerized stock, nursery growers and retailers typically sold their stock "balled in burlap." The plants were heavy and cumbersome, difficult to transport, and often needed to be sold in fall or winter when they looked bare and unattractive. John Ferrell, photographer, "Washington, D.C. Construction of temporary war emergency buildings on the Mall, near 16th and 17th Streets, N.W. Trees being prepared for transplanting to make way for buildings," March 1935. Photograph courtesy of the Library of Congress, Prints & Photographs Division, FSA-OWI Collection, reproduction number LC-USF34-011438-D-A.

often wrought with difficulty. Until the late 1940s, most American nurseries either raised plants in greenhouses (or "under glass") or grew them directly in the ground. Both methods had drawbacks. Greenhouses were expensive to build and keep up, and they could only hold a limited number of plants. As an alternative, a grower could raise plants directly in the ground (such plants are called "field stock"), a method with its own shortcomings. First, field stock had to be spaced amply to prevent root intermingling, and thus it required a large growing grounds. Second, when a customer bought a plant, a salesman needed to dig up the specimen by hand and carefully wrap its roots in burlap. The root balls were heavy and delicate, and they could fall apart during transport or when the customer replanted it in the yard. Many trees and shrubs came "bare root" (no soil against the roots), and, while there was no bothersome root ball to deal with, the specimen resembled little more than a bare stick. Finally, to avoid harming the plants, nurseries needed to sell a good percentage of their stock during winter dormancy, when the plants looked dead. A bare tree or shrub might transplant better than one in full leaf and bloom, but its bare branches offered little visual or sales appeal.

In 1949, nursery growers in Southern California devised a way to raise plants that was superior to greenhouses and field growing in almost every way.[18] The climate in the Los Angeles basin was similar to the glasshouse environment of the Midwest, East, and parts of the South, and nurserymen could raise a wide variety of species outdoors with little concern for frost. Key to the new technology was the use of tin canisters, which had numerous advantages over traditional growing methods. First, the cans—unlike terra cotta pots—were cheap and light, and they could be packed close together without danger of the rootballs intermingling. Growers could thus store far more container plants in their yards than they could field-grown ones. If a plant got too large, an employee simply transferred it to a bigger container. Second, growers could regulate the soil mix inside the container to optimize growth and flower color. It took some time to develop the right soil mixes, and early on many seedlings were damaged or killed by excessive concentrations of salts and bacteria. If a mix was too fertile, weeds could overrun the container and strangle the seedling; if a mix was too light, water ran right through the container, taking valuable nutrients along with it. Once growers solved these problems, however, plants could live in canisters for years. And, third, nurseries (especially those in coastal California and Florida) could sell container plants at most times of the year, particularly during spring and summer when the flowers and foliage were at their peak. By contrast, it was risky to dig a field-grown specimen out of the ground during the warm months when it was most bountiful. Containers were easy to ship from the growing grounds to a retail nursery, and homeowners could carry the plants home in their cars without leaving a pile of dirt and roots on the back seat. By comparison, transporting heavy, burlap-bound trees and shrubs was cumbersome and risky. Once in its new location, a containerized plant was much easier to install than one wrapped in burlap, as the root balls were lighter and slid easily from their canisters.

The Interstate and National Defense Highway Act of 1956, introduced by Congress, in part, to stimulate American truck commerce, benefited the nursery industry greatly. Rather than having to maintain diverse inventories, growers could specialize in plants that thrived in their own area and ship them cheaply to outlets all over the nation. Moreover, the lightweight soil mixes greatly cut down labor and trucking costs.[19] As a result, the California nursery industry quickly embraced national markets, and its methods and technology were copied—climate permitting—in every state of the country. In 1949, California surpassed New York, until then the biggest nursery state, in nursery sales. Since then, California nurseries have consistently topped the nation in sales, shipping plants to retail outlets all over the nation.[20]

Containers revolutionized the nursery industry after World War II, as suburban homeowners flocked to retail outlets to buy flowering plants for their new yards. By 1970, American nurseries were selling almost ten times as many ornamental plants as edibles, a complete reversal of turn-of-the-twentieth-century inventories which favored edibles over ornamentals at a ten-to-one rate.[21] Once a central part of mainstream garden manuals, advice on growing vegetable gardens steadily shifted to specialty

Figure 5.6. Workers planting field stock at Evergreen Nursery growing grounds in Sturgeon Bay, Wisconsin, in the 1960s. Photographer unknown. Photograph used by permission of Evergreen Nursery, Sturgeon Bay, Wisconsin.

Figure 5.7. The invention of containerized nursery stock in Southern California in the late 1940s revolutionized the retail nursery, allowing middle-class customers to buy a wide assortment of plants almost any month of the year, transport them home in the back seats of their cars, and plant them without the root balls falling apart. Photograph by the author, San Ramon, California, 2004.

publications, such as *Horticulture and Organic Gardening*, or to books by the *Sunset* Publishing Company dedicated solely to the activity. The enthusiasm for ornamental plants, on the other hand, spread faster than ever and not just along the West Coast; a 1973 survey of retail nurseries in the South revealed that beautification was the main reason people bought plants.[22] By the 1980s, it was common to find nurseries offering more than 3,000 species of plants, many genetically engineered to yield showy flowers and strong scent, long stems, uniformly straight trunks, rapid growth, extended germination periods, insect and disease resistance, and hardiness.[23]

Once in the ground, plants needed water to survive; if natural rainfall was insufficient for the task, then a family had to resort to irrigation. The problem was compounded by the fact that, due to the growth and diversification of the nursery industry, most retail plants in a given geographic area were exotic (imported, rather than native) and not always adapted to the climate of their new region. Frost could quickly kill off a species with poor hardiness, but thirsty plants slowly suffered when deprived of water, dropping leaves, browning, and drooping before finally shriveling up and dying. The effects were especially severe in states with arid climates, such as Texas, New Mexico, Arizona, Nevada, Utah, and California. Every part of the nation suffered drought from time to time, however, and plants could easily perish unless their owners gave them supplemental water. In addition, even in the wettest climates homeowners still needed to water newly installed species for several months to establish their roots.

The invention of so-called "plastic sprinklers" helped to provide a solution. Until the 1950s, it was rare to find irrigation systems in middle-class yards. Most homeowners instead watered by hand with pails, buckets, and the wide assortment of spinners, oscillators, spray guns, and rubber hoses available at house and garden centers.[24] Subsurface sprinklers had existed since the early 1900s but, due to their high cost and difficult assembly, were typically found only in public parks and gardens, large private estates, commercial properties, golf courses, and agricultural areas.

Most early sprinklers had evolved from an irrigation device invented in 1894 by an Ohio farmer named Charles Skinner.[25] In an effort to find a faster way to water his crops, Skinner drilled holes into a length of steel pipe, mounted the pipe on metal brackets, and connected it to a water tank. When he opened the tap, water squirted through the holes and out onto his crops. The system, called the "Skinner line," represented a major improvement over the traditional way of watering with furrows (ditches between crop rows). Furrows required enormous volumes of water, and the trenches had to be contoured carefully to equalize the distribution of water from one end to the other. Even then the water did not always spread laterally to sufficiently wet all the roots, forcing a farmer to over-water to guarantee coverage. Finally, the trenches had to be plowed at regular intervals to break up the silt that collected along the bottom.

Skinner continued to develop his product, adding levers to rotate the pipes and machining the nozzles to distribute the flow more evenly, and eventually he sold his invention to a company bearing his name. His systems quickly became popular with farmers, public works departments, city park managers, and the owners of large country estates. In the 1911 *House and Garden* column, "The Naturalizing of a City Man," the author—who remained anonymous in order to bestow more freely his opinions about the benefits of country living—extolled the mechanical sprinklers a neighbor had installed to irrigate a potato field. "This new system can run literally up and down hill and is practical for a quarter of an acre, four acres or fourteen; and the labor of applying it is almost nothing, as a man can keep right on with his work of hoeing, weeding or cultivating while attending to it."[26] Compared to lugging a bucket or wielding a hose, the artificial rain cascading over a private garden was wondrous. The author continued:

> The sight that awaited his curious eyes as they returned to the field seemed almost incredible. There was a slight breeze blowing—here and there in the broad fields it stirred up clouds of powdery brown soil. A parching, searing dryness was everywhere. Everywhere except just ahead of them, and there, for a stretch of 400 feet, two thin walls of water mounted, wavering and gleaming, into the air, broke gracefully and came down in a fine, drenching spray. It almost seemed a miracle. . . .[27]

House and Garden's anonymous writer spent $132 for a one-acre system in 1911, a sum affordable to a country estate owner but beyond most middle-class budgets. Moreover, the apparatus was heavy, prone to clogging and overspray, and it required a plumber to assemble it. Large commercial and public properties were more suitable candidates for the technology. Irrigation pioneers, such as John D. Ross of Pasadena (reputed inventor of the first pop-up lawn head in 1904), L. B. Harris (inventor of the "Harris Precipitator" in 1910), W. Van Thompson (inventor of the revolving arm roller sprinkler circa 1907), and L. R. Nelson (inventor of one of the first "traveling" sprinklers that propelled itself through greenswards) were instrumental in developing sprinklers for parks, cemeteries, and golf courses.[28] In 1910, Los Angeles claimed to be the first American city to use pressurized sprinklers. Spray heads—set flush with the grass for protection from an equally new invention, the gas-powered mower—

Figure 5.8. Early sprinkler systems were expensive and difficult to assemble and likely to be found only at public gardens and parks, large commercial properties and private estates, and golf courses and agricultural areas. Advertisement in *House and Garden* (July 1922): 61.

watered the lawns in the city's Central Square Park. Skinner lines watered the shrubs. The city boasted that the system, while expensive to install, saved eighty percent in labor costs over hand watering; a single attendant could water the park in two hours at a cost of seventy cents, versus two workers and a full day of labor at five dollars.[29]

New irrigation products appeared on the market from 1910 into the 1940s, including impact heads (popularly called "Rainbirds" and invented in 1933 by the Rainbird Company), gear-driven rotors, hydraulic valves, electro-mechanical controllers, and improved Skinner lines, many of which still operate today in city parks and along highways. It was not until polyvinyl chloride (PVC) appeared on the retail market place in the 1950s, however, that middle-class homeowners began installing irrigation on a large scale. Just as containerized nursery stock had made it easy to buy and install plants, PVC made sprinklers accessible and affordable to middle-class homeowners. Polyvinyl chloride was invented in Germany during the 1930s, and it had numerous advantages over galvanized steel and copper pipe, then the industry standards for irrigation conduit. The material was light in weight, strong, and much cheaper to manufacture than its metallic counterparts. It had excellent flow characteristics; where engineers gave corrosion-prone galvanized steel a design life of ten years, the inside walls of PVC remained smooth for decades. Most importantly, it was easy to install. Galvanized steel pipe was heavy and difficult to handle, and most homeowners needed a plumber to cut, thread, and assemble the pipe. Copper—though hydraulically efficient—was even more expensive than steel, and it had to be soldered with a gas torch. If a homeowner mistakenly connected it to steel pipe, both pieces could corrode and might even interrupt the home's electrical grounding. In comparison, a novice with a hacksaw and a can of cement could install PVC pipe.

Figure 5.9. A plastic pop-up sprinkler. Polyvinylchloride (PVC) helped to make underground sprinklers affordable to middle-class homeowners. Photographer unknown and photograph undated. Courtesy of Maddison Water Technology, Spalding, Lincolnshire, England.

In 1955 and 1956, *House Beautiful* and *Sunset* ran stories about an exciting new invention—the plastic sprinkler—that was beginning to appear in retail markets. These early systems, primitive by today's standards, relied on clamps, flexible pipe, and fixed-height heads, and they were buried but a few inches below the soil where they were vulnerable to lawn mowers and spades. Still, they were remarkably easy to assemble and operate compared to steel and copper equipment. Annotated photographs showed homeowners how to lay the pipe along the ground, clamp plastic sprinklers on at regular intervals, connect the pipe to a hose outlet, and then bury the whole system beneath the ground. An electric timer turned the water on and off automatically, eliminating the tedium of moving an oscillating sprinkler from bed to bed every half-hour or, worse, watering with a hose.[30] The residential irrigation market entered a period of remarkable growth, as suburban homeowners raced to local hardware stores to buy plastic sprinklers for their yards. PVC soon replaced weaker rubber pipe and greatly improved system assembly, strength, and efficiency. The Champion and Safe-T-Lawn companies introduced spring-loaded pop-ups in the early 1960s and added plastic nozzles with arcs fitting odd sized and shaped planting beds.[31] Meanwhile, professional plumbers watched with disgust as homeowners glued together their back yard piping.[32] By the 1970s, millions of sprinkler heads were popping up out of American yards on a daily basis, letting loose a torrent of precipitation two to three times stronger than the heaviest rains. The effect on the home grounds was dramatic, especially in the West, Southwest, and Southeast, the areas with the largest markets for the equipment: trees growing thirty feet high in five years, lawns needing twice-a-week mowing, hedges billowing into walks and patios, and ferns and philodendrons thriving in desert climates.[33] What was once an abhorred, time-consuming task now took place at 4 A.M. while the household slept. A family could leave for vacation without fear of returning to a dead yard. A homeowner's only concerns were to pay the water bill, keep the grass below the heads, avoid slipping on the wet driveway, and hope that nature forestalled the next drought.

While containerized nursery stock and PVC irrigation simplified yard installation and management, the biggest breakthrough to affect the home grounds was the development of lawn grass and the mechanized apparatus used to install and maintain it. After World War II, the lawn emerged as the uncontested surface of the American yard. By 2005, turf acreage in the United States had climbed to nearly 40,000,000 acres, an area larger than Pennsylvania. While this figure included public uses, private homes accounted for eighty percent of the total.[34] By the 1950s, grass was well on its way to becoming the most researched non-agricultural plant in the world. The U.S. Department of Agriculture, United States Golf Association, owners of professional sports teams, universities, and park and recreation departments across the nation all invested considerable sums in turf grass technology. Rutgers University alone developed more than 7,000 varieties of bluegrass that proved reliable in almost every part of the country, given adequate water and fertilization.

Homeowners considered numerous factors when choosing trees and shrubs for their home grounds. Grass, however, was a nearly perfect fit in most yards for three main reasons: the speed with which it could be installed, the ease with which it could be maintained, and the social activities it could support. Prior to the twentieth century, growing a lawn was a complicated endeavor. Homeowners first needed to buy or collect the seeds, and, if the retail market for such a purchase was limited by today's standards, collection in the wild was exceptionally difficult. Upon securing the seeds, an owner's next step was to work the soil into a level, arable plot, carefully distribute and cover the seeds, and keep the new shoots moist for four to six weeks until they rooted. Weeks passed before the shoots could support foot traffic, and, even then, the grass was subject to fungus attacks, preying birds, and infestations of insects, moles, and weeds. As an alternative, homeowners could journey the countryside to harvest a mature meadow. Upon locating a suitable stand, the harvester dug up sections of sod with a flat shovel or "turfing iron," laid them upside down in a box, and scraped and pounded them into even thicknesses. A typical segment might weigh thirty to forty pounds, and it could take more than 100 sections to fill a small yard. After lugging the sections back home, the harvester laid them atop the rolled and leveled soil and kept them watered until the turf took root. Both seeding and sodding were painstaking, time-consuming activities, and most lawns before the 1900s were patchy, lumpy, and weed-infested, despite the owner's best efforts.

The invention of the sod-kicker at the turn of the twentieth century marked a turning point in the ease of installing a lawn. The kicker, or "sod-cutter," consisted of a large blade sitting two to three inches below the grass roots, which operators kicked forward with their feet. As the blade thrust forward, it cut a thick, even mat of grass and roots, thereby reducing the need for turfing irons and box work. The kicker made it possible to harvest sod quickly and on a large scale, and before long companies were selling turf on the retail market. Just as home and garden centers emerged to serve the suburban home market, sod farms became a major fixture in the horticulture industry. By the 1940s, sod growers had developed gas-powered machines that accelerated harvesting times, added netting to bind the sod together, and were growing improved varieties of turf. By the 1960s, the operator of a single machine could cut, roll, and stack sod onto pallets for shipping anywhere in the nation.

Sod offered homeowners a remarkable option: they could roll out a front and back yard in a day or two, for less time and money than it took to carpet the house.[35] Shrubs and ground covers could take years to grow, by comparison. Turf growers enjoyed huge national markets during the housing boom following World War II.[36] By the mid-1960s, there were more than 1,000 turf farms in the United States; by 2002, the number had climbed to more than 2,000, with annual harvests exceeding 386,000 acres.[37] For a young family with a new suburban home surrounded by bare dirt—with children clamoring for a place to play, with parents wanting to put their best face forward to the neighborhood, and with the statistical likelihood that the family would move within four to five years—a sod lawn had no equal as a surface for the yard.

A second reason for the increasing popularity of grass was its suitability for mechanized care. Despite the horticulture industry's best efforts to simplify the task of gardening, yard care contained numerous pitfalls and obstacles. Even trimming a hedge was not as simple as it looked; an improperly clipped bush could thin out under its own shade, the leaf type had to tolerate shearing, and more than a few homeowners sliced through the power cord on their electric clippers while trimming their shrubbery. Advances in lawn mower technology, however, had made grooming a lawn almost as simple as cleaning the kitchen floor. Hand-operated reel mowers had been in use since the 1880s, but now they competed with fast, efficient motorized versions. Gas-powered cutters first appeared around the turn of the twentieth century, but high cost limited them to public, commercial, and estate properties. By the 1940s, however, power mowers had become smaller, lighter, more powerful, and, most of all, affordable. By the 1950s, they were outselling reel mowers by a ratio of nine to one.[38] The fully drivable mower appeared around 1960, a suburban icon as notable as the convertible and the built-in barbecue.[39] By the end of the twentieth century, lawn mowers of all types had become household necessities; in the mid-1990s, Americans owned 89,000,000 of them.[40]

Compared to the time and skill necessary to raise a flower garden, mowing a lawn was the epitome of simplicity. Even the ten-year-old next door could manage the job, a feat unthinkable when it came to tending a perennial border, a vegetable plot, or rose beds. Lawn care technology did not end with the mower. Once the grass was cut, a homeowner could buy a myriad of pesticides and fertilizers to keep it free of weeds, bugs, and diseases. One of the most popular was 2-4D. Introduced in 1944 by the American Chemical Paint Company, 2-4D was a "selective" herbicide, killing only broadleaf weeds (dicots) but ignoring grasses (monocots). Though later found to have potentially harmful side effects, 2-4D was at once hailed as a gardening miracle. No longer did homeowners need to spend their Saturdays on their hands and knees digging out dandelions with a weeding fork; a quick shot of 2-4D did the trick. No longer did a family cringe at the prospect of the clover-infested weed patch next door threatening their greensward. No longer did a household's lawn turn yellow from nitrogen deficiency, since most weed killers also contained powerful supplements to keep the grass a rich emerald green. 2-4D paved the way for an extensive array of chemicals for all garden plants. By 1992, Ortho (a division of Chevron) offered ninety-six weed, bug, and disease control products, thirty fertilizers, and even "Leaf Polish" to give foliage a lustrous sheen.[41]

The greatest reason for the popularity of grass, however, was not technological but its ability to withstand sustained human activity. Grass could endure a brutal trampling and recover in a week or two, as a suburban family quickly found out after hosting a back yard birthday party or barbeque. It could be flooded, driven on by cars and trucks, and covered for months with trash and firewood and then rejuvenate in the briefest period. No other plant came anywhere close in this capacity. It constituted as durable an outdoor floor as most built surfaces, and it was far more comfortable and climate-friendly than brick, flagstone, gravel, or concrete. It cooled the family during the summer, it absorbed annoying glare, and it was soft and yielding when children fell on it. It not only made sense as a cover for the home

Figure 5.10. Children playing on a front lawn in Washington, D.C., in September 1935. "These houses have both sweeping front lawns and clean backyards," wrote Carl Mydans, the photographer. By the 1930s, the lawn was becoming the outdoor carpet of choice for American home grounds. Library of Congress, Prints and Photographs Division, FSA-OWI Collection, reproduction number LC-USF33-000161-M1.

grounds; it was as indispensable to the yard as the floor was to the house. If habitability lay at the core of the American back yard, then the lawn was inseparable from that purpose.

The family orientation of the post-war home grounds served a population that was moving in vast numbers into new suburban homes with bare back yards crying out for development; a population having children in record numbers; a population that, if it had more than a passing interest in horticulture and gardening, did not have the time to pursue these activities for more than an hour or two a week. By the 1950s, house and garden publications had shifted their focus even further away from horticultural concerns to serve this changing readership. A generation earlier, such publications featured articles on raising camellias and rhododendrons, improving the soil, growing vegetables, and developing cutting gardens. While still offering such advice, articles of a whole new character were now appearing. *House and Garden* magazine's 1951 feature, "Children in the Blueprint," showed readers how to divide up their homes and yards to allow the kids to play in one area while their parents entertained guests in another.[42] The magazine's 1951 story, "36 Ideas Show You How To Use the Outdoors as Part of Your House," hardly made mention of plants, an orientation unthinkable a few decades earlier.[43] From 1946 to 1951, the table of contents in *House Beautiful* seemed to devalue rather than celebrate gardening, listing articles such as "Let Power Do the Work in Your Garden," "Why Make Gardening Such Hard Work," "We Believe Gardening Should Be Painless," "Now You Can Garden Without a Lick of Work," and "Landscapes Without Waiting."[44] Contrary to the traditional meaning of the word, the magazine's *Gardening* section frequently included family living features, such as "The Backyard—America's Most Mis-used Natural Resource," "You Have A Gold Mine in Your Backyard," "The Secret of a Useful Backyard: Privacy From Nosy Neighbors," "How to Have a Child-proof Backyard," and "Your Backyard Is a Room."[45]

In 1951, *House Beautiful* published an article entitled, "Why has America invented its own Style in Gardens?" The author gave five reasons why a national garden style was emerging, and day-to-day family concerns rather than horticulture were at the heart of each one.[46]

Reason number one stated:

> *The automobile changed our living habits.* Twenty-five years ago we abandoned our gardens to go for a Sunday drive. Today we seek refuge from bumper to bumper traffic. So we convert our back yards into comfortable areas for lounging, eating and entertaining.

The car was indeed shaping twentieth-century life. The sheer number of vehicles, however, combined with the nuisance of flat tires, breakdowns, accidents, and poorly paved roads, were reducing the appeal of recreational driving. No longer impeded by laundry lines, firewood, and trash cans, a family could find refuge in the back yard.

The second reason stated:

> *Houses are growing smaller.* Americans crave the luxury of spaciousness, but rising costs force us to shrink the size of the house. So we use big windows and livable gardens to make small houses seem larger.

With a post-war baby boom in full swing and tract homes often lacking big attics and basements, the yard was a promising outpost of household expansion, short of moving or tacking on an expensive addition.

House Beautiful's third reason behind the American style of gardens concerned mechanization:

> *Power equipment replaces the professional gardener.* The garden is now designed to eliminate the need for professional gardeners. This banishes all the fussy garden details that past generations loved. Lawns become big open sweeps edged with mowing strips. Flowers are confined to show areas.

Mechanical and technological innovations had indeed simplified the task of gardening. Moreover, middle-class yards were botanically simple compared to the grand estates the magazine used to feature, and, if a homeowner did hire a gardener, it was

Figure 5.11. A back yard in Brooklyn, New York, in 1948, arranged for comfort, entertaining, and leisure. By now, utilities occupied a much smaller portion of most middle-class home grounds, opening up the space to more refined uses. Photographer unknown. "Ullman Co., 319 McKibbin St., Brooklyn, New York. "Barbecue set-up IV," May 15, 1948. Photograph courtesy of the Library of Congress, Prints and Photographs Division, reproduction number LC-G612-T-53078.

probably to mow the lawn and cart off the clippings.

The fourth reason focused on lifestyle:

> *America's pace makes a place for relaxing essential.* Americans spend so much time on the run that they must have an adequate place for relaxing. Now the garden is being redesigned to serve as a quiet room for relaxing.

Many people feared that technology was turning American life into an ever-accelerating treadmill, with workers stuck on assembly lines, languishing in cubicles, and jammed into commuter trains. What could offer a better respite on weekends and summer evenings than a quiet back yard free from piles of bills, dirty dishes, and a telephone ringing off the hook? Furthermore, many public attractions that used to be located miles from home were now available right on the property itself. The television was competing with the movie theater, the radio with the music hall, the barbeque with the public picnic grounds, the Doughboy pool with the old swimming hole, and the croquet set and badminton net with the city playground.

House Beautiful's final reason for the nation's emerging garden style combined the first four reasons into a straightforward explanation for what the yard was finally becoming: an outdoor family room:

> *Americans are sun-lovers and fresh-air enthusiasts.* Everyone in America strives to live outdoors as much as possible. Most people, especially children, must do this right in their own back yards, so the garden takes on a new importance. It becomes a recreation spot useful to the whole family.

House Beautiful's analysis sent a clear message: middle-class Americans might never produce beautiful gardens on a wide scale, but neither were they about to let their yards go to waste. It was about the time people could enjoy their home grounds in ways that counted: for their simplicity, efficiency, and opportunities for day-to-day habitability. Suburban home ownership was first tied to household needs; if most families used their yards to raise children rather than plants, so be it.

Figure 5.12. By 1960, America was reaching the peak of a twenty-year baby boom. Many homeowners had to choose between gardening and domestic uses for their grounds, and most of the time family living won out. © Bill Keane. Reprinted with permission of King Features Syndicate.

Chapter Six: The Suburban Garden Under Fire

America's post-World War II exodus to the suburbs spawned an outbreak of criticism on the part of intellectuals, and the home grounds often lay squarely in the line of fire. Critics from all quarters decried the overbearing homogeneity in the homes and the occupants: never before had so many Americans so quickly come to look, act, and dwell so much alike. Songs, such as Malvina Reynolds's "Little Boxes" and Leonard Bernstein's operetta "Trouble In Tahiti," and books, such as *The Crack in the Picture Window, The Man in the Gray Flannel Suit,* and *The Lonely Crowd,* portrayed the suburbs as a breeding ground for mindless conformity. "In any one of these new neighborhoods . . . you can be certain all other houses will be precisely like yours, inhabited by people whose age, income, number of children, problems, habits, conversation, dress, possessions and perhaps even blood type are also precisely like yours," wrote novelist John Keats.[1] At 8:02 each morning, millions of suburban front doors opened to unleash a parade of gray-suited businessmen who commuted by train to the city, indulged in three-martini lunches, had affairs with their secretaries, and walked into the wrong homes at the end of the day. "By day the suburbs were nearly deserted by men, who had gone to the city, and the community, its culture and climate, became a woman's world," wrote *Harpers* editor Russell Lynes in 1948. "In the suburbs a man's home is his wife's castle."[2] Fraught with boredom, suburban wives gossiped endlessly, bought every latest kitchen gadget, and drank themselves into oblivion, reinforcing the worst stereotypes of American gender roles. "[They are] developments conceived in error, nurtured by greed, corroding everything they touch," wrote Keats. "They destroy established cities and trade patterns, pose dangerous problems for the areas they invade, and actually drive mad myriads of housewives shut up in them."[3]

The suburban home grounds, by now firmly established in the public mind as a household extension, became a major target of critical fire. Keats might have added that, on Saturday mornings, the husbands paraded out again, this time dressed in Bermuda shorts and straw hats, to tend the yard. By ten o'clock, the street was alive with the whir of electric hedge clippers, the roar of gas-powered mowers, and the sweet fumes of freshly cut grass mixed with two-stroke engine exhaust. Later that day, the husbands met at the edges of their properties—carefully marked by the grass height where each had each stopped mowing—to chat about the dreadful commute and the promise of weekend hunting and fishing trips, if only the yard work would let up. Later in the day, the family gathered for the weekly ritual: the barbecue. "Whatever outdoor living the suburban family does is done in the back yard, where the smell of charcoal dominates

Figure 6.1. Malvina Reynolds's 1962 song lyrics, "Little boxes on the hillside, little boxes made of tickytacky," satirized the cookie-cutter suburbs that had sprouted up across America since the mid-1940s. Were these dwellings a breeding ground for conformity or a new and wide-sweeping version of the home and grounds that simply needed time to mature? Photograph by the author, San Ramon, California, 2005.

the still air of a July night," wrote Scott Donaldson in his lively examination of post-war suburbia. "Here, then, is real suburban living, and if one is tempted to doubt it, he need only look on every side to discover that his neighbors, every one, are proclaiming their devotion to fresh air and the suburban, even American way of life by eating in the dark."[4] Landscape architect James Rose called the post-war American home grounds one of the "newest, largest, most expensive, most antiseptic slums in the world."[5] Bernard Rudolfsky lambasted suburban dwellers for reducing the grounds around their homes to waste space. "As a rule, the inhabitant of our climate makes no sallies into his immediate surroundings. His farthest outpost is the screened porch," Rudolphsky wrote. "The garden—if there is one—remains unoccupied between garden parties . . . . Evidently, the current variety of gardens is not intended to be more than an ornament."[6] Regarding the natural destruction builders left in the wake of housing tracts, Bill Vaughn remarked, "suburbia is where the developer bulldozes out the trees, then names the streets after them."[7]

The critical fire directed against the home grounds peaked at the mention of the front yard. Here was a space that zoning laws, traffic, the disappearance of the front porch, the invention of the radio, television, and air conditioning, and the domestication of the back yard had relegated to little more than a decoration for the street. Moreover, most front yards had come to look too much alike, regardless of where a family lived. What the civic beautification movement had started, in the way of lawns and foundation plantings, homeowners were now executing to near perfection through the assistance of power mowers, hedge clippers, fertilizers, weed killers, automatic sprinklers, sodded lawns, and the widespread availability of easy-to-plant nursery stock. One could literally drive for hours through American subdivisions and see the same front yards almost anywhere one looked. "Regional differences in taste have all but disappeared," wrote Russell Lynes in 1948, "and if you were to be put down blindfolded in the new suburbs of any American city it would be difficult to tell whether you were in the East or the West, the North or the South."[8]

That most front yards sat idle and unused was of particular distress to architects, city planners, and even the editors of house and garden magazines. Sam Bass Warner deplored the ubiquitous "handkerchief front lawns" that adorned American homes, and he urged owners to enclose their properties along the streetside to gain outdoor living space. "High walls and enclosed gardens and courtyards in the European manner," Warner argued, "would have enabled American residential neighborhoods to be used more comfortably by people of varying incomes and ways of life."[9] For years, *Sunset* magazine urged Westerners to rip up their front lawns and foundation plantings and replace them with walled courts in the Mission Revival style, with tiled patios, wall fountains, sheltering arbors, and outdoor furniture. *House and Garden* magazine featured photos of families dining in front yard privacy behind walls just three feet from busy sidewalks. *Better Homes and Gardens* told readers that walled and paved front yard courts not only provided private living space, but also eliminated the need for hedge clipping and lawn mowing. "People who really love their gardens and work and play in them," *Better Homes and Gardens* writer Estelle Reise remarked, "cannot get real garden comfort unless they are shut off from the outside world, any more than they could get true comfort from living in a room whose walls were all clear glass."[10]

Figure 6.2. Many critics dismissed the post-World War II American front yard as a gigantic waste of potential living space. Most residents, however, regarded the space as vital to neighborhood beauty, and many communities banned front yard fences to preserve open street views. Photograph by the author, Dublin, California, 2005.

Figure 6.3. When asked why they chose not to fence their front yards, *House Beautiful* readers responded in 1960: "I want people to see what my house looks like;" "People want to see the open vistas across the yards;" and "It's prettier to drive through a street with wide front lawns." Photograph by the author, Oakland, California, 2005.

In 1960, *House Beautiful* editor Elizabeth Gordon launched a campaign to privatize the front yard. Not only were homeowners wasting valuable living space, Gordon argued, but many cities were actually usurping personal liberties by forbidding or restricting front yard fences. In her provocatively entitled article, "Does Your Front Yard Belong to You or the Whole Neighborhood?," Gordon argued that the historical precedents for fence restrictions were flimsy and arbitrary, and she encouraged homeowners to rebel against local statutes. "What did you buy a house for? Shall the kind of life experienced in a house be no different from that of an apartment?" Gordon asked her readers. When Gordon's *House Beautiful* assistants went door to door to poll homeowners on the issue, however, they heard a different view: "I want people to see what my house looks like," "I want to know what my neighbors are doing," "People want to see the open vistas across the yards," "I like to look out and see what's happening," "It's prettier to drive through a street with wide front lawns," and "It's the custom in this town."[11]

Gordon's pollsters met squarely with a sentiment that had been growing since the onset of streetcar suburbs, the enactment of residential zoning regulations, and the spread of civic beautification campaigns, a sentiment affirming the front yard as a public entity in the American mind. Apparently the ideology of individualism and the promise of some additional living space were not fair compensation for the vista of front lawns and trees and the resulting feeling of community identity. Americans were not only clear in their support for the open front yard, but also quick to insist that their neighbors comply with community standards concerning yard care. Sociologist Herbert Gans lived in Levittown, New Jersey, for two years in the 1960s and found that residents complained not just of neglected lawns but ones that were too well cared for.

Gans noticed that homeowners urged one another to support neighborhood norms and deviate neither toward shabbiness (which might lower neighborhood values) nor elaborate yards (which raised the standard of maintenance and created more work for everyone). Those who did not comply with this norm—by either neglecting their lawns or working too hard on them—were the target of wisecracks by their neighbors.

Gans believed that peer pressure rather than interest in gardening prompted public compliance. "Everyone knows it is social control and accepts the need for it, although one year some of my neighbors and I wished we could pave our front lawns with green concrete to eliminate the endless watering and mowing and to forestall criticism of poor lawns."[12]

In retrospect, the sudden and widespread expansion of post-World War II suburbia had intensified much of the criticism directed towards it. In time, the ethnic compositions became more diverse. The identical strings of homes became more varied as owners tacked on wings, upper stories, and bigger garages. Spindly saplings grew into tall trees that shaded the streets and yards and provided a neighborhood with a sense of maturity. The exaggerated gender roles turned out to restate the familiar division of labor that husbands and wives had long worked out

around the home, only now magnified due to the addition of the back yard to the list of household responsibilities. In the late 1950s, Rolf Meyersohn and Robin Jackson surveyed more than 300 suburbanites for their study, *Gardening In Suburbia*, and they found that "usually the wife is the keeper of the culture, living or otherwise. But in accordance with 'togetherness', some division of labor is usually worked out, commonly one in which the husband is expected to do the heavy work."[13] Rachel Kaplan reached similar conclusions in her 1973 study, *The Psychological Benefits of Gardening*. On the basis of personal interviews, Kaplan found that many women sought the same kinds of satisfactions from growing a garden they might expect from caring for the house. "The Primary Gardening Experiences appear to be most salient among women home gardeners and among home gardeners who find

Figure 6.4. Despite enjoying a rich heritage of English garden tradition, most middle-class Americans have used their yards for domestic purposes rather than horticultural ones. Of those who prefer to garden—as numerous surveys and statistics have shown—women have outnumbered men (and continue to do so) by more than two to one. Photographer unknown. Photograph used by permission of the Chicago Historical Society, Chicago *Daily News* negatives collection, DN-0085840, circa 1928.

the greatest satisfaction from Nature settings," Kaplan wrote. "For these women, the home is the primary focus, and gardening may provide a rewarding change from the other demands placed on the housewife."[14] Because it was an extension of the house, Kaplan suggested, the yard was yet another room to be managed, and women were far more likely than men to assume that particular responsibility in our culture. Kaplan's findings mirrored a survey done the same year of retail nursery expenditures made by 840 Southern homeowners. The study showed that wives participated in seventy-five percent of nursery purchases and were twice as likely as their husbands to be the sole decision-maker for such purchases.[15]

Most telling about the post-war suburbs was the sheer number of people who chose to move there. By 1960, more than 26,000,000 Americans lived in new single-family homes, mowed and watered their front lawns every week, parked their motorboats and campers in the driveways, piled firewood in their side yards, took down the clotheslines, and converted their back yards into family rooms. Were these people's yards really, in Rudolphsky's words, "a gigantic waste of potential living space" or a new and wide-sweeping version of the home grounds that simply needed time to mature?[16]

Part Two
California Garden

Chapter Seven: California and the Inside-Out House

If family living rather than horticulture became the raison d'être for the middle-class home grounds, it was a purpose limited by geography. In most of the United States, the climate drove people indoors for a good portion of the year. There was the drizzle of the Northwest, so constant that the city of Seattle was known to declare civic celebrations when the sun finally poked through the clouds; there was the blistering dry heat of the desert Southwest, which nearly eliminated daytime street life in Phoenix and Tucson; there were the humid summers and freezing winters of Chicago, where high-rise apartment windows were sealed shut year-round and occupants had only a thermostat to control the temperature; there were the sweltering summers of the Southeast, where Sarasota homeowners sat inside screened porches to fend off gargantuan insects and swarming mosquitoes; and there were the thunder and lightening storms that sent New England picnickers running for shelter on summer afternoons. For most parts of the nation, the "comfort zone"—a temperature range of sixty-five to eighty degrees that physiologists find most people prefer—was difficult to sustain for extended periods.[1] *House Beautiful*, which regularly featured stories on indoor and outdoor climate control, reported that residents of the Ohio River valley near Louisville, Kentucky, experienced "comfort zone" temperatures less than one-third of the year.[2]

Americans' inability to come to terms with climate, warned Bernard Rudolphsky in the 1950s, was breeding architectural styles that turned their back on the outdoors:

> A New York journalist oncc proved to his immense satisfaction that he could live a normal, or at any rate, what is recognized as normal, busy week's life, go to work at his office, visit restaurants and theaters, shop, fill social appointments, without ever emerging into the open air. The news of this feat must have been received with great relief by all those people who feared that we had come to the end of progress.[3]

Rudolphsky was not far off the mark: industrial psychologists have estimated that average Americans spend ninety percent of their weekdays indoors.[4]

Rudolphsky's New York City journalist obviously did not live in coastal California, where, by the 1950s, residents were pursuing year-round outdoor living with a fanaticism unsurpassed anywhere else in the nation. The Pacific Ocean was a powerful moderator of climate: summer temperatures averaged from sixty-five to ninety degrees, and, apart from some Alaskan storms, temperatures seldom dropped below freezing for more than a handful of days per year. Rainfall was light, about ten to twenty inches a year, and only a small fraction (about one-sixth) of it fell between April and October. In January, while most of America huddled in wool overcoats, Californians were hiking, fishing, golfing, picnicking, bird watching, eating in sidewalk cafes, and relaxing in lavish back yards. "Even if you starved to death in California, you'd enjoy the climate doing it," remarked Los Angeles police sergeant Joe Friday on an episode of the *Dragnet 1969* television series.

In coastal California, the American yard—a place to kick a soccer ball, swim in a Doughboy pool, or hold a 4th of July barbecue—had the potential to become a full-fledged garden. Not in the English style, with tall hedges, flowering borders, and rockeries, though many California gardens included these things. Not in the Japanese style, with flowering cherries, bonsaied pines, and koi ponds, though such gardens were common among the state's Asian population. Not in the Mission Revival style, with gravel courtyards, trickling fountains, and stucco walls, though this style had flourished for decades in the southern part of the state. Not in the agricultural style, with squash, carrots, beans, strawberries, and herbs, since fresh vegetables were cheap and abundant at produce stands and grocery stores. The California garden was a furnished outdoor room where the family could eat, play, entertain, and relax for almost the entire year due to the mild climate. It was a place—unlike most American yards—made separate and private from the neighbors by walls, fences, and tall shrubbery. It was a place where the back yard air and scent might be as fresh as that at the beach or the mountains. It was a place where mild temperatures, rich soils, and a huge "green industry" contributed to an enormous distribution of plantings, even in the yards of people with no interest in gardening. By the 1950s, the middle-class California garden was arguably becoming an American yard that approached its full potential as habitable outdoor space.

The first step in the evolution of the middle-class California garden was the emergence of a dwelling that communicated intimately with the outdoors. The practice of indoor-outdoor living went back centuries. According to Madge Garland:

> the conception of the garden as an outdoor room, an extension of the house rather than a separate entity, has been extensively developed in Italy from Roman times to this day. An intimate connection between the house and garden was part of the classical tradition, and a garden room was included in the residences of most well-to-do Roman citizens."[5]

Outdoor rooms worked best in places with warm climates, such as Italy, Spain, and North Africa. Each of these regions produced house styles with strong indoor-outdoor connections, and, owing to its favorable weather, coastal California promised to do the same.

As a prominent household feature, the outdoor room would take time to develop. Almost all of the Spaniards and Mexicans who made their way into California during the eighteenth and nineteenth centuries lived in crude dwellings, few of which incorporated prominent connections to the outdoors. Settlers fashioned homes out of adobe blocks or straw and mud mixes, paved the floors with packed dirt, and sealed the roofs with asphalt. Families typically cooked their meals outdoors and heated their homes with pans of hot coals. Settlers planted few trees or shrubs around their homes, likely due to the heat and arid summers and the need to protect their households from surprise attacks and theft.[6]

One dwelling type, the mission, though limited in distribution, offered more comfort and portended the development of indoor-outdoor living. From 1769 to 1823, Spanish missionaries built twenty-one missions along the Pacific Coast. Each mission typically had a central courtyard that was walled from the summer wind, shaded by an arcade (a roof overhang supported by posts) along the edges, and featured a fountain to offer relief from the intense summer heat. The fountain, as was common in Islamic, Moorish, and Spanish gardens upon which the Mission Revival style (originating in the 1890s) was based, also celebrated the preciousness of water. Courtyards were a highly developed art in Moorish Spain and became a cultural insignia wherever Spaniards colonized the new world. The insignia worked especially well in California, as David Streatfield points out, where the rolling savannas of grasses and trees, the marine-influenced seasons, and the hot interior valleys resembled the Spanish landscape. "The Spanish and Mexican occupation of California is a typical example of cultural colonialism in a frontier environment," wrote Streatfield. "The familiar was recreated as rapidly as possible."[7] The private ranch and farm dwellings that followed the missions often copied the latter's style, incorporating arcades, small fountains, and walled courts paved with stamped earth or gravel where the families ate meals, did chores, and escaped the intense summer heat that collected inside the house.

Virtually no rain fell in California between May and October, and water was scarce. Settlers planted their land sparsely with fruits and medicinal herbs from Spain and Mexico, such as almonds, apples, apricots, avocado, cherries, chilies, figs, grapes, lemons, limes, olives, oranges, peaches, pecans, plums, quinces, raspberries, strawberries, and walnuts. Because of California's proximity to the ocean, sea-going traders often stopped along coastal ports and exchanged plants for supplies, bringing more exotics into the state.[8] The most prominent foreign contribution to California flora was perennial rye grass, a species that got there by accident. Spanish explorers inadvertently brought rye seeds in the mud caked on their supply crates and in the feed for livestock. The grass spread ferociously, crowding out over ninety percent of the state's native bunch grasses. When prospectors swarmed the Sierra Nevada in 1849 in search of gold, the foothills shimmered with brown rye grass. It was the color of the rye rather than gold which inspired California's nickname, the "Golden State."[9]

Ornamental plants around early California dwellings were especially scarce, limited to species with economic or practical benefits. Maureen Gilmer notes that eighteenth-century Mexicans brought begonias, cosmos, dahlias, daturas, marigolds, morning glories, and poinsettias as they traveled from mission to mission.[10] One of the most colorful plants around the missions was the native rose, *Rosa Californica.* Mission dwellers cherished the plant for its colorful flowers and for the leaves, which exuded a sticky oil that cured minor ailments. The California pepper became the signature tree of the missions. Popularly regarded today as a native, the tree actually originated in South America. A legendary Spanish sailor stopping in Peru stripped off some seeds from a Peruvian pepper and brought them to California. The seeds made their way into the hands of a priest, who planted them in front of his mission. Only one tree survived, but it purportedly generated enough seeds for pepper plantings at all the other missions, and the species eventually naturalized itself along the coastal foothills.

Another familiar mission plant was the date palm, a species that yielded branches for fences, roofs, and religious ornaments. Another was the prickly pear cactus, sometimes called "beaver cactus" owing to its beaver-tail-shaped leaves. The prickly pear not only bore edible fruit, but it made a thorny hedge, provided a paste to firm up mortar and whitewash, and harbored a microscopic insect that produced a rich, durable red dye for clothing. According to Dane Coolidge, certain plants marked the trails between the missions, each located about a day's travel apart: "It is said that the first padres as they traveled up the coast dropped mustard-seed to mark the Camino Real; and when the golden flowers sprang up, each in the form of a cross, the Indians looked upon it as a miracle."[11]

Spanish and Mexican settlers believed that certain native plants had magical properties. The California bay tree offered security, averting danger and trouble for anyone who dwelt beside it. The elderberry warded off evil spirits, and a sprig concealed on a grudge holder removed all powers of evil. A branch of Monterey cypress placed on a casket moved the deceased's soul out of purgatory and into heaven more quickly. New brides and grooms often planted a Toyon to determine who would rule the household. If the Toyon languished, the husband would prevail; but, if it flourished, the wife would rule the home.[12]

The plants introduced by Spanish and Mexican settlers, though diverse, were few in number and had little visual impact on the landscape. The territory was vast in size, and the population remained small for nearly a century after the Spanish and Mexicans arrived. The hot, dry summers made extensive farming impossible, and settlers instead engaged in low-impact enterprises, such as raising cattle, sheep, goats, and pigs and exporting hides and tallow. The peace, however, was not to last. In 1849, news flashed across the United States of the discovery of gold in the California foothills. Within a few months, 80,000 prospectors arrived by wagon and sea in search of fortune. Some journeyed by mule train over the Sierra Nevada, while others sailed from the East Coast, a voyage that included an arduous trek across the Isthmus of Panama. Upon arriving, prospectors en route to the foothills abandoned thousands of boats in San Francisco Bay, many of which the city of San Francisco commandeered for housing and firewood. The Sierra foothills teemed with newly formed tent cities populated in the thousands. A few prospectors struck it rich; the rest barely scraped by. The gold rush mostly burned out in three years, but by then California had become firmly inscribed in the American mind as a modern-day paradise, a land of beauty and opportunity.[13]

In 1869, the Union Pacific Railroad completed the transcontinental railway, setting the stage for a steady migration to California that has yet to stop. Real estate speculators launched vigorous campaigns to lure Easterners to the Pacific Coast, publishing pictures of rugged coastlines and white beaches, of luxurious California homes framed by orange orchards and snow-

WINTER SCENE IN OAKLAND.

Figure 7.1. A winter scene in 1885 in Oakland, California. The mild Pacific Coast climate, with its promise of luxurious plant growth and year-round outdoor living, lured millions of Americans west. From *Oakland and Surroundings: Illustrated and Described, Showing its Advantages for Residence or Business* (Oakland, Calif.: W. W. Elliot, 1885), 40.

capped peaks, and of avenues lined with robust palms. Travel journals portrayed a land where the temperature never froze, where people picked fresh fruit year-round, and where plants from every corner of the world flourished. In 1887, a railroad fare competition allowed people to travel from Kansas City to Los Angeles for one dollar, and newcomers arrived in droves. In less than ten years, the population of Los Angeles rose from 11,000 to 80,000.[14]

If East Coast streetcar suburbs were a pleasant alternative to city life, coastal California was akin to paradise. "The purity of the air of Los Angeles," an enthusiast wrote in 1874, "is remarkable. Vegetation dries up before it dies, and hardly ever seems to decay. Meat suspended in the sun dries up, but never rots. The air, when inhaled, gives to the individual a stimulus and vital force which only an atmosphere so pure can ever communicate."[15] And the *San Francisco Call* hailed Berkeley as a "byword for climatic perfection throughout the world."[16] So healthful was the Oakland climate, boosters bragged, that the death rate was less than half that of Cleveland, Chicago, Detroit, and other Eastern cities.[17] Journalists even hailed the chilly, damp fog of San Francisco for its health-giving ozone, "which conduces to the tone and vigor of the physical, mental, and nervous forces."[18]

The first post-gold rush dwellings built by newly arriving Americans often mimicked the styles from their homelands: to paraphrase David Streatfield's observation, another recreation of the familiar.[19] Early neighborhoods in Oakland and San

Figure 7.2. A California dwelling in the Mission Revival style. The long, low rooflines and single-story construction pre-dated the ranch style that emerged in the 1940s. Photograph by the author, Palo Alto, California, 2003.

Figure 7.3. A California back yard in the Mission Revival style, with a broad courtyard, vine-laden arcade, and tall shade tree. Photograph by the author, Palo Alto, California, 2003.

Francisco revealed block after block of Victorian, Colonial Revival, Shingle, and Eastern Stick homes, structures that stood high off the ground and had few connections to the grounds other than front porches and foundation plantings. Front and back yards contained broad lawns dotted with evergreens, elms, and maples, but they revealed few opportunities for outdoor living. Architects and builders were soon to respond to the mild coastal climate, however. The turn of the twentieth century saw the construction of thousands of white-plastered Spanish and Mission Revival dwellings, especially in the southern part of the state, with red-tiled roofs, arcades, and walled patios in which the family could sit and enjoy the outdoors. The patio would quickly become a signature feature of California gardens, appearing in many types of gardens in the coming century.

The next major house style to emerge was the California bungalow, a small middle-class dwelling that emphasized simplicity and economy and that contained both symbolic and literal connections to the outdoors.[20] A combination of traditional bungalow and Japanese influences, the style came closer to expressing regional conditions than did the derivative Mission Revival dwelling.[21] In keeping with California's mountains, rugged coastline, and frontier-like character, the bungalow incorporated various links to the outdoors. The homes were usually single level and built close to the ground. The siding consisted of naturally finished or lightly stained wood, and the moderately pitched roofs culminated in wide eaves that shaded the windows and porches. The dwellings contained many "mountain camp" references, such as rough-hewn timbers, exposed fieldstone foundations, cobblestone chimneys, and sometimes log or pebble-dash accents and decorations, all of which suggested an interweaving of nature and structure. The style caught on rapidly, according to Kenneth R. Trapp: "Although the prime years of bungalow promotion were 1905–15, the *Los Angeles Examiner* reported in May 1904 that every street in Pasadena had a bungalow, and Los Angeles and Hollywood abounded in the wide-roofed dwellings as well."[22]

The California bungalow had two important features that linked the house to the yard. The first was a broad veranda that extended across the front facade and often well back along the sides of the dwelling, providing a sizeable outdoor sitting area accessible from the rooms inside. The porch was more than just a pleasant place; it was a symbolic connection to nature, a place where "the indoors and outdoors might be said to join hands," according to an advertisement in *Radford's Artistic Bungalows.*[23] Second was a patio. The Southern California climate was comfortable almost all of the year, and the patio—like the mission courtyard—provided valuable living space. Patios were not as common as porches but represented an important precursor to the outdoor room style that would soon sweep the state. Though used loosely in ordinary conversation to mean any sort of paved terrace, the term "patio" literally describes an outdoor space framed by walls. A bungalow's patio typically abutted two or more sides of the house, and some sat directly in the house center, not just acting as outdoor living areas but also providing passage between rooms. Patios ranged in size from quite large (often found in U-shaped houses where the patio abutted many of the rooms) to less than eight by ten feet, but most were similar in size to the living room of the house. Many featured ceilings in the form of vine-laden pergolas and floors of brick, tile, or concrete (often called "cement"). On larger properties, patios often extended past the house and well into the garden, and they included grass, trees, and flowerbeds. Most of all, patios provided sunlight, fresh air, and opportunities for outdoor living, and owners often furnished them with chairs, tables, hammocks, and outdoor rugs.[24] Arthur Jerome Eddy, a lawyer and YMCA leader, hired an architect to design a bungalow for him, and soon he became an avid booster of indoor-outdoor possibilities of the style:

> . . . for a house in Southern California without a patio is no house at all. It is just a decorated box wherein people swelter. The patio serves three vital purposes; it lets in sunshine in winter; it gathers the breeze in summer; it affords a place for the family to lounge in perfect seclusion or lazily sleep to the soft sound of the splash of water from the fountain.[25]

The interior of the bungalow often included the same rustic elements as the exterior, such as stone chimneys and thick wooden beams, features that further enhanced the indoor-outdoor associations. Moreover, the moderate coastal winters allowed architects to include lots of windows, increasing connections to the outdoors even further. The California bungalow was affordable, and plans in pattern books cost as little as $5. "When you see a cozy one or one-and-a-half storied dwelling, with low-pitched roof and very wide eaves, lots of windows and an outside chimney of cobble or clinker-brick half hidden by clinging vines—that is a bungalow, whatever other houses may be," wrote Charles Francis Saunders of his bungalow in a 1913 issue of *Sunset* magazine.[26]

The era of the bungalow paralleled the emergence of a related style, the Arts and Crafts garden. Arts and Crafts gardens were not so much distinguishable by looks as by common approaches and philosophical underpinnings. Practitioners of the style ranged widely from architects, horticulturists, and nurserymen to poets and writers. The designs they proposed, though varied, shared the common premise that the house and grounds should be treated as a single unit rather than as separate entities. Arts and Crafts gardens borrowed from many styles. Japanese

Figure 7.4. A California bungalow in Oakland, 2005. The style featured rough-hewn timbers, exposed stone foundations, and broad front porches where, as promotional brochures put it, "the indoors and outdoors might be said to join hands." Photograph by the author.

gardens provided models for integrating nature into the confines of the property, for establishing strong connections with the house, and for the design small outdoor spaces. The California missions and early ranch houses contributed the walled court, a common form in Mediterranean architecture that provided protection, privacy, passive climate control, and outdoor living space. North African courtyard gardens provided the inspiration for colonnades, pools, and fountains. The designers of Arts and Crafts gardens, however, were not content simply to copy elements from other countries, but they endeavored to create regional character by using local stone, lumber from native trees (especially redwood), and indigenous plants.

Common to the style was the naturalistic use of plants to unite landscape and house. Gardener and architect Charles Frederick Eaton believed that houses should fit seamlessly into the surrounding landscape, and he selected plants to highlight the bronze colors of the grassy hills surrounding his home in Santa Barbara. Horticulturist Kate Sessions used native and Mediterranean plants to create hillside gardens suited to the dry climate of San Diego County. Berkeley poet Charles Keeler worked with architect Bernard Maybeck to turn a Berkeley neighborhood into a continuous garden filled with lavish plantings from all parts of the world. Keeler's horticultural enthusiasm, like that of his Arts and Crafts contemporaries, was possible, in part due to the mild coastal climate, which allowed plants to grow with minimal danger of freezing.[27] While the owners of most Arts and Crafts gardens were well-to-do professionals, the style was steadily trickling down to the middle class. In 1914, Eugene O. Murmann published *California Gardens,* a pattern book for bungalow gardens. Typical of garden books of this era, *California Gardens* included a photo showcase of lavish estates with grounds large enough to contain entire neighborhoods of working-class homes. But Murmann went on to present fifty designs for bungalow homes and lots, many of which were within the means of ordinary homeowners. The designs addressed the practical needs of the household by placing vegetable plots and service areas near the back of the lots and screening them from view, naturalistic shrubbery around the perimeters for privacy and beauty, and open lawns in the centers for family living and children's play. "There are many back yards in a great metropolis or a small town which are used as assembly places for clothes poles, ash cans, and similar things. Such an unsightly 'back yard' can easily be converted into a charming garden without great expense," Murmann advised.[28] Readers who saw something they liked could buy a set of drawings—complete with plant names—for as little as $1-2 from the author. Between 1909 and 1924, John McLaren, horticulturist and designer of San Francisco's Golden Gate Park, released three editions of *Gardening in California: Landscape and Flower.* Mostly a horticultural guide, the book also contained an array of garden plans showing homeowners how to transform their grounds into livable space. Similar to those in Murmann's book, the drawings included plantings (most of which are still popular in the nursery trade today) from the world's five Mediterranean climate zones and open lawns for family living and children's play.[29]

By the early twentieth century, garden writers were commonly calling for homeowners to remodel their back yards, and the mild costal climate encouraged such conversions in California. One such writer was Ernest Braunton, who for twenty-five years was Garden Editor for the *Los Angeles Times Sunday Magazine.* In his 1915 book, *The Garden Beautiful in California,* Braunton argued that the back yard was not just an area to assemble ornamental plants but an extension of the living space of the house itself. While many parts of the home grounds were rightly given over to ornamentation with plants, he believed, the back yard was a "family affair. . . . Here is the part upon which to lavish your homely affections. Have a place in which to swing a hammock and have at least on arbor or covered seat or a playhouse for the children, and if there is sufficient room, have them all, and more."[30] Echoing Braunton's sentiment was architect Charles E. White, whose 1923 book, *The Bungalow Book,* advised readers not only on house layout, but also water service, sewage disposal, site planning, and garden design. "The back yard is a place most frequently wasted in American grounds," White wrote. ". . . Unfortunately some house owners use it as a sort of dump for ashes: a neglected place hidden from public view, where neatness is not always the chief end." He advised readers to make the space beautiful and useful by planting grass for lawn games, installing trees and shrubs to create pleasant views from inside the house, and in general bringing it up to the level of the rest of the grounds. "Cause it to yield of its best for the benefit of the family, just as much as the front yard," he urged.[31]

While converting a back yard into family space made good sense, many of the solutions designers put forth revealed only minimal connections to the homes. Murmann's and McClaren's lawns and terraces often sat near the back of the lot rather than near the house and—through no fault of their own—were often only reachable by narrow side or back doors. Moreover, the curvaceous lawns and meandering shrubbery commonly found in design books, while more beautiful than ash barrels and trash cans, appeared more derivative of English garden design principles than a regional style. At the same time, architects such as Myron Hunt, Elmer Grey, and Irving Gill were experimenting with an "outdoor room" style of building that better linked the indoors with the outdoors and appeared more house-like than gardenesque. Gill's clean, spare designs presaged the modernist movement by nearly two decades. He believed that nature and architecture were related and commonly designed his San Diego homes around patios and garden spaces. Gill drew openly from the hacienda style in his use of sleek, modern arches, ramadas, and walled courts furnished with easy chairs, dining tables, hammocks, and rugs. Describing how San Diego's historic Casa De Estudillo ranch home had inspired his work, he remarked, "In California we have liberally borrowed this home plan, for it is hard to devise a better, cozier, more convenient or practical scheme for a home. In the seclusion of the outdoor living rooms and in their nearness to the garden, the arrangement is ideal."[32] Gill further linked architecture and nature by using plants to create living roofs, to break up the severity of large surfaces, and to play off the walls of his homes, which he sometimes painted with primary hues to enhance the flowers' colors. He often collaborated with horticulturist Kate Sessions, who sympathized with Gill's simplified architectural forms. Eloise Roorbach, an avid promoter of Gill, wrote, "The garden is so essential a feature of his homes that he includes the designing of them in the house plan and this should be the case with every architect. Garden and House are one and indivisible in his mind. Not only this, but he makes the garden take a second blooming upon the walls of the room."[33]

No California house style, however, matched the popularity of the ranch house and the opportunities it presented for outdoor living. Southern California architect Cliff May introduced the ranch style in the 1930s. May, a colleague of California architect William Wurster, admired the sheltering eaves and open interiors of Frank Lloyd Wright's horizontal Prairie style homes and the courtyards, low roof lines, and simple layouts of the Spanish ranchos which had once dotted the state. More than any other regional style up to that time, his homes encouraged outdoor living. The absence of frost allowed May to put the homes on slabs, where they hugged the ground. High foundations were common in the East, where soils heaved in the cold of winter and required a builder to hoist the house floor far up off the ground. Slabs, on the other hand, sat within inches of the ground. "I wanted the concrete slab to keep the house low to the ground. . . . You can't get . . . continuity . . . to the garden if you are looking down steps at it," May explained.[34] With the interior floor at the same level as the patio, getting from house to yard was as simple as walking from room to room. "If you can't walk out of the living room or kitchen onto the ground," May said, "why, you're not living like a real Californian."[35]

May's homes contained big, plate-glass windows that brought the yard into view from almost every room of the house. Plate glass also contributed to the popularity of garden lighting, as landscape architect Garret Eckbo noted in his book, *The Art Of Home Landscaping.* When a room was fully lit from inside, it cast annoying glare against the windows. A family could always close the drapes but only at the expense of shutting out the view to the outdoors. Garden lights, however, reduced the reflection by lessening the contrast between the inside and out. A person standing indoors could see right to the edges of the garden, and, as a result, the house and yard could appear that much more spacious.[36] Once outdoors, the owners of a ranch home often enjoyed a generously sized patio, a feature May often included in his house plans. May believed that the outdoors was a living area every bit as important as the rooms inside, and it made no sense

Figure 7.5. A California ranch house in Danville, 2005, with a split-rail fence enhancing the style's Western imagery. Photograph by the author.

for the architect to stop at the house walls. He extended ceiling beams and walls to the outside and interrupted thresholds and moldings where doors opened to the yard. These devices, according to Clark Clifford, "make the structure fraternize with nature and create a sense of interior and exterior unity."[37]

The ranch home was more than a shelter—it expressed May's enthusiasm for a casual, Western way of life. Though the roots of the United States were strongly agricultural, May saw that Californians wanted no dooryard full of steaming manure and scratching chickens. The ranch house had a rambling informality, giving the impression, according to *Sunset* editor Dan Gregory, that "the designer has simply reared back and swung his lariat out over a hilltop, lassoing oak trees and boulders at will, roping them into his plan, like dogies at the rodeo."[38] Such Western imagery still prevails in the naming—if not always the appearance—of new housing tracts throughout the state, such as Circle B Ranch, Golden Eagle Farm, Ponderosa Landing, and Wildhorse Ranch. In 1993, "Tapestry of the Vineyards" promised Bay Area residents a return to the sprawling ranchos of the eighteenth century:

> Tapestry returns to California living the way it was intended to be. Grand 4 and 5 bedroom ranch style homes, spacious and sprawling, surrounded by golden flat stretches of land. Lots of land. Tapestry's traditional ranch styling features a forgotten signature of gracious living, a front porch, where you can sit and appreciate the scenic beauty of rural Livermore.[39]

The imagery continues to prevail today, with real estate agents offering San Francisco Bay Area residents homes in subdivisions named Dublin Ranch Villages, Alden Meadows, Gale Ranch, Pheasant Ridge, and Sunflower Estates.[40]

Sunset's 1946 best-selling book, *California Ranch Houses by Cliff May,* set off a chain reaction in house building lasting more than fifty years.[41] From 1948 to 1955, builders constructed more than 1,000,000 ranch homes each year. Nor did Cliff May's influence stop at California. John Jakle, Bob Bastain, and Doug Meyer found that ranch homes constituted more than a third of all

Figure 7.6. A ranch-style backyard in Danville, California, 2005, with an interior floor nearly flush with the patio. "If you can't walk out of the living room or kitchen onto the ground," architect Cliff May said of the style, "why, you're not living like a real Californian." As quoted in Dan Gregory, "The Ranch House Rides Again," *Sunset* (March 1992): 89. Photograph by the author.

house styles in twenty-one Midwestern, Eastern, and Southern towns in the 1980s, an impressive figure considering the limitations that climate put on indoor-outdoor living in these regions.[42] Thick walls, double windows, and insulated roofs could protect a home in Ohio or New York from harsh weather, but warming the yard was another matter. Architects experimented with solid patio roofs, glassed-in courtyards, and gas heaters to maximize a yard's comfort zone. Careful site planning could maximize the comfort zone by optimizing exposure to the sun, choosing materials with an appropriate albedo (the amount of light an object reflects), and using arbors, walls, and trees to provide shade and direct breezes.[43] Though it was an expensive solution, a family could use radiant heat to warm the patio, a system that promised to provide comfort when air temperatures were low enough to make one's breath steam. Cliff May embedded electric coils in his own Southern California patio and achieved impressive results. The high cost of heating the concrete (twenty-five cents an hour in 1951 U.S. dollars) was more than offset, May confided, by reduced wear and tear inside the house, as his family spent nearly all of their time on the patio.[44] High costs and the narrow, fifteen-degree range of the comfort zone, however, limited the usefulness of such techniques, and most Americans were left with a four-month window in which they could comfortably inhabit their yards. Could climate control technology have gone further, there is every reason to assume that Jakle, Bastain, and Meyer would have found California-style gardens in the yards of ranch homes throughout the East, South, and Midwest.[45]

Chapter Eight: *Sunset* Magazine and the Outdoor Room

Mission Revival, bungalow, and ranch style architecture helped millions of Californians move from house to yard. Once outside, a homeowner's work had just begun. A poorly placed patio could get blistering hot in summer or miss a beautiful view of surrounding scenery. An inappropriate tree could drop messy fruit on the chaise lounge or lift the driveway with its roots. A hastily laid lawn could puddle, deer could chew shrubbery to the bone, and an unfenced yard invited the stares of nosy neighbors. Play equipment had to be changed as the children got older. A mishmash of materials could render the yard cluttered, confusing, and, worst of all, tasteless. The question facing a homeowner was straightforward and simple: how could one best organize the yard into an efficient and beautiful space that provides optimal room for outdoor living?

The so-called "modern movement" (the style that Tom Wolfe caricatured in his book, *From Our House To Bauhaus*) of the 1930s provided many of the answers middle-class Californians were looking for.[1] An outgrowth of similar movements in architecture and industrial design, modern gardens reacted against the symmetry, classical ornamentation, and elitist symbolism of the Beaux Arts gardens of the City Beautiful era. A Beaux Arts garden would likely feature a walkway or strong axial corridor down the center, with a gazebo, fountain, or temple positioned prominently at the end. Formally clipped yews, cypress, or poplars might line the path, with identically shaped beds extending out to either side. As a setting for a public museum, courthouse, or a Greek Revival mansion, such symmetry was appropriate; as a zone for middle-class outdoor living, it made little sense. Not only was its purpose largely symbolic and visual, but it ignored nearly every rule for achieving human comfort. In the endeavor to attain symmetry, Beaux Arts designers paid little attention to the orientation of the sun, wind, or other site conditions affecting the "comfort zone." They laid out space according to geometric principles rather than ground form or house shape, and they often forced people to walk along axial paths rather than take more direct routes to their destinations. Modernists sought to rid their designs of such traditional, pre-ordained elements and instead believed that the form a design took should depend on site conditions and actual use. Most middle-class people used their yards in domestic ways. If form really followed function, as the modernist credo asserted, the designer's task was simple: a yard should look and work like an outdoor room of the house.

Two California landscape architects helped to lay out the modernist formula for outdoor habitability: Thomas Church, the author of the influential and widely read *Gardens Are For People,* and Garrett Eckbo, whose thoughtful and entertaining book, *The Art of Home Landscaping,* got right inside the heads of new homeowners as they laid out their grounds.[2] Both authors promoted the garden as a social space, structured around family use rather than horticulture. No longer were readers inundated with plant names, soil amendment options, propagation techniques, and composting advice. Instead, Church's and Eckbo's recommendations included plenty of paving and furniture, wooden pergolas and trellises, swimming pools, whirlpool spas, contemporary sculpture, and lots of privacy in the way of fences, walls, and hedges. According to Eckbo, building architects put too much emphasis on the house to the exclusion of the grounds. The outside spaces were, in their own way, just as important to day-to-day life as the ones inside, and a designer should consider the exterior from the outset to maximize a property's usefulness. Eckbo wrote:

> It is a mistake to follow the standard practice of designing the house as a box of living space, placing it more or less appropriately *on* the lot, and then landscaping it (adding beautification, or exterior decoration). It

> is more sensible, and productive of better results for the residents, to plan the use of the entire lot at once, as a coordinated series of rationally connected and related indoor and outdoor rooms.[3]

Key to the modernist garden formula was a material, as opposed to a botanical, underpinning: concrete, tile, plastics, metals, stone, and wood all predominated over plants, especially when located close to the house. Eckbo's book, *Landscape For Living*, regaled the reader with photos and descriptions of so-called "hardscape." In one garden (the captions read), "Paved entrance court combines approach by car and afoot." Nearby, "Shady area and badminton court surfaced with fine rolled crushed rock. . . . Pergola and split redwood fence extend house into garden on dining room side." Another garden featured an "Intimate patio with living and bedroom glass walls on three sides, Lucite pool, paving and foliage, louvered screen." In still another, the ground was "paved and cuts retained in the brick to reduce maintenance. Extension of existing tall trellis on the house into the garden was suggested and a system of free screens of split redwood around service area was developed." Yet another garden featured a prominent cinder block wall at the edge of a paved pool deck. Eckbo continued:

> The wall, of brick, pumice blocks, and bottles, endeavors to extract a maximum expression from the materials by an expanded structural-sculptural-mural treatment. Pattern of paving and pool intended to expand the sense within the structural enclosure. . . . Paving combines brick, concrete with crushed brick aggregate ground smooth, and plain concrete. Redwood screens on south side and around diving board meet and mingle with masonry in the bathhouse.[4]

Many an Eckbo garden contained enough materials and fixtures to furnish a good portion of the house.

Church and Eckbo both conceived of gardens as abstract art, in which contours of form and space were just as important as the contents of the garden. Eckbo used a cubist approach, where interweaving spaces and shifting focal points replaced a traditional axial design, the latter which took all mystery out of

Figure 8.1. Thomas Church's curvaceous swimming pool—a celebrated icon of "modern" garden design—at the Donnell Estate in Sonoma County, California. Photograph by the author, 2004.

the composition by instructing one exactly where to look. James Rose, a prominent modernist who was expelled from Harvard University for rebelling against the Beaux Arts style, remarked, "Being in a garden should be like being inside a piece of hollow sculpture."[5] One of Church's most famous designs was the Donnell swimming pool in 1946. The pool, which sat in a hilltop terrace overlooking San Pablo Bay, resembled a work of art more than a recreational spot. The coping curved around a series of changing radius points and parabolas—not unlike a figure in a Miro painting—and an abstract sculpture sat perched on a middle island. Church explained that the curves, radical for their time, mimicked the estuaries of the river delta in the valley below. The Donnell pool would become arguably the most photographed swimming pool in America, appearing on the cover of *House Beautiful* in 1951 and in nearly every book that mentioned pools or the California garden for the next fifty years.

Plants were neither absent from modern gardens nor were they the primary objects of focus. Referring to them abstractly as "plant materials" or sometimes just "materials," modernists such as Church and Eckbo used plants to screen views, provide shade, and help shape the horizontal, vertical, and overhead planes (floors, walls, and ceilings) of the garden. In an article promoting Modernism, *House Beautiful* editor Elizabeth Gordon advised:

> . . . it is fatal to allow yourself, or him [your husband] to think in terms of favorite plants. Instead . . . ask what it is that you both wish the plants to do. . . . If your favorite plants will play their roles in the whole correctly and do what is needed, where they are needed, when they are needed, then it is all right to use them. But if they won't, to drag them in regardless is the surest way to spoil your garden.[6]

It was time for Americans to turn away from the decorative planting schemes of old, she continued, and to look towards "an architectural, functioning design."[7] Garden journals of the era admired Eckbo, Church, and other modernists, and they routinely published their work, invited them to serve on advisory boards and judge garden contests, and helped to build many careers. If landscape architects were relegating plants to a service function, the point was often moot. By the time one subtracted the patio, deck, paths, play area, swimming pool, service yard, carport, entry walk, and other "hardscape" from the garden, there was little soil left in which to plant anyway.

A garden by Church or Eckbo did not come cheap; many cost more than an entire middle-class home. Still, the premise of outdoor living held great appeal, and, if people could not afford Thomas Church, there was always *Sunset* magazine. Of all the popular voices championing the garden as an outdoor room, *Sunset* was—and arguably remains—the most compelling. *Sunset* began as a travel journal for the Southern Pacific Company in 1898. Early issues lured travelers west by rail with accounts of snow-capped mountains, pastel deserts, blue lakes, and craggy shorelines. Articles described enticing real estate opportunities, and gossip columnists chronicled the daily activities of famous visitors. In the teens and twenties, the magazine became a literary review. In 1928, Lawrence W. Lane bought the journal and recast it as the "Magazine of Western Living." Lane focused on four areas of domestic life: home design and decoration, cooking, gardening, and travel, all presented from a uniquely "Western" point of view. In order to preserve the magazine's regional focus, he launched Pacific Northwest, Northern and Central California, Southern California, and Desert Southwest editions. Eventually, he expanded the Western focus to include the mountain states, Alaska, and Hawaii, but he went no further east than Colorado.[8] After World War II, *Sunset* magazine and its popular do-it-yourself books could be found everywhere in the West: on newsstands, in doctor's waiting rooms, garden center counters, hardware stores, supermarket racks, and, according to the magazine's editor, in nearly half of all middle-class homes. In 1954, the editors claimed that one out of every two Western households received the publication. *Sunset*'s fierce dedication to the West distinguished it from *House Beautiful, Better Homes and Gardens, House and Garden, Southern Living,* and other house and garden magazines. In 1954, the magazine ran a set of editorials letting readers know they were a breed apart from the rest of Americans:

1. The West's climate encouraged Westerners to build differently, to open up their houses to the outdoors (the patio house).
2. Western gardeners could grow plants they couldn't grow elsewhere and enjoy their gardens for more months of the year.
3. The geography of the West offered mountains, oceans, and desert nearby—all invitations to the Westerner to travel and spend more of his and her leisure time in outdoor recreation.
4. The West's climate and the diversity of its early settlers presented a much wider variety of foods and culinary lore than is usual elsewhere in the nation—Scandinavian influences in the Northwest; Spanish and Mexican foods in the Southwest; and along the coast the cooking traditions brought by early settlers of Italian, French, Chinese and Japanese ancestry.[9]

Another editorial made sure that there was no confusing the nation's two coasts:

> We make no concessions in our pages to those good people in the East where gardens are out of action in winter, who must travel 2,000 miles through farmland and factory towns before they reach desert or high

country, who must retreat behind storm shutters in winter, who consider that artichokes and abalone are culinary curiosities.[10]

The editors poked fun at the rest of the country by pronouncing that, along with superior climate, geography, and culture, Westerners had more money, better health, and taller children.[11] Despite frequent requests, *Sunset* refused (and still refuses) to sell its magazine at newsstands east of Colorado, to maintain an undiluted, unduplicated editorial service.[12] *Sunset* continues to assert that Westerners are a special breed. In a 1998 article entitled "100 Years Of *Sunset* Magazine," *Sunset*'s CEO and President, Steve Seabolt, himself originally from the East, wrote, "Westerners in general, and *Sunset* readers in particular, are open to trying new ideas. In contrast to Southerners, who believe strongly in tradition, Westerners are not brand-loyal . . . and they constantly ask whether there's a better way to do things."[13]

Sunset ardently promoted the notion of the garden as an outdoor room in its magazine and many of its how-to-do-it books. "Western gardening is based upon the Western way of life. It is bringing the outdoors into the home, and actually projecting the rooms of the home into the outdoors," the 1948 *Sunset Western Flower Book* stated. "The Western garden is more than a burst of color and fragrance; it is a number of outdoor rooms in which to work, play, relax, and live."[14] The message was familiar to most people, given the steady conversion of back yards to family living areas over the past half century. Outdoor rooms, however, worked best where the weather remained mild enough to sustain a sixty-five-to-eighty-degree comfort zone, and few places other than coastal California could meet that requirement year round, the magazine noted:

> If you had a sum of money in the savings bank on which you received interest only 4 months of the year, you would consider it a poor investment. If you had a yard or garden (even a tiny one) here on the Pacific coast, in which you have flowers only 4-5 months out of the year, that likewise is a poor investment. With a little careful planning we who live on the Pacific coast can gather flowers every day in the year from our gardens.[15]

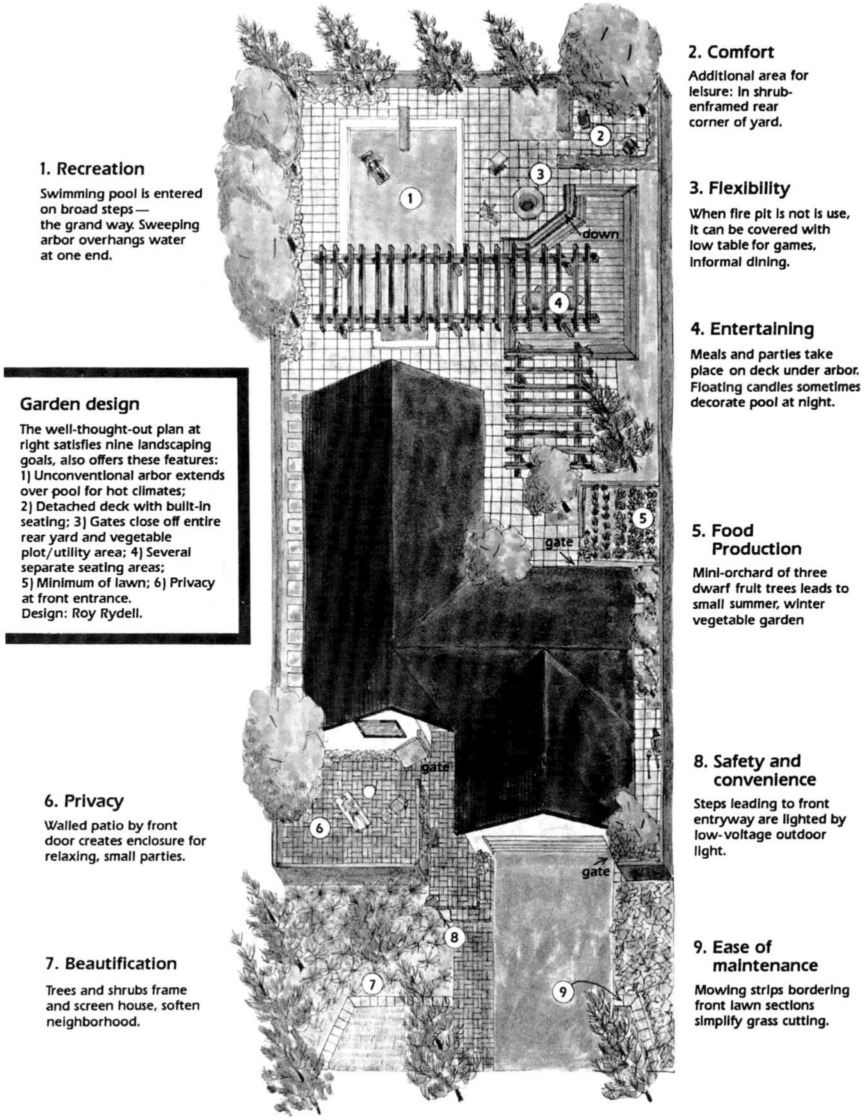

1. Recreation

Swimming pool is entered on broad steps— the grand way. Sweeping arbor overhangs water at one end.

2. Comfort

Additional area for leisure: In shrub-enframed rear corner of yard.

3. Flexibility

When fire pit is not is use, it can be covered with low table for games, informal dining.

4. Entertaining

Meals and parties take place on deck under arbor. Floating candles sometimes decorate pool at night.

Garden design

The well-thought-out plan at right satisfies nine landscaping goals, also offers these features: 1) Unconventional arbor extends over pool for hot climates; 2) Detached deck with built-in seating; 3) Gates close off entire rear yard and vegetable plot/utility area; 4) Several separate seating areas; 5) Minimum of lawn; 6) Privacy at front entrance. Design: Roy Rydell.

5. Food Production

Mini-orchard of three dwarf fruit trees leads to small summer, winter vegetable garden

6. Privacy

Walled patio by front door creates enclosure for relaxing, small parties.

8. Safety and convenience

Steps leading to front entryway are lighted by low-voltage outdoor light.

7. Beautification

Trees and shrubs frame and screen house, soften neighborhood.

9. Ease of maintenance

Mowing strips bordering front lawn sections simplify grass cutting.

Figure 8.2. *Sunset* magazine diagrams the modern garden. The suggested uses—recreation, comfort, flexibility, entertaining, food production, privacy, beautification, safety and convenience, and ease of maintenance—favored family needs over traditional gardening. From *Landscaping and Garden Remodeling* (Menlo Park, Calif.: Lane Publishing Co., 1978), 8. Used with permission of the Sunset Publishing Company, Menlo Park, California.

If *Sunset* championed the outdoor room, its readership did not need much persuading. In 1955, two of the magazine's writers swooped over properties in Palo Alto, California, in a helicopter to observe the improvements taking place below. Everywhere they looked, homeowners were converting their grounds into useful domestic space. On the Zinke property, the writers saw not one but "two separate patio areas . . . each shaded from the sun." On the Kelley property, "the patio is generous . . . and sheltered." On the Culliton property, they saw "generous paved areas and a green lawn close by, and front fences and locked gates provide pool security." The Dudley A. Zinkes's "worked for 18 straight months, every weekend . . . they built two patio roofs. They laid 3,800 bricks in sand and mortar. They built fences; they installed raised beds; they planted trees, shrubs, vines, groundcovers." Based on hours of flyovers and follow-up interviews with the families, the writers concluded that "a remarkable change is taking

Figure 8.3. Rosemary, a Berkeley homeowner, says: "We use this everyday, if the weather permits. It's a very important part of our house, because our house gets quite dark. It's like an additional room. I think that's why we wanted it smooth enough for furniture." Photograph by the author, 1981.

place in the old-fashioned back yard . . . family after family has by now developed its plot for outdoor living, outdoor working, outdoor playing. Space is carefully divided, and every square foot put to use."[16]

The authors' conclusions went right to the heart of habitability. According to *Sunset,* garden design started with the notion that the yard was first an opportunity to be outdoors. What people did there once they arrived was a matter of individual preference, and human concerns were no less important than horticultural ones. "Western landscaping's first concern is people—their activity and their comfort in the garden," the 1968 edition of *Landscaping For Western Living* proclaimed. "The measuring stick of Western landscape design is people—men, women, and children in pursuit of ways to satisfy their varying interests out of doors."[17] The human body was a yardstick for how tall trees and shrubs should be, for how high a fence should be, and whether a fence was for privacy, screening, or simply to separate areas from one another. The width of the human body and the length of the stride determined the proportions of a garden. "People in motion outdoors require more space than they do when moving through a house," the design manual continued:

> Two people can walk side by side on a 4′ garden path, but a 5-foot width gives them freedom to stroll and raise their eyes from the path. The width of a wheelbarrow measured from knuckle to knuckle, the width of the clothes basket from elbow to elbow—these measurements determine the width of gates, passageways, and other openings.[18]

Sunset's emphasis on outdoor habitability forced a balancing act between the needs of people and plants. Plants played a critical role in a garden, even one designed primarily for human activities. From a monetary point of view, trees, shrubs, and groundcovers were much cheaper to install than patios, walls, and fences, and along the mild Pacific Coast they thrived with little care. Most importantly, plants provided sensual effects that made the garden different from the interior rooms of the house. Where else could one enjoy the scent of roses and lilacs, chirping birds, the beauty of butterflies, the warmth of the sun, the splashes of color no wallpaper could match, the sweet smell of fresh air, and cooling afternoon breezes on a hot summer afternoon? Domestic uses notwithstanding, what made the garden unique was that it was outdoors, and plants were central to the ambiance. Plants, however, also played the role of spoiler. Not only did they require ongoing maintenance, but they seemed to have the capacity—due to the mild Pacific Coast climate—to insert themselves into a garden whether or not the owner wanted them there in the first place. Many new homeowners not only inherited a garden left by previous owners, but watched plants establish themselves on the property from wind-born seeds, bird and squirrel droppings, underground runners, stump sprouts, and by simply climbing over fences and walls from adjacent lots. Coastal California homeowners, regardless of their interest in gardening, had to develop a strategy for managing the botanical menagerie surrounding their homes.

From the outset, *Sunset* was happy to offer gardening advice, and the magazine devoted a fair portion of each issue to such concerns. Ultimately, however, the editors made it clear that the magazine addressed "the reader who chooses or chooses not to garden." *Sunset* believed that the garden was a place "to accept or reject gardening; to be absorbed in the arrangement of flowers, shrubs and trees, or just to sit in the shade; to enjoy close communion with plants, or people. . . ."[19] To this end, the editors developed a style that balanced the needs of people and plants, the "low-maintenance garden."

The low-maintenance garden had two components. First was the use of plants to reinforce structurally the spatial layout and function of the garden. However pleasing plants might look, their primary purposes were to create spatial definition, screen unpleasant views, cast shade, provide privacy, and define entries and exits. Plants with formal, architectural qualities—Grecian bay, Italian buckthorn, English laurel, Japanese privet, and Irish yew—served this purpose well, but many other species also worked if properly placed and maintained. The second component was the selection of plants that needed little care. Aware of its readership's diversity, *Sunset* directed its popular *Low Maintenance Gardening* book "to the man who values his put-

Figure 8.4. A low-maintenance yard in Albany, California, 2005. According to *Sunset* magazine, the low maintenance garden is for "the man who values his putter and driver at least as much as he does his rake and shovel." As quoted in *Sunset Low Maintenance Gardening* (Menlo Park, Calif.: Lane Publications, 1974), 4. Photograph by the author.

ter and driver at least as much as he does his rake and shovel."[20] The writers recommended species—such as tam juniper, algerian ivy, rhaphiolepis, escallonia, lantana, photinia, agapanthus, marguerite, and star jasmine—that grew fast, tolerated poor soil, were resistant to insects and diseases, stood up to abuse and neglect, stayed green year round, and had minimal leaf-drop. Many of these plants needed little pruning, and, when they did, they were easy to shear or cut back. The magazine featured stories on a regular basis about versatile plants, such as shiny xylsoma, a pleasant-looking species with numerous uses: "Buying a xylosma is like buying an all-in-one landscaping kit. Whatever you need—a tree, shrub, espalier, hedge, screen, ground or bank cover—xylosma will serve beautifully with a little pruning and directing of the branches."[21] Xylosma, like many low-maintenance plants, remained virtually unchanged throughout the West Coast's four seasons, but most homeowners were more than willing to accept this limitation in exchange for less yard work. The magazine frequently ran features on container gardens, showing owners how to raise flowers and small bushes in terra cotta pots, window boxes, and half wine barrels. In many ways, container plantings epitomized low maintenance. They were a quick way to decorate a paved yard, the plants never spread out of control, and the "garden" could be carted off in a moving van along with the dining-room set when the family—in all statistical likelihood—moved every five years.[22]

Photographs in *Sunset* books and magazines occasionally showed people dressed in overalls with their hands plunged into fresh soil. Aware that most people spent no more than two hours a week caring for their yards, however, the editors were more likely to photograph casually clad people serving refreshments to guests, sunning by the pool, or playing with their children against a backdrop of English laurel or other low-maintenance greenery. Thomas Church, whose designs appeared regularly in *Sunset* throughout his career, remarked in the 1950s, "I am sorry our way of life seems to produce fewer clients who love gardening, and that the old-fashioned garden, filled with flowers and overgrown shrubs and charm, is disappearing."[23] *Sunset* and Church had their fingers on the pulse of the West. Most of the gardens they endorsed, though delightfully planted, were more distinguished for their patios, decks, walls, pergolas, and furniture. Not only were such features icons of outdoor living, but they could be photographed in any season and right after they had been installed. The low-maintenance landscape did not foretell the demise of the home garden but rather addressed readers who had never made horticulture a priority in the first place. In this respect, Californians were proving to be very much like other Americans who had, for half a century, put family needs ahead of plants when it came to their home grounds.

Sunset featured numerous designs by Church, Eckbo, Lawrence Halprin, Douglas Baylis, Ted Osmundson, Robert Royston, and other California-based landscape architects.[24] While showing off expensive, professionally prepared work, the magazine also spoke to a middle-class readership looking for practical, affordable advice. According to *Sunset* editor Dan Gregory, "*Sunset* has always been for the person who builds one of our benches or plants their own flower bed, not someone who has to hire out the work."[25] *Sunset*'s commitment to the ordinary reader was a huge reason for its success. Newsstands already abounded with magazines such as *Fine Gardening* and *Architectural Digest* that featured homes and gardens far beyond middle-class budgets. *Sunset* writers, however, got down in the trenches with their readers and talked about design in plain language. On the subject of lawns, the *Sunset Complete Garden Book* assured that "simplicity is beauty. We no longer clutter our lawns with iron deer, crowded flower beds and intricate paths." On the task of planting a parking strip—a narrow, awkward space at best—the writers suggested Irish Moss "for something different and in good taste for your parking." On whether or not to install a front yard fence they advised that "most follow the friendly American custom of allowing neighbors an unobstructed view of the house." On the established practice of foundation plantings they recommended the gardener "always group them. A shrub standing alone against a foundation is a depressing sight."[26] For homeowners struggling to convert their grounds into useful and

Figure 8.5. *Sunset* magazine's 1955 feature, "Landscaping the Subdivision House," helped millions of California homeowners transform bare suburban lots into family living spaces. From "Landscaping the New Subdivision House," *Sunset* (May 1955): 66. Used with permission of the Sunset Publishing Company, Menlo Park, California.

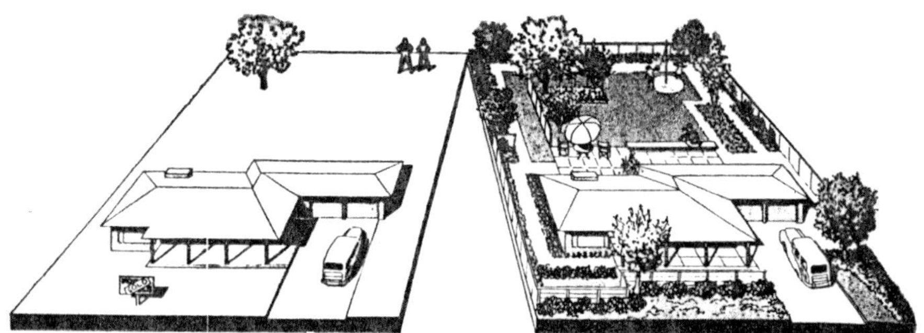

If you want to get from this . . . within three years or so . . . to something like this

STEP ONE: THE PAPER WORK

Do you have a notebook ready? A measuring tape? Some string and stakes? Here are questions you should ask yourself . . . facts to note down . . . measurements to take . . . choices to consider . . .

Figure 8.6. Even today, developers often leave the yards bare around new tract homes, allowing buyers to turn to magazines, such as *Sunset,* for design advice. Photograph by the author, San Ramon, California, 2005

manageable space, such instructions were a clear and welcome substitute for an expensive professional design.

In 1955, *Sunset* published a groundbreaking series of articles under the heading, "Landscaping the New Subdivision House."[27] The message, as the title suggested, was aimed at the millions of owners of new tract homes, people who were unfamiliar with their physical surroundings, knew few of their neighbors, and whose yards were little more than pads of graded earth. "Landscaping the New Subdivision House" was a convincing treatise on suburban garden design. The reader went step by step, from a bare lot to a finished landscape, with professional techniques, tricks, and secrets explained in plain terms. Owing to the magazine's editorial policy, the authors avoided endorsing historical styles, opting instead for the "form follows function" directive of the modernists. First of all, style detracted from usefulness, the very foundation of a modern garden: " . . . Let's forget the outmoded styles, such as formal gardens and gardens with an Italian motif," the authors wrote. ". . . Instead of following traditional landscape gardening rules, let us base our garden planning on human needs." Homeowners were better off focusing on practical issues, such as how big to make a back yard patio: ". . . The secret in designing an outdoor room is to close it in as much as necessary for comfort and privacy, but as little as possible to keep from losing the feeling you are outdoors. . . . A California patio works best if it is at least twice the size of the living room." Style was tricky, containing pitfalls and traps that could vex an inexperienced designer: "Beware of curves in paving or structures. Not all curves are pleasing, and any curve is difficult to install. Often it is wiser to stick to straight lines for patio paving and fencing." Free-form layouts, odd angles and especially triangles were "dangerous for the amateur." Style was also pretentious and could backfire on a naive homeowner who might buy an inappropriate statue for the garden at a pottery outlet. It was safer to adopt solutions that copied nature, as this advice on incorporating sculpture into a garden suggested: "For sculpture in keeping with today's Western gardens, we turn more often to forms found in nature than to statuary done in the classic traditional style (E.G., a large boulder, a piece of driftwood, a bird or animal, gnarled bark)."[28]

Though focusing most of its attention on the back yard, the magazine still took care to advise readers on front yard etiquette. Over the years, *Sunset* had run many stories on making front yards more useful, even advocating that homeowners enclose them—in the Mission Revival style—behind stucco walls, an unneighborly solution in most other regions of the nation. The editors drew the line, however, when it came to planting vegetables in the front. A 1981 article warned readers: "As food prices continue to climb, a few brave souls have considered making the front garden a food-producer by growing vegetables there. On occasion, this experiment has been handled with taste and style, but often the result has been unsightly and the neighbors have been understandably upset."[29]

By the 1970s, Lane publications had supplemented its magazine with how-to-do-it outdoor building books on decks, patios, fences, barbecues, pergolas, swimming pools, spas, vegetable gardens, lawns, flower beds, fish ponds, and garden lighting and many more on room additions, bathroom and kitchen remodels, cooking, decorating, plumbing, carpentry, skylights, and almost every other matter pertaining to Western homes and their grounds. Lawrence Lane had begun *Sunset*'s book program in the 1930s, when he offered readers cookbooks as premiums to their subscriptions. In 1946, Lane formed a separate book division, and sales rose dramatically from $4 million a year in the 1950s to $50 million by the end of the 1960s. By 2000, *Sunset* had published more than 400 titles showing readers how to cook, remodel their homes, plan vacations, and design their yards.[30] Landscape architect Doug Baylis and his wife, Maggie, were instrumental in the development of the book series during the 1940s and 1950s. Baylis, whose designs often appeared in the magazine, was passionately committed to helping homeowners who could not afford the services of a landscape architect. He and Maggie—who worked as a journalist and graphic artist for *Sunset* before she met her husband—developed a "how-to" series of articles and books showing homeowners ways to design their yards on reasonable budgets and how to install them using simple building techniques and ordinary tools.[31] This commitment to the common reader became an underlying theme for every new *Sunset* book and magazine issue; to be sure that the advice worked, employees tested all the projects, recipes, and gardening techniques at the *Sunset* headquarters, called the "Laboratory for Western Living."

Figure 8.7. A back yard in Palo Alto, California, designed for outdoor cooking and dining. Photograph by the author, 2003.

Sunset's owners and staff lived and worked by the advice they gave to readers. The magazine's 1951 Menlo Park headquarters was designed by Cliff May to resemble a ranch house, with a long, low roof and broad eaves, sheltering arcades, sliding glass doors, movable walls that opened to the garden, and a generous patio, in all a larger-than-life counterpart of the homes owned by many of their readers. The patio opened onto an expansive back yard filled with popular plants, curvaceous paths, and a putting green for employees to use on lunch breaks. Designed by Thomas Church, the garden meandered through a progression of West Coast microclimates spanning Seattle to San Diego. The planting beds included many of the species featured by the magazine in the garden, and, in the spirit of democratization, the groundskeeper labeled them by common name alone (Latin names appeared in the 1980s).

Mirroring the suburban family further still, *Sunset* often portrayed wives as the overseers of the garden. When construction of the headquarters was complete, Lawrence and Ruth Lane commissioned an artist to paint their portrait to hang in the lobby. The artist positioned Mr. Lane in front of the ranch-style headquarters. Ruth was to the right, the *Sunset* garden in full bloom behind her. "When the portrait was planned, Mr. and Mrs. Lane could not agree on the setting," a tour guide explained. "Mr. Lane was quite involved in the construction of the building and insisted it be in the painting. Mrs. Lane loved the garden and wanted it included. The artist compromised: he put the front door behind Mr. Lane and the garden behind his wife."[32]

Chapter Nine: A Private World

Upon laying out their back yards for outdoor living, California families needed to complete an important step to maximize habitability: insuring their privacy. Domestic life, whether it took place in the kitchen, the rec room, or the back yard, was difficult to conduct if carried on under the nose of the neighbors. Homeowners with vegetable gardens or dog runs might not care if people looked into their yards, and some citizens might actually invite passersby to stop and admire their front lawns and foundation plantings. But for the Zinkes, Cullitons, and other families over whom *Sunset*'s helicopter pilot flew in 1955, fences were as fundamental to habitability as were the walls to the homes. The magazine's 1968 book, *Landscaping For Western Living,* drew the parallels well:

> Once you think of a garden as a space to live in....you expect and desire the same visual privacy you would enjoy in an indoor living room. No matter how friendly you are with your neighbors, you have no right to embarrass them by making them watch your outdoor activities. For outdoor dining, entertaining, sun-bathing, or just sitting and talking with a friend, you need at least a semblance of privacy.[1]

Privacy meant fences, however, and fences represented a break with the long-standing American tradition of the open yard. By the end of World War II, residential fences had been out of favor for nearly a century, and the unfenced yard showed little sign of disappearing, despite an onslaught of pressure to eliminate it. In the 1950s, house and garden magazines—in response to the emergence of the back yard family room and in a tone similar to *Sunset*'s position on the subject—launched a campaign to bring back garden fences. The suburbs promised relief from crowding, noise, and crime, but they did not always shelter residents from the eyes of the neighbors. Many families found themselves in fish bowls, with trees and hedges too small to screen the houses to either side, with the occupants next door staring into their bedrooms from second-story windows or watching them splash half-naked in the Doughboy pool. The concern was widespread; as late as the 1980s, a Harris poll revealed that, by a three-to-one margin, Americans felt they had less privacy in the suburbs than in the city.[2]

In 1950, *House Beautiful* ran a series of provocative stories urging homeowners to break with long-standing customs and fence their back yards. The provocative titles of the articles—"Good Living Is NOT Public Living," "Privacy—the Right to Be Alone," "How to Make the Neighbor's Disappear, " "Good Fences Make Good Neighbors," and "Do the Neighbors Know Your Business?"—underscored the tension brewing between the need for privacy and the tradition of open yards.[3] In an uncharacteristically militant tone, the writers declared that privacy was an unabridged right. A full-page quote, set in script to resemble a hand-penned document by Benjamin Franklin or another notable founding father, asserted:

> Privacy . . . the right to be alone
> the most comprehensive of rights
> the right most valued by civilized men
>
> — Louis D. Brandeis,
> Justice United States Supreme Court[4]

The article, "Good Living Is NOT Public Living," reminded readers that they had moved to the suburbs in the first place to get distance from their neighbors:

> People who live in apartment houses or row houses automatically must accept less privacy by their choice of abode. In such close quarters the sights and sounds and smells of neighbors cannot be screened

> out. It is the price people in such dwellings must pay in return for not having to cope with other people. For them we have nothing but sympathy—and no suggestions except to seal their windows and buy air-conditioning units.[5]

A homeowner should be free to run about the garden barely dressed, not have to smell the neighbor's lunch and not even be seen if he so chose, wrote author Dr. Joseph E. Howland. "If you can't walk out in a negligee to pick a flower before breakfast without being seen from the street or by the neighbors, you have not fully developed the possibilities of good living."[6]

In 1952, *Better Homes and Gardens* voiced a similar message in the article, "Privacy Is Worth All That It Costs." Author Robert Jones assured readers that privacy did not mean "vegetating in some dark cell." It was instead synonymous with self-determination, free rights, and private property:

> Privacy is your fundamental right to live your own life as you see fit, in undisturbed peace and quiet. It's the biggest thing you could buy the day you decided to move out of that blankety-blank apartment and lay cash on the line for a home of your own.... You should be able to putter around your garden, dressed in shorts, soaking up sunshine, without starting a neighborhood buzz about your bowlegs.[7]

Howland, Jones, Elizabeth Gordon, and others promoted their fence campaigns vigorously, but few readers responded to the cause. Most homeowners continued to let their yards flow from one to the other as had been the tradition for nearly a century, interrupted only by intermittent plantings, clotheslines, vegetable gardens, and some low, neighbor-friendly pickets or rails. The sentiment went beyond the bounds of custom, with many communities passing ordinances restricting or prohibiting front and back yard fences. In the late 1970s, the Nacoochee Valley National Register in Georgia campaigned for the preservation of unfenced back yards on the grounds they were key historic features. In a related cause, a Georgia group called the "New South Landscape Movement" promoted unfenced yards in order to recapture the "picturesque randomness" reminiscent of the state's Victorian-era landscape.[8]

In coastal California, on the other hand, developers and homeowners alike were erecting six-foot-high fences around back yards as fast as their houses went up. The visual impact on the residential landscape was so pronounced that many newcomers counted it (and continue to do so) as one of the defining differences between the state and the places from which they had moved. Between 1980 and 1995, I interviewed San Francisco Bay Area residents who had recently relocated from other parts of the country, and each one was struck by the number of fences in his or her new neighborhood. Before relocating to Berkeley to practice law, an attorney named Tom lived in Chicago, Connecticut, New York, and Arizona, and in each place the properties flowed uninterrupted from one to the next. "When we lived in upstate New York, one of the nicest aspects

Figure 9.1. A suburb in Yonkers, New York, with back yards flowing unobstructed from one to the next. Arthur Rothstein, photographer, ca. 1942. Photograph courtesy of the Library of Congress, Prints & Photographs Division, FSA-OWI Collection, reproduction number LC-USW3-005434-D.

was the open back yards," he remarked. "People would occasionally have a hedge—and only partway—and you could go between the yards to your neighbor's." Tom loved his brown shingle house in Berkeley, but he felt hemmed in by the grape stake fence that enclosed the back yard. "I don't want you to think I'm into communal sharing of territory. Just get rid of the fence, so it changes the visual image. If there were some way that people could have dogs that got along with everybody, I'd get rid of all the fences."[9]

Brian, a computer programmer, moved from Michigan to Danville, California, in 1990. His three-quarter-acre lot backed up onto a wooded canyon extending for miles beyond his property. His first inclination was to take down the six-foot redwood fence enclosing his back yard so he could enjoy the scenery, and he was astonished when his homeowner's association refused to allow him to do so. "It's blocking a wonderful view of the canyon. They won't even let me replace it with an open iron one. In Michigan, they won't let you put up a fence. In California, you can't take one down!" Brian's second-story rooms looked out onto a sizeable portion of his subdivision, and, while every back yard was fenced, no homeowner was allowed to enclose his or her front yard.[10]

Figure 9.2. Fenced back yards in a new development near Danville, California, in 2005. Due to the newness of many communities, comparatively high densities, and the intimate ways in which homeowners use their yards, fences are common in the state. Photograph by the author.

Tim was a college student who moved from Minnesota to California in 1997 and could not adjust to the fenced yards in his neighborhood in Oakland. "I've studied it very carefully, and everywhere I look Californians are hiding themselves behind fences," he exclaimed a few months before moving back to the Midwest. "This is *so different* from where I grew up, where you can walk for miles and not see a single fence. I think Californians must have a pathological need for privacy."[11]

At least three factors accounted for the fencing of backyards in California: the relative newness of the communities, the comparatively small lot sizes on the West Coast, and the extent to which residents were developing their yards as habitable space. With respect to newness, the number of California households was increasing at a far greater rate than anywhere else in the nation. The state's population nearly tripled from 1930 to 1960, a period during which time the rest of the country's population increased by only fifty percent.[12] New housing tracts were appearing almost daily, occupying land that just a year or two earlier had been given over to orchards, marshes, cattle, gophers, and rattlesnakes. In 1974, Helena Worthen, a graduate student in landscape architecture at the University of California, Berkeley, studied front and back yards in the community of Springtown, a new development near Livermore, California. Within months of the initial groundbreaking, families from all over the world had settled into new homes, and Worthen interviewed them about how they designed their grounds. One of the first steps Springtown owners took was to mark the edges of their properties.

> Although most boundaries between inhabited homes were marked with headers or plants, some were identified by a negative line where one homeowner mowed his lawn at a different blade height or fertilized with a different fertilizer. Many edges were precisely planted with rows of shrubs or flowers. More emphatic were the edges marked with a dozen or more Monterey Pines. . . . New homeowners were acutely conscious of property lines. One woman said 'Well, it's actually here', and put her foot into the middle of some pansies that her neighbor had planted.[13]

Springtown was typical of thousands of new California developments in which literally and figuratively the residents shared little common ground. Not only were the majority of the families from out of state (or country), but many of the surrounding towns were less than a decade or two old. The newness of such communities contrasted starkly with older Eastern, Midwestern, Southwestern, and Southern communities, where the history might go back hundreds of years, where residents had become familiar with each other's habits and lifestyles over generations, where the population was often bound by long-standing traditions and customs. Historical icons, such as the small farm, the town square, and the 4th of July or Cinco de Mayo parades, reminded citizens of their roots. The open, unfenced back yard was an intimate part of this heritage, a common thread between private properties, a tradition citizens were unlikely to change until they had good reason to do so. Unrestricted by a long-standing status quo, however, newly arriving Californians were freer to experiment with lifestyles, including the way they dressed and spoke, the political views they embraced, and the way they designed their back yards. Post-World War II Californians were earning the reputation as individualistic and iconoclastic, a population that delighted in breaking the rules to which most middle-class Americans politely adhered. Just as immigrants to America had done for the past 400 years, most of the state's population had pulled up roots, abandoned their birthplaces and communities of origin, and come in search of a different life. It was no surprise under these circumstances that newcomers would feel free to fence themselves off from their neighbors in order to live as they pleased.

If newcomers to California chose to live as they pleased, they likely had less yard space in which to do it. Residential lots in the West were significantly smaller than the national average.[14] A post-war New England property averaged around 32,000 square feet, lots in Mid-Atlantic states averaged about 15,000 square feet, and those in the South and the Midwest averaged about 13,000 to 15,000 square feet. Properties in California, however, averaged 6,500 square feet, half or less than the national average.[15] Such small properties seem improbable given the state's

Figure 9.3. Workers building a privacy fence around a front yard in Berkeley, California, in 2005. Photograph by the author.

enormous size (only Alaska and Texas are bigger). Moreover, California had earned a notorious reputation for suburban sprawl, with the fastest growing areas—Los Angeles, San Diego, and San Jose—sporting densities significantly lower than comparable cities nationally. Yet, the picture was misleading. First, most of the population was concentrated along the coast, with the interior valleys, deserts, and mountains that made up the majority of the state more sparsely inhabited.[16] Second, forty percent of the population—double the rate of New York, Pennsylvania, and New Jersey—resided in smaller suburbs with populations of 10,000 to 100,000, the densities of which matched or exceeded the national average. Put simply, post-war California suburbs were not always the bastions of low-density sprawl that critics made them out to be.[17]

Accompanying the limited size of California lots was a daunting house-to-lot size ratio. In the 1990s, the average American dwelling allotted about 675 square feet for each occupant. Homes in the West were slightly smaller, at about 635 square feet per occupant, or ninety-four percent the national average. Moreover, family sizes in the state were among the highest in the nation—six percent bigger than New Jersey, seven percent bigger than New York, and ten percent bigger than Pennsylvania. The combination of large family size, lots that were sixty percent smaller than the national average, and houses that were six percent smaller than the national average all added up to one thing: Californians were packed together far more closely than were average Americans.[18] California families faced the prospect of waking up to the sound of their neighbors mowing the back lawn, or smelling the fumes from the barbeque, or listening to the dog barking next door, all but a few feet from their lot lines. By comparison, homeowners in Kansas or Illinois, with 20,000 square-foot lots, enjoyed ample distance from the houses to either side and 100 feet or more to the rear neighbor's house. In every major American city of the past century, the areas of greatest residential densities have revealed the highest number of fences.[19] The open front and back yards common to most American suburbs are as much a response to low density as to tradition and neighborliness. Given the small lots in which most Californians found themselves living, fences were hardly selfish luxuries but practical and logical necessities.

The newness of the communities, small lot sizes, and heightened ethic of outdoor living all made back yard privacy a high priority in the state. On top of those factors was the monetary investment many Californians were making in their back yards, an amount which, if nothing else, warranted the protection of their belongings. The majority of suburban Americans, despite enjoying the advantage of superior lot size, lived in regions where humid summers and freezing winters limited back yard development. Families could play croquet or badminton on the lawn when it was not too muggy or hang a bug light to fend off mosquitoes and dragonflies during a barbeque or birthday party. They could grow some apples and plums and tend to vegetables and flowers for about four months of the year. They could read outdoors between summer thundershowers and minimize the humidity with an electric fan on the back porch. When the first signs of frost appeared in October, they drained the portable pool, tied up the swing set, and carted the patio furniture into the garage. The lawn browned as the air cooled, and the elms and maples that shaded the family during the summer covered the yard with leaves. One by one the flowers died back, the lilacs lost their foliage, and by Thanksgiving ice and snow covered the grounds. For the next six months, no one went into the yard much, except to collect some logs for the fire, or to walk the dog, or to free up a frozen pipe.

Californians, however, used their gardens year-round in ways that rivaled the house itself. They not only ate, drank, relaxed, swam, and played there, but also soaked in hot tubs, meditated under Japanese maples, exhibited expensive sculptures, built

Figure 9.4. A garden courtyard in Oakland, California, in 2005, screened from the street by a six-foot privacy fence. The owners spend many hours in the front eating, entertaining, relaxing, and playing with their children, all but a few feet from the public sidewalk. Photograph by the author.

ponds and waterfalls, cooked on elaborate outdoor ovens, sat on furniture as comfortable as that in the living room, listened to music emanating from speakers concealed in rocks, sat bug-free under Craftsman lanterns, and even ran around stark naked.

The extent to which residents developed their yards was reflected in the latter's costs. Insurance companies have typically placed the value of average American home grounds at around two and one-half percent the value of the house. A 1986 real estate study funded by O. M. Scott & Sons (a prominent lawn care company) in Ohio found that nicely tended home grounds might represent three to four percent of the house value.[20] In California, however, these percentages were just the starting point. According to real estate agents, insurance brokers, and landscape architects, a simply planted home grounds in the post-World War II period was (and continues to be) worth about five percent the cost of an average home. The figure quickly rose to ten percent or more with the addition of a paved patio or redwood deck, shade arbor, portable electric spa, lighting, durable fence, and other accoutrements of outdoor living. Nor was it uncommon for affluent homeowners to invest fifteen to twenty percent of their house value in improving the grounds, especially if they purchased a swimming pool.[21]

It would be most unusual to see a California garden in an unfenced middle-class suburb of Chicago, New York City, Washington, D.C., or any other metropolitan area in the Midwest, South, or East, exposed to view in the summer and covered with snow and icicles in the dead of winter. And it would be just as unusual to find a California garden along the Pacific Coast without a tall fence, the owners swimming, eating, relaxing in the spa, and conducting the intimate activities of their lives in full view of their neighbors.

Chapter Ten: From Garden to Desert

When *Sunset* magazine announced in 1955 that, "providing you irrigate, plants respond generously in our climates," suburban Californians had rarely questioned whether there was enough water for their gardens.[1] During the arid summers, homeowners let their sprinklers pulse for hours a day, the runoff cascading across the yard and driveway and out into the gutter. Families washed their cars on weekends, showered until the water turned cold, and flushed their toilets after each and every visit to the bathroom. And, as earlier generations had done for nearly a century, homeowners filled their gardens with a myriad of exotic plants that drank up water as fast as the sprinklers could get it to them. The water supply appeared bottomless, despite the limited rainfall, and shortages seemed out of the question; drought was something that happened on cattle drives in John Wayne westerns.

Drought is a term that is popularly linked both to precipitation levels and the demand that people put on their water supply. Wet winters and summer drought are normal parts of California's Mediterranean climate (a climate that the state shares with Western Australia and New Zealand, Chile, South Africa, and parts of Southern Europe). Rainfall rates in the coastal cities average from ten to twenty inches a year, almost none of which falls between May and September. This five-month period, strictly speaking, constitutes a drought. Much of the population has relied on water from the Sierra snow pack, which builds during winter and steadily feeds rivers, lakes, and reservoirs as it melts. The state has undergone numerous periods of low rainfall, but drought is a relative term. Until the 1970s, the population was still too small to be jeopardized by the limited water supply. In the winter of 1976–1977, however, California endured the worst drought since officials began keeping such records. Almost no winter rain fell in the West, and the Sierra Nevada snow pack dwindled to barely fifteen percent its normal depth. Hetch Hetchy Reservoir, San Francisco's main supply of water, dropped low enough to make John Muir turn in his grave: jutting from the muddy Yosemite floor were the stumps of hundreds of trees Muir had fought in vain to save sixty years earlier, trees cut down during the dam's construction and buried beneath the Tuolumne River which filled the valley.

The snow pack was indeed low, but more telling was the fact that the state's population had outgrown the water supply. Public panic ensued, especially in the northern part of the state which, unlike Los Angeles, had no Colorado River or Mono Lake from which to draw. Good citizens took "Navy showers" (wet down, soap up with the water off, and rinse off), dropped bricks into their toilet tanks to reduce the volume of each flush, and proudly complied with the popular credo, "if it's yellow let it mellow, if

Figure 10.1. California water districts began rationing water during the drought of 1986–1991, prompting many homeowners to abandon one of the enduring icons of the American yard: the front lawn. Photograph of a San Diego, California home, circa late 1990s or early 2000s, courtesy of Joel Michaelsen, University of California, Santa Barbara.

it's brown flush it down." Newspaper articles described how to irrigate gardens with "gray water" left over after family members had bathed or washed the dishes, and many bathtubs sat full while the occupants tried to figure out how to get the tepid suds into the garden. Restaurants started serving water only by customer request. Bechtel engineers unfurled a scheme to tow icebergs (the polar icecaps hold seventy percent of the world's fresh water) to Long Beach with slow-moving tug boats; after the two-to-three year trip, what remained of the bergs would be moored alongside the Queen Mary and slowly melted for drinking water.[2] Water districts routed pipelines to underserved communities and bought water by the acre-foot from districts in wetter, less populated counties. Residents in Marin and Monterey counties—where water was scarce due to especially tight development restrictions—watched their yards shrivel up and die as water boards limited households to less than 200 gallons per day, about enough for a Navy shower and a glass of water with meals for each family member. Affluent residents spent hundreds of dollars per month paying tank-trucks to spray their front yards, while their less fortunate neighbors watched helplessly as their own gardens browned. Most Northern Californians held to the cause, however, and elevated water rationing to a high ideal, the proud emblem of which became the dirty car. All the while, San Francisco Bay Area television stations enraged viewers with footage of Southern California residents leisurely sprinkling their lawns and washing their cars while their garden hoses ran full tilt into the gutters.

The drought affected domestic life in numerous ways, from people's bathroom habits to the cleanliness of their cars, to how often they did the laundry, and particularly to the condition of the plantings in their gardens. About eighty-five percent of the state's water supply went to agriculture and another five percent went to businesses. That left ten percent for private homes, and a substantial portion of that amount was going into yards to irrigate thirsty, exotic species, such as azaleas, camellias, rhododendrons, birches, roses, perennials, and especially Kentucky Bluegrass lawns, plants which required several times more water than normal amounts of rainfall provided. According to East Bay Municipal

Utility District (East Bay Mud) statistics, families in Berkeley and Oakland used about one-fourth of their water in their yards, a somewhat low figure due to the moisture-laden fog that hovered near the bay on summer days.[3] But a few miles east, in the hotter and drier bedroom suburbs of Lafayette, Walnut Creek, and Concord, homeowners were putting forty to fifty percent of their water into the yards, especially to water lawns. Moreover, lots were substantially bigger in these communities, increasing the water consumption even further. Suddenly the true cost of California's exotic flora was revealing itself, and the sizeable investment people had put into their gardens was at risk.

For the next year, Northern California newspapers printed list after list of so-called "xeriphytes" (plants that thrived on little water). Before long, poppies, ceanothus, manzanitas, sages, lavenders, and ornamental grasses began to appear in parks, median strips, commercial buildings, and front yards. Retail nurseries began setting up "drought-tolerant" sections. Succulent and cactus gardens became the subject of numerous magazine

Figure 10.2. A family in Albany, California, replaces its front lawn with gravel after the drought of 1977. Photograph by the author, 1982.

articles. *Sunset* magazine showed readers how to replace dying lawns with gravel, a popular scheme in the cactus-filled front yards of Tucson, Las Cruces, and, to a lesser extent, Albuquerque and Phoenix. The editors even cautiously suggested that homeowners could allow their grass to die and then spray-paint it green—a practice more common in the East where warm-season grasses, such as Bermuda, St. Augustine, and zoysia, browned out each winter, but a practice dangerously close to the green-painted concrete found in working-class yards. The drought became a day-to-day topic of conversation, and in the back of the public's mind was the fear that, if conditions stayed dry, front yards would soon be full of saguaro cactus, animal skulls, and mounds of shifting sand.

Homeowners did not have to worry for long. The rains returned from 1978 through 1986, furiously enough to wash coastal homes into the sea, precipitate landslides that toppled hillside properties, and generate dramatic plant growth. Fueled by a low-pressure system called "El Niño," the winter of 1982–1983 saw more precipitation in California than in Seattle, a city that typically received more than twice the rainfall of the San Francisco Bay Area. Sierra reservoirs filled to overflowing within a year, brown lawns quickly reverted to green, and popular commentary about drought disappeared, save the warnings—mostly ignored—of a few experts that water shortages were only going to get worse as California's population grew. The experts were right. In 1986, rains waned again, this time for six years, the longest drought in modern California history. East Bay Mud began rationing water and implored homeowners to replace their dying gardens with xeriphytes. Most surrounding water districts followed suit, even slapping flow restrictors on the meters of homeowners who refused to ration. The California state legislature in 1990 passed Assembly Bill 325, a law requiring every community to adopt a water conservation policy. Assembly Bill 325 not only resulted in numerous restrictions on the plantings of lawns and ornamentals, but produced a slew of calculations and paperwork with which developers and designers needed to comply to obtain building approval. In one of the drought's biggest scandals, the *Oakland Tribune* leaked an East Bay Mud "hit-list" of the district's top water-wasters. One of the worst offenders was using a garden hose to fill a 2,000,000-gallon artificial lake on his twenty-five acre property, an event taking more than two months and drawing more than 20,000 gallons of water a day. The rest were affluent homeowners who simply overwatered their huge properties. The district sent out counselors to encourage big users to replant their yards, offering free design services and tempting financial incentives to those who complied. Overall, homeowners did too good a job of rationing. So great were individual cutbacks that East Bay Mud revenues from water bills plummeted. The agency, which had just raised rates to encourage cut-backs, had to raise them even further to cover losses stemming from the public's over-zealous commitment to conservation.

Water conservation offered a temporary solution, but it did not address the heart of the problem. During the droughts of 1976–1977 and 1986–1992, landscape architects, geographers, ecologists, magazine editors, and politicians alike suggested that water shortages were illuminating a bigger problem that had been growing since the gold rush: California landscapes were "inappropriately" planted. Since 1849, the state had been invaded by millions of outsiders—mostly from the Northeast and Midwest—who brought with them the desire to recreate the wet, green landscapes of their homelands. "From Maryland, Missouri, or Connecticut families leave their homes and the expanses of lawn to live in Novato or San Bernardino," landscape architect Russell Beatty wrote in 1977. "Either they, or the developers, make the transition easy by duplicating the lush landscape of their home towns."[4] Beatty was one of the first professionals to frame the drought in broad, cultural terms. Despite California's beautiful coastline, rugged mountains, rolling coastal hills, and scenic rivers, many of the builders, architects, prospectors, speculators, and entrepreneurs who had populated the state during the past century were little pleased by the arid climate and dry landscape.

One such individual was Stephen Nolan, a nursery grower who moved to California from the East in the late 1800s. Disenchanted by the brown hills surrounding his East Bay growing grounds (and no doubt intrigued by their commercial poten-

Figure 10.3. After enduring water shortages during the 1970s and 1980s, many Californians feared they would have to replace their front yard plantings with cactus, animal skulls, and mounds of shifting sand, as seen in this Oakland, California, neighborhood. Photograph by the author, 2004.

tial), he reforested them with thousands of eucalyptus, an exciting new species from Australia. ". . . The eyes of our friend lighted with enthusiasm of Nature's poet as he pictured the day when that landscape would be relieved and the whole country fertilized by these magnificent trees," Nolan said of his plans.[5] One of the first persons to bring Eucalyptus to California was clipper ship captain Robert Waterman. Waterman's dream upon retiring was to plant a "heap o' trees," and he did not have to wait long to get his chance. The captain, who moonlighted as a city planner, prepared the plat maps for the California cities of Fairfield and Cordelia in the 1850s, and he planted each city with blue gum seeds brought from Australia.[6] Nineteenth-century horticulturists hailed the species as a "miracle tree" capable of solving California's firewood shortage, providing lumber for building, pulp for paper, medicinal herbs and ointments, cures for respiratory ailments and malaria, and promising to green up the brown state.[7] San Francisco nurseryman William C. Walker was one of the first to sell Eucalyptus seeds, and his Golden Gate Nursery was

Figure 10.4. Many newcomers to California, especially from a greener East, disliked the dry, brown landscape and filled their yards with lush, green, and thirsty exotic plants that contrasted visually and ecologically with the surrounding native vegetation. Photograph by the author, East Bay Area foothills, 1991.

regarded as one of the best in the state.[8] Elwood Cooper of Santa Barbara, an Australian plant enthusiast, put in more than 150,000 eucalyptus near Santa Barbara in the 1870s. In 1905, the Judson Powder Plant planted blue gums on Albany Hill (along the east shore of the San Francisco Bay) to muffle the company's dynamite explosions. So many of the trees appeared by the turn of the twentieth century that parts of the San Francisco Bay Area appeared to be more Australian than Californian.[9]

The campaign to green-up the dry California landscape came from all quarters. In 1866, landscape architect Fredrick Law Olmsted developed a master plan for a College of California in Berkeley, and he took a quick dislike to the dry, brown hills surrounding the proposed school. Olmsted was strongly committed in his work to preserving an area's regional identity, but he nonetheless advised the city to cover the hills with thick green foliage to ameliorate their bleakness. "I can think of nothing to which the imagination turns with more eagerness in the bleak and open scenery, and the exceeding and all pervading lightness of the daylight of California," he wrote, "than to the memories of shady old lanes running through a close and overarching bowery of foliage. . . ." Olmsted, who later celebrated the arid climate of the region by using paved courtyards and sparse plantings in his design for Stanford University in nearby Palo Alto, recommended that the Berkeley roadsides be "draped over with living foliage" and that lush private gardens replace the "harsh, brown surfaces" that lay between homes and roads.[10]

By the turn of the twentieth century, the combined effects of mild climate, rapid population growth, and civic beautification campaigns prompted coastal Californians to adorn their homes, parks, and businesses with plants of every description. Charles Lummis, an East Coast transplant and avid booster of California living, wrote superlative accounts in his journal *Land of Sunshine:*

> [of] heliotrope hedges 15′ high, geraniums clambering up the second story of a house, a night-blooming cereus completely covering the side of a residence and fast enclosing the entire structure . . . callas growing by the acre and roses boasting thousands of blooms to a single bush. . . . That the trunk of an Acacia could measure six inches in diameter in just three years from seed and a eucalyptus could attain a height of 75′ in 8 years was a source of wonderment even to experienced horticulturists.[11]

Almost overnight, the streets of Los Angeles filled with olives, citrus, figs, and palms. Visitors to public parks enjoyed drifts of elms, liquidambars, lindens, maples, and other deciduous trees that barely turned color or dropped leaves during the gentle winters. The yards of affluent citizens ballooned with an array of flora unmatched anywhere in the nation, if not the world, plantings that were hailed as the keystone of the region's beauty. Even the yards of middle- and working-class citizens were notable, if only for plants which thrived in spite of the owners' inattention. As Art Commissioner John Mitchell wrote in 1910:

> Los Angeles already has the reputation of being a beautiful city. . . . What causes this impression? Is it wide, well-kept streets and boulevards? Is it handsome, well-proportioned public buildings, making a civic center? Is it galleries of art and museums, testifying devotion to education, art and science? No. . . . It is the private homes and gardens, erected and maintained by the home-lover, with a striking and attractive architecture of those dwellings great and small, and the well-kept lawns and private grounds, with the perennial growth of trees, shrubs and flowers.[12]

Despite the cooler climate, Northern Californians adorned their homes and cities with the same botanical fervor exhibited by their neighbors to the south. In his 1904 book, *The Simple Home,* Berkeley poet Charles Keeler advocated that builders position homes carefully on their lots to maximize garden space. Lamenting that too many homeowners wasted their back yards on clothes drying and trash barrels, Keeler recommended a blend of naturalistic and formal garden layouts containing liberal quantities of bamboo, palms, dracaenas, magnolias, oranges, bananas, eucalyptus, acacias, pittosporums, grevillias, araucarias, and "innumerable other fragrant or showy plants of New Zealand and Australia, of Africa, South America and the Indies . . ." While Keeler was sympathetic to the use of native plants, he felt constrained by their limited numbers and availability. "By having a choice of all the plants of the temperate zone, the landscape gardener is given limitless power of expression in his art," he wrote.[13]

Because of its rolling hills, wooded ravines, stately homes, and magnificent views to the Golden Gate, Berkeley was poised to become the San Francisco Bay Area's premiere garden city. In 1915, the city hired German city planner Werner Hegemann to help create a master plan. Hegemann, a proponent of the Garden City movement in Europe, extolled Berkeley's huge trees and overgrown shrubbery and urged every effort be made to save them in the face of modernization. "No stronger contrast to the architectural ideals of the old centralized city and its stone beauty could be imagined than this kind of residential neighborhood," he wrote, "where the walls and roofs of human shelter have returned to Nature under the influence of rapid transit and modern ideas about hygienic life."[14] The German planner advised the city to plant large numbers of street trees, adopt curving roads in the fashion of Frederick Law Olmsted's Riverside, Illinois, and—to dissuade estate owners from subdividing their land—exempt large gardens from taxation. "Any new city, especially cities in so happy a climate as California, must be real garden cities instead of repeating the congestion of homes of the old cities," he wrote.[15]

A garden city did not come without costs: ". . . water—and water in abundance, must be provided for a garden," John McLaren warned, "for unless there is an ample supply during our long Summer, gardening in general cannot be successful."[16] If most of the plants introduced into California required water in abundance, people were willing to pay the price. As the West grew, so did the numbers of dams and reservoirs, and by the 1920s California cities were providing pressurized water to most of their citizens. Household plantings flourished, and the press took note. "Santa Rosa is considered one of the garden cities of this district, and most of the claim to this title may well be credited to the free uses of water for lawns and gardens," wrote D. W. Cozad in 1918.[17]

While homeowners were busy filling their yards with plants, a few Californians, including Lockwood de Forest, Theodore Payne, Lester Roundtree, and Kate Sessions, questioned the consequences of unrestrained water use. Sessions operated a nursery that "resembled the gardens bordering the Mediterranean in Southern Italy." [18] She was responsible directly and indirectly for numerous public and private plantings in San Diego County, and she quickly realized that drought-tolerant species were far better suited to her dry environs than were water-loving ones. She was one of the first nursery growers to offer California native plants, such as Matilija Poppy, Fremontia, and California Lilac, and she lobbied for the use of xeriphytic plants in journal articles.[19] In a 1924 *Garden Magazine* article, Santa Barbara landscape architect Lockwood de Forest questioned the use of lawns both on ecological and aesthetic grounds. Most garden designers, he argued, proposed greenswards as a matter of course, even though few owners were willing to bear the expense of frequent mowing and irrigation. As a result, many lawns looked weedy and half-green. Moreover, much of California's natural landscape turned golden brown during the dry months and clashed with the deep green hues of irrigated grass, destroying visual harmony between homes and natural surroundings. "Because of the low annual rainfall, which comes only during the winter months, the natural scenery is brown for most of the year. The result . . . is of an overturned can of green paint," de Forest wrote.[20]

Kate Sessions and Lockwood de Forest foretold some of the problems the drought of 1976–1977 would reveal, but, in the meantime, the mild Pacific Coast climate, the availability of single-family homes, the growth of the state's nursery industry, the invention of automatic sprinklers, and the tremendous population growth all contributed to an extensive proliferation of plants in California. Whether or not the population was more adept at gardening than was the average American was a point fast becoming moot; plants grew so easily and quickly that even the disinclined could enjoy a garden. The distribution of urban flora, as a rule, is not well documented, but two studies suggested just how prolific such plantings had become. In 1971, James Schmid surveyed the vegetation in residential front yards in Chicago and found sixty-two species of trees, seventy-one species of woody shrubs and vines, and thirty species of herbs spread out over 812 houses.[21] Two years earlier, University of California, Berkeley, graduate student William Derrenbacher surveyed yards in four separate Berkeley neighborhoods and counted seventy-eight species of trees, 120 species of woody shrubs and vines, and eighty species of herbs spread out among 113 houses on sixteen city blocks.[22] The difference between the two cities was dramatic. Derrenbacher found seventy-one percent more species in Berkeley on less than one-seventh the number of Schmid's Chicago properties. Moreover, many Berkeley gardens contained fifty to 100 species. The Chicago yards that Schmid surveyed, on the other hand, contained far less diversity. More than forty percent of the 22,500 shrubs he recorded were either privets or yews, and a fifth of the 809 trees were elms.

Derrenbacher's findings portended the warnings professionals would issue seven years later during the 1976–1977 drought. Most of the plants growing in Berkeley gardens transpired water at a considerably higher rate than the region's rainfall and, as a result, required plenty of supplemental water to perform according to people's expectations. The fact that twenty-five to fifty percent of the water used by Bay Area residents was going to irrigation confirmed this discrepancy. These plantings represented not just a water liability, but a huge financial investment in the state's billion dollar "green industry," and a sustained

Figure 10.5. By the 1990s, California garden centers offered close to 4,000 species of plants, most of which required irrigation to survive. Photograph by the author, Berkeley, California, 2004.

drought promised to wreak economic havoc.[23] The proper response, the garden intelligentsia warned, was for people to abandon their desire for lush, green landscapes and learn to love California in its natural, arid condition. The state had a rich cultural history of missions, with their sparsely planted figs and olives, trickling fountains, and gravel courtyards; of rancho dwellings, with tiled patios and sheltering arbors; of fields of poppies and golden brown grasses; of a diverse native flora that survived on natural rainfall alone. In his article, "Browning of the Greensward," Russell Beatty advised Californians to start by replacing their front lawn with a courtyard, patterned after the missions of the 1800s:

> A front patio enclosed by a fence or wall would be a more usable family space as well as a pleasant entry forecourt. Here small beds of flowers, azaleas and other "thirsties" could be grown satisfactorily. Such interior-oriented gardens would be low water users compared with planting

> the entire front yard. The exterior could be planted with a combination of suitable Mediterranean species selected for both appearance and drought tolerance.[24]

The same qualities that made many xeriphytes appealing, however, also made them suspect. California's native flora had evolved in an environment of summer heat, clay, fire and drought—hardly the kind of conditions homeowners desired in their yards. To limit evapo-transpiration, natives, such as the bush monkey flower, had drab, resinous foliage and emitted unpleasant odors. The majestic California buckeye was one of several species that began dropping leaves in mid-July to save water, rendering it bare and dead-looking for a good portion of the year. Natives, such as ceanothus and fremontia, had short life spans and quickly rotted when watered along with conventional garden plants. The matilija poppy was one of several species that could only reproduce if wildfire scorched its seeds. The live oak, the statuesque tree symbolizing the state's native flora, was vulnerable to verticilium wilt, crown rot, sudden oak death, and caterpillar invasions that, when treated, could leave thousands of larvae wriggling and writhing on a homeowner's patio. Despite the barrage of articles and promotions in newspapers, books, and magazines, indigenous species were slow to take off. In 1995, Ross Hutchings, of the California Association of Nurserymen, reported that natives still constituted only two percent of the state's billion-dollar nursery sales.[25]

Practical factors notwithstanding, much of the resistance Californians have shown to adopting water-saving landscapes may take years to change. Stephen Nolan, Robert Waterman, and Charles Keeler were representative of millions of Californians born and raised out of state whose expectations for a home landscape were both formed at a very young age and unlikely to be overturned by one or two droughts. During the years 1981–1990, I interviewed more than 200 people in the San Francisco Bay Area about their yards, and in nearly every case the respondents remarked that their favorite plants were ones they knew from childhood. Tom, a Berkeley lawyer, was attached to the plants in each of the areas where he grew up. "I learned to appreciate bougainvillea in Arizona. I learned to like lilac trees in Illinois. We had a beautiful maple in Connecticut. And I like the forested areas where we lived in New York, especially deciduous ones." Tom's law practice left him little time to garden, but, upon moving into his new Berkeley home in 1980, he went straight to the nearest nursery to buy these plants for his yard.[26]

Nora's Kensington, California, yard overflowed with shrubs and flowers that bloomed without interruption from February to November. Her favorites, however, were those she remembered from childhood walks through the woods in Ohio in the 1920s. "I don't relate to new plants nearly as much as ones I knew when I was a girl, like four-leaf clovers or nasturtiums, the first plant I ever grew in my own garden," she recalled. "A friend brought me a rhododendron, but it doesn't mean nearly as much as the patch of ratty nasturtiums in the back yard. I hate gladiolas and rose of Sharon . . . . The little boy across the street drowned and the old ladies in the neighborhood brought those plants to the funeral."[27]

"I have a sentimental attachment to forsythia," said Jerod, an Albany, California, writer who was one of many people to mention this plant as a childhood favorite. "It grows in the Midwest where I came from. And I love the way lilacs smell in the Midwest."[28] Jim, an Oakland, California, school teacher, had vivid memories of swamp cypress and palm trees from his childhood home in Florida. "Every town in Florida had streets with rows of stately palms. I remember the royal palm the most. There were magnolias, cedars, and cypress growing in lagoons of artesian water, with Spanish moss drooping from the branches. It was like paradise."[29]

Virginia was a psychology Ph.D. student living in a two-bedroom shingled bungalow in Albany. Nearly every plant in her yard was a reminder either of a person she had known or a place she had once lived. "All the plants and flowers from the rock garden my father had made when I was growing up have significance. There's snowdrops, which my father's mother always loved and planted under an oak tree in our back yard—two acres. And they mean my grandmother to me. I've always resented stiffer flowers. Geraniums are a negative plant—my stepmother loved

Figure 10.6. Nearly every plant in this graduate student's yard reminded her of a person or place. Photograph by the author, Albany, California, 1982.

them, and I didn't like her. They almost seem like a shrub, not fragile or something. There are some plants I have a real prejudice against, because they remind me of a person I don't like. It's crazy. . . ."[30]

"My ironwoods mean Santa Catalina to me, and the back yard is Los Angeles," said Harry, a retired landlord who filled his Berkeley garden with the philodendrons, birds of paradise, and tree ferns he knew as a boy in Southern California.[31] Henry, an Albany grocer whose front yard contained boulders, moss, bonsaied pines, and a gravel creek bed, explained his garden simply: "I just like the Japanese landscape, that's all. I'm Japanese."[32] Romana grew up in Italy and, upon moving to Berkeley as a young woman, decorated her yard with ceramic sculptures set among apricots, persimmons, fuchsias, roses, dahlias, and herbs. "I'm a sculptor. When we moved from Italy, my daughter was a baby. I was so depressed—all there was for children to see in this country were those little flags around used car lots. In Italy we had sculptures everywhere—fountains, lions, and all kinds of marvelous things. So I started making things for my kids."[33]

People described their attachments to garden elements other than plants. Stephen, a San Francisco landscape designer, had a client who was originally from Massachusetts and who hated the orange Bay Area bricks slated for his front entry:

> We got samples from every manufacturer in the Bay Area, and the Richardsons would accept none of them. They hated the orange color. Then he went to Boston on a business trip and returned home with a purplish brick he especially liked. It was the sort of brick he had seen every day as a boy. We sent it to all the brick yards in the Bay Area and none of them could match it; the soils here simply could not produce the right color. So finally we had the Boston brick, over 20,000 of them, shipped by rail at twice the cost of the local ones.[34]

Even people with little or no interest in gardens have vivid recollections of plants from childhood. Nina lived in an Oakland apartment with a grassy courtyard shared by seven tenants and tended by hired gardeners. She had not lifted a rake or shovel in more than twenty years and had no desire to have her own yard. "I've never wanted to have a garden," she admitted. "But ever since I was a kid I've loved to get down on my hands and knees and look into lawns and see a miniature forest of grass, weeds, insects and butterflies. I still do this today sometimes." Nina had vivid recollections of walking home from grade school in Palo Alto "past fields of brilliant magenta-colored ice plant" and picking loquats in neighbors' trees. "When I see loquats for sale at the produce market they look ratty and unappealing. But when I see them on a tree I still get excited. I've fantasized about going out some night with a ladder and picking loquats off the trees in front of Safeway." Nina spent two years as a teenager in East Africa, where she was surrounded by tropical plants of every description. "The plants were much more memorable than the buildings . . . . I remember especially the taste and fragrance, and there were always monkeys in the trees, just like you see squirrels here in Oakland. We ate so many papayas, I get nauseous just seeing one now."[35]

Susan was a computer consultant living on the top floor of a San Francisco duplex. She never liked gardens or, for that matter, even being outdoors. "I'd like to live further up on the hill, with a better view, and have piles of blankets. I've always found lots of land sort of scary." Susan never wanted a yard, although during what she termed the "house plant craze" of the 1970s she had seventy plants, now down to fewer than a dozen. "I associate a garden with clutter, and I don't do well in a cluttered environment. A garden is an obligation, like having a pet. I had a dog once and it died, and I have to admit I felt better being free from the obligation." Still, she had fond memories of playing in the fields around her childhood home in Illinois. "Our house was surrounded by corn fields, and I was always playing in them. My parents got me excited by growing things, like raspberries and rhubarb. We used to have hollyhocks, and my mother would make dolls out of them for my sister and me."[36]

Studies involving children's responses to outdoor environments suggest why plants might evoke vivid childhood memories. In 1991, Rachel Sebba interviewed several hundred adults to learn the origins of their environmental preferences. When asked to recall favorite childhood places, more than ninety-five percent of the adults described outdoor areas, even though Sebba never stipulated that the place be outside. Moreover, the things that people recalled most fondly were natural rather than built: trees, rocks, bushes, sand, puddles, and sky.[37] Sebba's respondents were Israeli, but Americans give similar answers. Clare Cooper-Marcus has asked hundreds of adults to prepare drawings of ideal childhood places, and eighty-five percent have depicted outdoor spots.[38] When the same people were later asked to describe or draw present-day places that they considered ideal, their responses strongly resembled their childhood drawings.

The post-World War II California garden was a product of many forces: the spread of affordable suburban homes, the comfortable climate, the state's paradisiacal reputation, the need for outdoor living and family raising space, and the development of horticultural technology and irrigation. The garden was also a product of the westward migration of millions of Americans who brought with them notions of landscape beauty formed in much wetter climates. California offered stunning coastal and mountain scenery matched in few other states. It also offered small, fenced lots, many of which were little more than bare ground awaiting inscription by the new owners. In the absence of a strong regional garden style and a deep cultural history, it stood to reason that homeowners would plant species with which they were already familiar and had cherished since they were children. To paraphrase David Streatfield once again, they sought to recreate the familiar.[39]

In his seminal essay, "Axioms for Reading the Landscape," Peirce F. Lewis remarked that people will not change a landscape unless they are under pressure to do so.[40] Garden solutions responding to the state's climate, rainfall, and native flora now are appearing with more and more frequency. Some twenty years after writing "Browning of the Greensward" in 1977, Russell Beatty re-evaluated California gardens in his article, "Greening of the Brownsward."[41] Beatty found more drip irrigation systems

Figure 10.7. A xeriscape (drought-tolerant) garden in Studio City, California, in 2005. Water boards, house and garden magazines, landscape architects, and nurseries have worked hard, especially in the past thirty years, to convince Californians that dry gardens—that is, gardens requiring little or no irrigation—can be beautiful. Photograph by the author.

(a low-flow irrigation method developed in Israel in 1949 to water desert farmland), more nurseries carrying xeriphytes, and more designs in the Mission Revival style, with gravel courts in place of lawns, walls in place of hedges, arbors in place of trees, and mulch in place of ground cover. Two major droughts, water rationing, the passage of Assembly Bill 325, and a sustained public education campaign on the part of newspapers, magazines, and water districts deserve credit for many of these changes. Another change, perhaps more significant, also occurred in those twenty years. By 1998, the population of California—for the first time since the gold rush of 1849—included more native-born residents than non-natives. A native-born population has more opportunity to build upon common roots, more opportunity to develop and share traditions, and more opportunity to form strong attachments to its region. It is no coincidence that the Japanese and English gardens—arguably two of the world's most highly regarded styles—evolved on islands, isolated for centuries from sustained contact with other cultures. If it takes time for people to develop fondness for the place in which they dwell, then perhaps, as more and more of California's population becomes native born, so will its residents welcome gardens that more closely reflect regional conditions.

The emotional attachments children form for plants are not necessarily sufficient to propel them into a life of gardening, but these sentiments have contributed significantly to the concepts of habitability around which people arrange their yards. California is still a young state. As the number of native-born residents grows, people's memories of wet, green landscapes will give way to images of brown hills dotted with oaks, courtyards of gravel and tile, gray-green shrubs dotted with pale yellow and blue flowers, and rough meadows that only faintly resemble groomed lawns. The shift, which is already occurring, will come from more than just the requirement to save water. It will come from intrinsic attachments to the landscape instilled early on in life. Suki, who grew up riding horses in the foothills near Mount Diablo, is one of the native-born Californians ready for such a garden. "I think the dry brown hills are beautiful, and I love the heat," she said of a region near her home so bare one could walk for miles and see only a handful of trees and scrub. "I grew up in the Bay Area and used to ride my horse around the trails near Clayton. There were not even any trees, just brown grass waving in the wind. It was wonderful. I've never understood this attitude of sticking plants in everywhere."[42] As time passes, the arid landscape that once repelled newcomers will become a bigger part of the population's shared history, allowing the ideal and the real to converge into a more fully formed regional garden.

Part Three

Outlook for America's Home Grounds

Chapter Eleven: The Common-Interest Landscape

As Americans change their dwellings, it is reasonable to assume that they will also change their yards. Leisure and family activities have been cornerstones of the American dwelling since the end of World War II, and they continue to shape the contents and uses of most middle-class yards. The profile of the family is changing, however. In 2001, less than twenty-five percent of households in the United States consisted of married couples with children, down from a high of forty-five percent in 1960.[1] About sixty-five percent of mothers now work full-time, and some thirty percent of all newborns have unwed parents.[2] In the past twenty-five years, there have been more double-income families, single-parent families, same-sex households with and without children, and homes that sit empty for weeks or months while the owners are traveling or working in distant locations. By the 1990s, Americans were working about ten percent more hours than they were in the 1950s, according to economist Juliet Schor.[3] As a result, people have been spending less time in their homes and yards, and both spaces are changing as a result.

In the past century, most Americans have preferred to live in detached homes, a dwelling type in which the home grounds have contributed significantly to day-to-day habitability. Increased mobility, high home prices, and family structure, however, are challenging this preference. For the last two decades, more and more families have chosen to live in "common interest" developments, such as townhouses and condominiums, where walls are jointly owned, driveways are shared, outdoor space is held in common, and private yards are often tiny or non-existent. By 1994,

Figure 11.1. A townhouse community in Oakland, California, 2005. Most of the grounds are commonly held and maintained, creating the impression of an expansive, communal front yard. Photograph by the author.

one out of seven Americans lived in common-interest communities, and such dwellings accounted for more than one-half of the market of new homes. By 2005, seventy-five percent or more of new housing units were condominiums, cooperatives, or controlled by homeowner associations, and nearly 52,000,000 Americans resided in such dwellings.[4] *Sunset* magazine no longer advises, as it did in 1954, that a patio be "twice the size of the average living room." The magazine is, instead, publishing small-space design manuals where the "yard" consists of an enclosed eight-by-ten-foot concrete platform for a table and chairs, with plants in pots or espaliered flat against the fence. "Small gardens have advantages over large ones. The atmosphere is usually by necessity intimate and secluded, and every detail of a pot or flower can be appreciated up close," wrote the authors of *Landscaping Small Spaces*. "You can perhaps indulge a love of fine materials and objects and be glad you only need a few. Most important, a small yard offers the best chance of experimenting playfully or artistically with what you learn and what you like, while leaving you a little free time simply to sit outdoors in the fresh air." Still holding true to the magazine's editorial philosophy that a garden is primarily a social space, the authors warned against filling it with too many plants. ". . . If you want the garden to be used and appreciated, commit yourself to allocating a generous amount of it to paths and sitting areas," the authors advised.[5]

Common-interest dwellings are often set amid shared grounds planted with trees, lawns, and large swaths of low maintenance shrubs and groundcovers. Much of the terrain is mounded into berms (artificial mounds), and residents rarely use it to picnic, toss a ball, or relax on the grass. Professional gardeners maintain the grounds, and codes forbid residents to modify the plantings. Outdoor living, if the busy professionals who live there have time for it, occurs around the complex's pool and spa. Capriana Townhouses in the San Francisco Bay Area promises:

> Young & Restless . . . to be able to pursue your active lifestyle and own a home that allows you that freedom is every young person's dream. To take off skiing, biking, traveling or whatever you choose, knowing you'll be coming back to a home where the yard and exterior maintenance are all taken care of. Because when you're young, you have better things to do.[6]

Common-interest communities, through the vehicle of homeowner's association boards, often control everything within the street view (and even things concealed from it): house color, exterior light fixtures, mailboxes, trash can locations, open garage doors, on-street parking, holiday decorations, and the placement of numbers on the door. The Woodbridge Association in Harbor Bay Isle, an Alameda, California, subdivision built in the 1970s, gives new owners a two-inch-thick manual listing its rules and regulations. Most of the manual concerns the legalities of joint property ownership, but it also includes a strict list of landscape guidelines.[7] Woodbridge prohibits or discourages signs on the houses or in their windows, pergolas over eight feet tall, visible clothes-drying structures, dog runs, open garage doors, on-street parking, and patios that are "too large" in proportion to the rest of the yard, a judgment call enforced by a design review board. The association forbids above-ground swimming pools and allows spas only if they are thoroughly concealed from the neighbors. Rules require that wood structures be made from naturally weathered redwood or cedar, and they expressly prohibit red-painted or stained wood. The mailbox guidelines alone are five pages long.

Figure 11.2. Owners of townhouses, condominiums, and other common-interest communities often have little private outdoor space other than small courtyards and balconies, but they also enjoy freedom from yard work. Photograph by the author, 2006.

Woodbridge is as restrictive about plantings as it is about mailboxes. The association has banned bamboo (underground runners), blue gums (limb breakage, messy appearance), various grasses (wind-born seeds), and discourages more than forty-five species of trees and shrubs.[8] Woodbridge also bans unleashed pets, as one resident discovered upon receiving a ticket for letting her cat out one night.[9] Such rules are not unusual. Edward Blakely and Mary Snyder surveyed homeowner associations across the nation when researching their book, *Fortress America.* Along with the above-mentioned restrictions, they found prohibitions against window air-conditioners, back yard swing sets, satellite dishes, streetside trash cans, and even indoor furniture visible through the window of the house.[10] Blackhawk, a gated community in Danville, California, prohibits door-to-door solicitation, a rule that has forced Girl Scouts to sell their cookies to drivers queuing up outside the guardhouse. This onslaught of regulations, Blakely and Snyder have observed, could stem, in part, from the newness of such places, especially in Phoenix, Houston, Atlanta, and other rapidly developing areas. Residents of such common-interest communities, the authors surmise, have perhaps imposed codes, covenants, and restrictions governing public expression and behavior because such regulation has simply not had time to develop informally through person-to-person interaction.[11]

Restrictions have been especially strict in subdivisions located in natural areas, a practice that beckons back to Haskell's and Davis's efforts in 1853 to preserve the picturesque scenery of Llewellyn Park in New Jersey. A good example is the widespread effort many California communities have made to preserve oak-bay forests, one of California's revered plant communities. Oaks and bays have been fast disappearing due to the encroachment of agriculture, grazing, and housing developments. From 1900 to 1990, hardwood forests dominated by oaks became twenty-seven percent smaller in San Luis Obispo County, thirty-eight percent smaller in Los Angeles County, and forty-two percent smaller in Santa Barbara County.[12] As a result, local planning departments often require developers to save a high percentage of the trees (especially oaks) by restricting grading practices, limiting lot sizes to very large parcels, and banning tree removal. The best trees often get a "heritage" designation, and a developer who removes or kills one can pay a steep fine. The codes

Figure 11.3. A gated development in Alamo, California, 2005. Homeowner associations in such communities often pass strict rules regulating how residents may plant, build, and use their yards. Photograph by the author.

often have strong ecological underpinnings, such as those at Golden Eagle Farm in Pleasanton, California, where yards must blend with the "majestic Oaks, grassy hillsides weaving through the wooded area and natural ravines supporting riparian plant life."[13] Portola Valley Ranch, an affluent subdivision built in the mid-1970s on the peninsula south of San Francisco, has some of the strictest planting regulations to be found. To provide harmony with the woodland surroundings, the developer left half of the 450-acre property untouched and sited the houses serendipitously amid the native oaks and bays. Landscape architect Nancy Hardesty divided the unfenced grounds around each home into zones, each with its own list of permissible plants. Hardesty allowed homeowners to plant the largest number of species—up to about ten—close to the house. As one moved farther away from the homes into the rolling fields and meadows behind the homes, the list got shorter until it included only oaks, bays, and madrones. Hardesty's plans allowed the residential landscape to blend smoothly with its natural surroundings, an effect that contrasted sharply with nearby tracts planted with juniper, agapanthus, daisies, ornamental pears, and other popular exotics. Her zones were more than polite suggestions; they were written into the deeds of the homes. "The native planting at Portola Valley Ranch provides a sweep of continuity from forest to front door. And the bonus is . . . no lawns to mow," Hardesty promised. Today, oaks, manzanitas, buckeyes, and ceanothus weave between the wooden houses in a remarkably naturalistic manner. Storm runoff flows into rock-lined creeks—called "drainage easements"—resembling mountain streambeds more than concrete culverts. Parking spaces are labeled "auxiliary parking easements" or "apes," as the residents call them, and they are widely spaced to prevent any traces of "Manhattanization."[14]

Common-interest housing and the forces that produced it have opened the door to a new version of the home grounds, one in which private space is at a minimum, outdoor areas are largely shared among the residents, planted scenery takes the place of functional space, and community needs often preside over individual ones. The common-interest garden is not the only way in which yards are changing, however. During the 1980s and 1990s (and continuing to this day), a wave of commentary

Figure 11.4. A house in Portola Valley Ranch, California, 1981. Homes and their grounds, owing to exacting design guidelines, are meant to blend seamlessly with the surrounding natural landscape. Photograph by the author.

appeared, suggesting it was time for Americans to re-evaluate the cornerstone of the home grounds: the lawn. The criticism fell into four basic categories: that the sheer amount of chemicals homeowners were pouring on their lawns was threatening regional ecosystems; that lawns were taxing water supplies, especially in the arid West and Southwest; that lawns represented an unhealthy urge to control nature; and that, in a frontal assault to the premise of the home grounds, Americans would be better off gardening than mowing grass. The commentary raised significant questions regarding practices in which Americans engaged in order to maintain their home grounds. With respect to pollutants, Ted Williams revealed that Americans were dumping more fertilizer on their grass than India used for all its agriculture.[15] Grass clippings had gotten voluminous, to the point of constituting one-third of public landfill waste. Even worse, the power mowers that were used to generate the clippings were producing up to five percent of the nation's air pollution, and the gas that homeowners spilled filling their mower tanks in a given year exceeded the Exxon Valdez oil spill.[16]

Residents in the arid West and Southwest were, without question, giving their lawns plenty of water. But the effort that homeowners were making to green-up their otherwise arid surroundings was only part of a larger desire—especially among men, wrote Virginia Jenkins—to wage war against nature:

> On the American front men use power machinery and chemicals, the tools of war, to engage in a battle for supremacy with Mother Nature. Men have made front lawns into engineered spaces with rigid boundaries and hard edges . . . . This battle, openly declared in the late forties, was the ultimate declaration of masculine ownership of the lawn.[17]

Jenkins also revealed that she never cared much for lawns and suggested that, deep down, most Americans would agree, had the turf industry not persuaded them to think otherwise. "Lawns were not a need expressed by consumers that was then met by producers," she wrote. "The need was fostered by producers, who continued to raise the standards of what constituted a good or acceptable front lawn. Americans were taught to value lawns and were sold the equipment and supplies to care for them."[18] Whether by choice or manipulation, Americans were indeed pouring money into their lawns. According to Turfgrass Producers International, turf grass represented a $147 billion dollar industry in 2005.[19]

A huge turf grass industry—as much as three times larger by various estimates as all other household gardening expenditures combined—translated to a residential landscape dominated by grass, the sheer amount of which raised even more hackles. In a 1995 piece describing the "new urbanism" movement in the United States (a cause dedicated to replacing suburban sprawl with higher density, mixed-use communities), *Newsweek* writer Jerry Adler proclaimed the ornamental lawn "the single most useless form of plant life in all botany."[20] Michael Pollan, former editor of *Harper's* magazine whose book, *Second Nature,* has become a modern classic on the ethics of gardening, went even further, suggesting that Americans might be better served spending their time cultivating plants rather than mowing grass. Pollan developed an enthusiasm for gardening when, upon buying a farmhouse in Connecticut, he found that a traditional American yard did not suit him. Nearly every act of gardening in which he engaged—from the moral imperatives of composting (produces "more virtue than beauty") to the obligation of weeding ("to weed is to bring culture to nature"), to planting a tree ("a utopian enterprise")—taught him something, with the exception of mowing a lawn. "If lawn mowing feels like copying the same sentence over and over, gardening is like writing out new ones, an infinitely variable process of invention and discovery."[21]

Pollan's words illuminate the dichotomy that has long existed in the American mind regarding the home grounds: the tension between gardening and family activities. In many respects, the lawn stands squarely in the middle of this dichotomy, serving at once as the symbol of the garden and the family room, the dividing line between those who are horticulturally inclined and those who are looking for additional living space. In their book, *Redesigning the American Lawn,* F. Herbert Bormann, Diana Balmori, and Gordon T. Geballe ask, "Can I manage or redesign my lawn in ways that minimize its negative impact on the environment and yet create an environment that meets my aesthetic and recreational needs?"[22] If such change is to come, all indications are that it will be in the way of lawns that are less chemical-dependent rather than smaller or fewer in number. In the past decade, turf growers in the West have introduced numerous new strains that not only need infrequent mowing and fewer fertilizers, but also have water requirements barely exceeding those of regional xeriphytes. Moreover, seed growers are selling more and more "meadow-mixes" that blend grasses with clover, wildflowers, and other species that previous generations took great pains to weed out. The Environmental Protection Agency now promotes pollution control for power mowers, and companies such as Toro advertise gas-powered mowers with low emissions. Until Americans adopt a more widespread interest in gardening, however, or until a plant comes along that is as comfortable and durable as grass under foot, it is hard to envision the demise of the lawn. Contrary to assertions regarding the uselessness of grass, there is reason to believe just the opposite is true: that, in making 30,000,000 acres of land potentially habitable, no other single plant has contributed so much to American life, public or private.

Changes in family size and make-up, the spread of common-interest communities, redefinitions of the lawn, and a mobile population have each led to transformations in American home grounds. Despite these changes, the basic association of house and grounds has remained constant. Until such time as this connection ends, it is likely that the majority of people will continue to organize their yards around day-to-day habitability.

During the past two centuries, the house and yard in America have been shaped by closely related circumstances. Initially, the *agricultural yard* embraced livelihood as its basic purpose, a purpose that extended from the doors of the house to the farthest reach of the fields. Whether used for growing vegetables, repairing a wagon or plow, raising animals, canning fruit, or growing medicinal herbs, the house and grounds were critical to the survival of the household. If flowers and ornaments had a place, they were limited to a few, special spots around the house, often on the sides visible to the public. In this respect, the front yard has changed little to this day as a symbol of individual property ownership and community beauty.

The second incarnation of the home grounds, the *urban utility yard,* was indispensable to the house in a different but equally critical way. In comparison to spacious rural parcels, city lots during the mid-to-late-1800s were tiny and closet-like, with few traces of agriculture uses. The poor state of American cities, with their high densities, rampant diseases, slow transportation, and meager level of public services, left most residents little choice but to use their back yards to store water, dispose of trash, hang laundry, dig a privy, and perform other household services necessary to obtain a minimal level of habitability. Then, as the nation began its first major thrust to suburbanization, two important shifts occurred in the home grounds. The first was the emergence of the front yard as an expression of civic beauty, a place that provided uninterrupted vistas of tamed greenery for citizens to enjoy. The second was the gradual replacement of back yard utilities with commercial and city-supplied equivalents, a process that steadily freed up space behind homes for family living. These two events helped to solidify what had long been poised to occur: the division of the home grounds into distinct public and private spheres.

The third incarnation of the American yard, the *outdoor family room,* was as closely related to the dwelling as its predecessors, but its focus had shifted from basic necessities to a higher level of habitability. By the end of World War II, the nation was primed for a new version of the home grounds. The economy was on a huge upswing, the number of families was rapidly growing, and Americans were moving in great waves into detached homes in new suburban tracts. Free from the vestiges of agriculture and utility and buoyed by an increase in leisure time, greater financial security, and a baby boom, homeowners were free to organize their back yards for children's play, family entertaining, and leisure. This version of the yard, while limited by climate in most regions of the nation, found its most pronounced expression in California, where the mild climate, enormous nursery industry, and ethic of outdoor living promoted by *Sunset* magazine encouraged residents to raise their yards to a new standard of livability.

If a fourth version of the home grounds is poised to emerge, it could well be scaled back in size—in order to fit with the reduced living space found in common-interest dwellings. It could have a smaller lawn—especially in front yards—since more people are questioning the long-term benefits of ornamental grass. It could have more regional plants, especially in places where mobility rates have decreased and where nurseries are stocking native plants. It could have more focus on nature, as concepts of ecology and sustainability become more and more integrated into mainstream American culture. Magazines such as *Sunset, Better Homes and Gardens,* and *House Beautiful* are currently running more and more articles about attracting birds and wildlife into back yards, replacing off-property drainage with dry creeks and vernal pools, selecting regional plants, adopting low-flow irrigation, and using recycled wood, broken concrete, and other environmentally friendly materials. Though hardly a return to the horticultural recommendations such magazines espoused a century ago, this advice nonetheless portends an evolving understanding of the role of nature in the home grounds and a re-evaluation of "tamed scenery."

Like so many other instances of American culture, traces of past home grounds are still evident all around us. One can drive not thirty minutes from Oakland, California, and find agricultural yards tucked into the valleys in the foothills surrounding San Francisco Bay's plain. Though vastly more modern than farms a century or two ago, these properties still contain barnyards, dooryards, and vegetable plots in the style of their predecessors. Cattle graze the surrounding hills, perched on the narrow "terracette" footholds they have carved into the steep grassy slopes. Barns and fenced yards line the roads, dooryards are alive with activity, and road signs advertise dog and horse boarding, well drilling, chickens and rabbits, firewood, and fresh produce. Cell phones, pickup trucks, and water mains have replaced messengers, horse-drawn carts, and wells, and one can see well-manicured lawns and flower gardens in front of the homes. Still, the workings of such properties remain closely linked to a family's livelihood, and the grounds reveal it in numerous ways.

One can then turn and drive to the inner-city neighborhoods along the flat of the bay and find yard after yard resembling early twentieth-century urban properties, where utility and neglect recall the wasteland wrought by rapid industrialization and meager public services. Broken appliances and trash sit uncollected in tiny yards surrounded by fences topped with razor wire. Vegetables grow out of raised wooden beds that age has split at the seams. Laundry flaps on clotheslines stretched above

Figure 11.5. This front yard in Palo Alto, California, achieves an effective balance between plantings, household use, privacy, connections to the street, and water conservation. Photograph by the author, 1982.

cracked, concrete terraces. Used lumber, saw horses, and rusty tools rest against back porches. Occasionally one comes across a yard developed for family living, but most are plain and functional, the doors and windows that look out onto them covered with steel security bars.[23]

In the nearby Berkeley and Oakland hills and in the neighboring suburbs of Orinda, Lafayette, and Walnut Creek, copies of *Sunset* magazine arrive in mailboxes each month. Lawn and pool care vans make their rounds, while hired gardeners build stone walls, lay sprinkler pipe, and haul off piles of clippings in their pickup trucks. Residents open their *San Francisco Chronicle* and *Contra Costa Times* to gardening sections filled with advertisements for spas and rain-forest friendly wooden benches, schedules for garden tours, and advice on pruning fruit trees and cooking with home-grown herbs. Children play on swings and slides on back yard lawns. Families dine under vine-laden arbors, enjoy scenic views from their redwood decks, and relax in hammocks under statuesque oaks. Grass and flowers abound, watered by automatic sprinklers that whoosh to life before the families rise to take their morning showers.

Although the agricultural yard, urban utility yard, and outdoor family room vary significantly in form and content, the one thread they all share in common is an intimate connection with the house. During the past two centuries, the home grounds in America have acquired the popular reputation as a measuring stick for the horticultural talents of the owners. When a yard does not rise to the level of a beautiful garden, we tend to look the other way and often miss where its true value lies. This is not to say that plants and beauty are insignificant to American yards, or to deny the importance of the vast nursery industry throughout the nation, or to overlook the millions of citizens for whom gardening is a beloved and passionate endeavor. Horticulture and gardening are compelling activities, but, in terms of common yards, they are part of a much larger picture. First and foremost, the home grounds are about how people dwell and about the effort that Americans have made collectively and individually to transform their dwellings—inside and out—into habitable space.

Notes

Prologue

1. Thomas Church, *Gardens Are for People*, 2nd ed. (1955; New York: McGraw Hill, 1983), 7.

2. Fred Schroeder, *Outlaw Aesthetics: Arts and the Public Mind* (Bowling Green, Ohio: Bowling Green University Popular Press, 1977).

3. Interview with the author, 1981.

4. My previous writings on the subject include "Social Meanings of Residential Gardens," Master's thesis (University of California, Berkeley, 1983); "Gardens for California Living," *Landscape*, Vol. 28, No. 3 (1985): 40–47; "The Well Tempered Garden," *Landscape*, Vol. 30, No. 1 (1988): 41–47; and "Social Meanings of Residential Gardens," in Mark Francis and Randolph T. Hester, editors, *The Meanings of Gardens* (Cambridge, Mass.: The MIT Press, 1990), 178–83.

Introduction

1. John Brinckerhoff Jackson (better known professionally as J. B. Jackson or John B. Jackson), "Nearer Than Eden," in *The Necessity for Ruins and Other Topics* (Amherst: University of Massachusetts Press, 1980), 19. Put another way, most garden literature is directed to garden enthusiasts, a group which in nearly every respect is different from average homeowners looking for ways to manage their yards.

2. Peirce F. Lewis, "Axioms for Reading the Landscape," in D. W. Meinig, editor, *The Interpretation of Ordinary Landscapes* (New York: Oxford University Press, 1979), 12.

3. See, especially, J. B. Jackson's writings in *Landscape* magazine, which he founded in 1951 and edited and published until 1968. Although *Landscape* is no longer published, its articles still make for excellent reading. See, also, D. W. Meinig, *The Interpretation of Ordinary Landscapes* and the *Journal of Popular Culture.*

There are also interesting books available on "folk art" gardens and dwellings in which the owners have built homes out of bottles, excavated caves on their properties, and decorated their yards with found objects and unusual pieces of sculpture. Though not exactly ordinary, these homes and gardens reveal aspects of the common landscape often ignored in more formal studies. See Jim Christy, *Strange Sites uncommon homes and gardens* (Madeira Park, B.C.: Harbour Publishing, 1996); Jennifer Isaacs, *Quirky Gardens* (Berkeley: Ten Speed Press, 1995); Charles Jencks, *Bizarre Architecture* (New York: Rizzoli, 1978); and *Daydream Houses of Los Angeles* (New York: Rizzoli, 1978 and Academy, London 1978); Bryce Muir, *Lawn Wars* (Bowdoinham, Me.: Bowdoinham College Press, 1988); Jane Owen, *Eccentric Gardens* (New York: Villard Books, 1990); and Jan Wampler, *All Their Own* (Oxford, London, New York: Schenkman Publishing Company, 1977).

4. The English, probably due to their deep garden tradition, tend to regard the grounds around the home as a garden, and they use it as such. Hannah, a landscape design student at Merritt College in Oakland, California, grew up near London and found the American distinction between yard and garden curious. "In England, if there is any planting around the house we call it a garden," she told me in 1996. "A yard to us is a place where a builder stores lumber. It seems you Americans feel something has to be very special before you call it a garden. Perhaps it's humility or a need to aspire to something grand." (Interview with the author, 1996).

5. Quotes taken from Paul Groth, "Lot, Yard, Garden, American Distinctions," *Landscape,* Vol. 30, No. 3 (1990): 29–35. This article is a "must read" for anyone interested in the structural foundation of the common yard.

6. A former director of the American Society of Landscape Architects offered the same interpretation, only more curtly: "LANDSCAPING. Probably no other word in the English language has done more to degrade the profession than this one. It has come to mean the orna-

mental arrangement of plants, especially shrubs and bushes. It is used every day to describe the foundation spinach around a bungalow or bunches of spirea to hide an ugly monument or garbage can." See "A Note From the Executive Director," *Landscape Architectural News Digest* (April 1962): 3. After World War II, landscape architects began to turn away from residential design, partly on the grounds that they believed garden design was elitist and partly because more and more wealthy landholders were subdividing their estates and it was getting harder to get big contracts. A 1981 survey showed that residential design constituted just fifteen percent of all work for 100 randomly selected firms. "Survey Reveals Trends Among Landscape Architects," *Weeds, Trees and Turf* (April 1981): 25.

7. For a cost accounting of home vegetable gardening in America, see "The Joy of Gardening (And Also The Tedium, Rage and Sheer Hard Work)," *Newsweek* (July 26, 1982): 50–53; and Bruce Butterfield, *Gardening in America* (Burlington, Vt.: The National Association For Gardening, 1982).

8. See Wilbur Zelinsky, *The Cultural Geography of the United States* (Englewood Cliffs, N.J.: Prentice-Hall, 1973).

9. I studied gardens principally in Albany, Berkeley, and Oakland, California. While my conclusions were broad-based, I found differences in gardens that could be traced down to the block level.

Chapter One

1. John Brinkerhoff Jackson, "Nearer Than Eden," in *The Necessity for Ruins and Other Topics* (Amherst: University of Massachusetts Press, 1980), 21.

2. See Amelia Leavitt Hill, "The Cape Cod Cottage Garden," *Better Homes and Gardens* (May 1937): 26, and Rudy F. Favretti and Gordon P. DeWolf, *Colonial Gardens* (Barre, Mass.: Barre Publishers, 1972). Ornamental plants have been virtually synonymous with gardens in the public mind for the past century or more. As notable features in ordinary middle-class properties, however, they are a twentieth-century phenomenon.

3. *U.S. Census, Population: 1790–1990* (Washington, D.C.: U.S. Department of Commerce, 1990).

4. Daniel Boorstin, *The Americans: The Democratic Experience* (New York: Vintage Books, 1973), 330–31.

5. *U.S. Census, Population: 1790–1990.*

6. Kenneth Jackson, *Crabgrass Frontier: The Suburbanization of the United States* (New York: Oxford University Press, 1985), 11 and 185.

7. Charles Mulford Robinson, *The Width and Arrangement of Streets* (New York: The Engineering News Publishing Company, 1911), 35.

8. Ash barrels were usually used for making soap, a time-consuming activity generally performed by the wife of the family in the back yard. After filling the barrel with the residue of burnt logs, she slowly poured water into the barrel, where it became a sticky slush. Next, she poured the slush through a sieve into a vat and removed the impurities that had collected. Finally, she molded the slurry into soap for bathing, dishwashing, and cleaning clothes.

9. John B. Jackson, *American Space: The Centennial Years 1865–1876* (New York: W. W. Norton and Company, 1972), 221.

10. Juliet B. Schor, *The Overworked American* (New York: Basic Books, 1992), 45.

11. As quoted in Beth Bagwell, *Oakland, The Story of a City* (Oakland, Calif.: Oakland Heritage Alliance, 1994), 76.

12. As quoted in Anne Holler, "Backyard Archeology," *New York Times*, Section 8, June 11, 1978. See, also, Matthew J. Belson, "Bottle Brigade," *Archaeology* (January/February 1996): 100. Belson, whose business card reads "Urban Archaeologist—Artifact Recovery: Cisterns-Privies-Attics-Crawl Spaces," digs up urban back yards to search for household artifacts that early owners once discarded into privies.

13. Adrian Praetzellis, and Mary Praetzellis, eds., *Putting the 'There' There: Historical Archaeologies of West Oakland* (Rohnert Park, Calif.: Anthropological Studies Center at Sonoma State University, 2004).

14. Margaret F. Byington, *Homestead The Households of a Mill Town* (1910; Pittsburgh: University of Pittsburgh Press, 1974), 131. See, also, Andrew S. Dolkart, *Biography of a Tenement House in New York City: An Architectural History of 97 Orchard Street* (Santa Fe and Staunton: The Center for American Places, 2006).

15. Jackson, *Crabgrass Frontier*, 129.

16. Prior to the invention of balloon framing in the 1830s, homes and barns were "brace-framed," a method in which heavy timbers were attached with carved joints (laps, dados, mortise and tenon, and similar joints). The method required large timbers, an experienced carpenter who could cut and fit the joints with proper tools, and several workers to hoist the framing into place. The balloon-framed house was easier to build on almost every score. Balloon framing, sometimes called "platform framing" or "stick-style," used thin, light members, such as two-by-fours made possible by the invention of the power saw, drill, lathe, and other mechanically powered woodworking equipment. No longer did one need a barn-raising party to hoist 300-pound timbers into place or to tilt up a wall; even a child could lift a two-by-four. According to Harold Kirker, the balloon-framed house received little respect at first from seasoned builders, who claimed that the light structures would blow away "like balloons in the wind." See Harold Kirker, *California's Architectural Frontier* (Salt Lake City: Peregrine Smith Books, 1986), 59. Bryce Muir remarks that balloon framing allowed everyone to get in on the act of house building: "The stick-built house was invented by a contractor in Chicago who couldn't find any skilled labor. Once any idiot could throw up a house out of 2x4s, lots of them did." Bryce Muir, *Lawn Wars* (Bowdoinham, Me.: Bowdoinham College Press, 1988), 4. For a good account of the development of the balloon-framed house, see Jackson, *Crabgrass Frontier*, 124–28.

17. See Jackson, *Crabgrass Frontier*, 104–09. Transportation has significantly affected the shape of the dwelling and its grounds. The three stages of the American yard—agricultural, utilitarian, and domestic—correspond to the means of transportation at each time: horse and wagon, trolley, and automobile.

18. Bagwell, *Oakland*, 201.

19. Jackson, *American Space*, 126.

20. Christopher Tunnard and Boris Pushkarev, *Man Made America, Chaos or Control?* (New Haven: Yale University Press, 1963), Part Two, Chapter 3. *Man Made America* gives a good account of the role that city planners, architects, landscape architects, and civil engineers played in shaping twentieth-century America.

21. Richard Untermann and Robert *Small, Site Planning for Cluster Housing* (New York: Van Nostrand Reinhold Company, 1977).

Cluster housing projects, sometimes called "common interest communities" due to the fact that residents share house walls and most of the land, have transformed the home grounds into a largely visual entity. See Chapter Eleven of this book for more details.

22. This siting is described well by Roger Barnett, "The Libertarian Suburb," *Landscape* (Summer 1978): 44–48.

23. Many political theorists point out that early immigrants to the United States had come out of a desire to define themselves independently of the rules, customs, and laws of their home countries. As a result, these people were responsive to a form of government that emphasized individual rights.

24. John Locke's political philosophy can be found in his 1690 work, *Two Treatises of Government* (Cambridge: Cambridge University Press, 1960). Locke's theories are generally regarded as the basis for our country's ethic of individualism. Geographer Wilbur Zelinsky believes that individualism has been an enduring characteristic of the American character (the other three being mobility, perfectionism, and a mechanistic worldview). See Wilbur Zelinsky, *The Cultural Geography of the United States* (Englewood Cliffs, N.J.: Prentice-Hall, 1973).

25. See Hamilton, Madison, and Jay, *The Federalist Papers* (New York: Penguin Putnam Inc., 1961).

26. Much has been written by and about Thomas Jefferson. For starters, see Adrienne Koch, *The Life and Selected Writings of Thomas Jefferson* (New York: Random House, Inc., 1998). See, also, Merrill D. Peterson, editor, *Thomas Jefferson: Writings* (New York: The Library of America, 1984). Jefferson himself was an avid gardener and sometimes is regarded as one of America's first landscape architects due to his design for his estate, Monticello, overlooking Charlottesville, Virginia. see Edwin Morris Betts, ed., *Thomas Jefferson's Farm Book* [1774–1826] (Charlottesville: University Press of Virginia, 1987) and *Thomas Jefferson's Garden Book, 1766–1824* (Philadelphia: The Amercian Philosophical Society, 1944).

27. Thomas Jefferson, in a letter to Dr. Benjamin Rush dated September 23, 1800, as shown on "Thomas Jefferson Letters," Positive Atheism, http://www.positiveatheism.org/hist/Jeff1080.htm (accessed January 3, 2006).

28. As quoted in Christopher Tunnard and Henry Hope Reed, *American Skyline* (New York: A Mentor Book, 1956), 52.

29. As quoted in Lucia White and Morton White, *The Intellectual Versus the City: From Thomas Jefferson to Frank Lloyd Wright* (Cambridge, Mass.: Harvard University Press, 1962), 27.

30. Don C. Seitz, *Horace Greeley* (Indianapolis: The Bobbs-Merrill Company, 1926), 55.

31. As quoted in White and White, *The Intellectual Versus the City*, 193.

32. Alma Lutz, "Concerning Apartments," *House Beautiful* (November 1919): 293.

33. Paul Groth, "Streetgrids as Frameworks for Urban Variety," *The Harvard Architecture Review* 2 (1981): 68–75. See, also, Hildegard Binder Johnson, *Order Upon the Land: The U.S. Rectangular Land Survey and the Upper Mississippi Country* (New York: Oxford University Press, 1976).

34. As quoted in Stanley K. Schultz, "City Planning," Houghton Mifflin, http://college.hmco.com/history/readerscomp/rcah/html/ah_016900_cityplanning.htm (accessed January 3, 2006).

35. Sam Bass Warner, *Street Car Suburbs: The Process of Growth in Boston, 1870–1900* (New York: Macmillan Publishing Company, June 1969). Warner's classic study concerns Boston, but many American suburbs followed a similar course. See, for example, Eric L. Holcomb, *The City as Suburb: A History of Northeast Baltimore since 1660* (Santa Fe and Staunton: The Center for Amercian Places, 2005; updated edition, 2008).

36. C. E. P. Gerard, "How to Build a City," (Philadelphia: Review Printing House, 1872), http://www.library.cornell.edu/Reps/DOCS/gerard.htm (accessed January 3, 2006). John W. Reps, Professor Emeritus at Cornell University, has posted Gerard's writings on the Web.

37. Most cities have for decades enforced strict ordinances that give fire fighters access to side and back yards and that govern building along property lines to slow the spread of fire.

38. See Sigrid Arnott, *Twin Cities Sanitation History*, From Site to Story, http://www.fromsitetostory.org/sources/papers/tcmsanitation/tcmsanitation.asp, January 1996 (accessed December 6, 2007).

According to Arnott, "For city residents of the late nineteenth century, drainage of standing waters was almost as important as the removal of sewage, and ordinances illustrate the concern that city fathers had that putrid odors caused by decaying organic wastes were causing actual danger to city residents." Sanitarians later determined that germs rather than odors were the real problem, but fear of the latter persisted for years.

39. "Set-Back Lines as an Aid to Better and Cheaper Street Layouts," *American City* (February 1917): 144.

40. Gary A. Tobin, "Suburbanization and the Development of Motor Transportation," in Barry Schwartz, editor, *The Changing Face of the Suburbs* (Chicago: University of Chicago Press, 1976), 99–103.

41. "Before the Peoria Duryeas, 1890–1897," Duryea Manufacturing Company, http://www.duryea-peoria.com/cduryea2.htm (accessed January 3, 2006).

42. Good Roads Improvement Company (Cincinnati), "Dust-Disease-Death," *American City* (May 1910): 291–92. For another example of public concern over dust, see Fredrick L. Hoffman, "The Prevention of Disease by the Elimination of Dust," *American City* (January 1911): 213–16.

43. Michael Southworth and Erin Ben-Joseph, *Streets and the Shaping of Towns and Cities* (Washington, D.C.: Island Press, 2003), 56.

44. Peter Rowe, *Making a Middle Landscape* (Cambridge, Mass.: The MIT Press 1991), 4.

45. Paul Groth and Marta Gutman, "Worker's Cottages in West Oakland," *Sights and Sounds, Essays in Celebration of West Oakland* (California State Department of Transportation, 1997), 46–50.

46. Schultz, "City Planning." See, also, Jon A. Peterson, *The Birth of City Planning in the United States, 1840–1917* (Baltimore: The Johns Hopkins University Press, in association with the Center for American Places, 2003).

47. Southworth and Ben-Joseph, *Streets and the Shaping of Towns and Cities,* 82.

48. Robinson, *Width and Arrangement,* 3.

49. Schultz, "City Planning."

50. Marc A. Weiss, *The Rise of the Community Builders* (New York: Columbia University Press, 1987), 13.

Chapter Two

1. John B. Jackson, "Ghosts at the Door," *Landscape* (Autumn 1951): 6. This is one of the best essays I have found on the broader meanings of the American yard.

2. H. Clay Tate, *Building a Better Home Town: A Program of Community Self-Analysis and Self-Help* (New York: Harper & Brothers, 1954), 73.

3. John B. Jackson, *American Space: The Centennial Years 1865–1876* (New York: W. W. Norton and Company, 1972), 103.

4. For an engaging history of the Columbian Exhibition, see Eric Larson, *The Devil in the White City* (New York: Crown Publishers, 2003).

5. Witness Lady Bird Johnson's 1960s Clean Up America and anti-billboard campaigns, the spread of municipal anti-blight ordinances, and the flower bouquets that adorn light poles in nearly every large American city. See, also, William H. Wilson, *The City Beautiful Movement* (Baltimore: The Johns Hopkins University Press, 1989).

6. David P. Handlin, *The American Home, Architecture and Society, 1815–1915* (Boston: Little and Brown Company, 1979), 193–94.

7. Alexander Barker, *To Landscape the Easy Way* (Kelownia, B.C.: Orchard City Press, 1970), 6. Barker's expression of civic beautification came decades later, revealing the enduring power the movement left in its wake.

8. Elizabeth Russell, "Civic Sloth," *House Beautiful* (August 1917): 159.

9. J. L. Dana, "The Woodstock Improvement Society," *House Beautiful* (May 1919): 268.

10. Dana, "Woodstock," 268–69.

11. Catherine Beecher, *The American Woman's Home* (Hartford, Conn.: Stowe-Day Foundation, 1975), 19.

12. As quoted in Patricia Tice, "The Plant Committee: How Garden Clubs Grew," *Garden Design* (Winter 1989/1990): 70.

13. Olive Foster, "Garden Clubs and Their National Meaning," *House and Garden* (March 1936): 58.

14. Mrs. Edwin F. Moulton, "Municipal Housekeepers," *American City* (March 1913): 123.

15. Harlean James, "The Baltimore Flower Market," *American City* (April 1913): 392. James's sentiment recalled Andrew Jackson Downing's belief that, "when smiling lawns and tasteful cottages begin to embellish a country, we know that order and culture are established, as quoted in Russell Lynes, *Tastemakers (*New York: Harper Brothers, 1954), 22.

16. O. R. Geyer, "Cleaning and Beautifying a City: The Famous Yard and Garden Contests of Davenport, Iowa," *American City* (April 1917): 365–66.

17. Russell, "Civic Sloth," 161.

18. As quoted in William J. Leonard, "Fire Prevention Window-Displays," *American City* (July 1920): 12.

19. "Furthering City Beautification Thru Exhibits," *American City* (April 1917): 368.

20. S. Mays Ball, "The Suburbs Beautiful," *House and Garden* (May 1909): 166.

21. Ball, "The Suburbs Beautiful," 169.

22. Fences were not for protection alone. According to Ann Stillman, they also served to justify a settler's claim to his land. See Anne Stillman, "Fences and the Settlement of New England," in Gregory K. Dreicer, editor, *Between Fences* (Washington: National Building Museum and Princeton Architectural Press, 1996), 13. In this respect, fences reinforced the emerging American ethic of individualism. As J. B Jackson wrote, "a fence or hedge served as a visible sign that the land was owned by one particular man and not by a group or community" (Jackson, "Ghosts," 8).

23. Jackson, *American Space,* 65.

24. Marion Nicholl Rawson, "The Return of the Garden Fence," *House Beautiful* (October 1930): 419.

25. Andrew Jackson Downing, *A Treatise on the Theory and Practice of Landscape Gardening, Adapted to North America; with a view to the improvement of country residences* (New York: Wiley and Putnam, 1844; originally published in 1841), 295.

26. J. H. Prost, "How To Judge Garden Contests," *American City* (April 1913): 372.

27. Werner Hegemann, *Report on a City Plan for the municipalities of Berkeley and Oakland,* 109.

28. Frank Waugh, *Everybody's garden; the how, the why and especially the wherefore of the home garden, with emphasis upon the interests of the average American* (New York: Orange Judd Publishing Company, Inc., 1930), 19.

29. For more information on Llewellyn Park, see Kenneth Jackson, *Crabgrass Frontier, The Suburbanization of the United States* (New York: Oxford University Press, 1985); Philip and Nancy Volkman, *Landscapes In History* (New York: Van Nostrand Reinhold, 1993); and John Reps, *The Making of Urban America* (Princeton, N.J.: Princeton University Press, 1956).

30. Reps, *The Making of Urban America,* 344.

31. Fredrick Law Olmsted, as quoted in Reps, *The Making of Urban America,* 344.

32. As quoted in Michael Southworth and Erin Ben-Joseph, *Streets and the Shaping of Towns and Cities* (Washington, D.C.: Island Press, 2003), 32. Olmsted evidently foresaw Frank Lloyd Wright's observation that architects can always cover their mistakes with ivy. Wright, in fact, designed several houses and a unique gardener's cottage in Riverside.

33. Southworth and Ben-Joseph, *Streets,* 34. I have heard people variously refer to sidewalk planting strips as parking strips, curb strips, verge strips, devil's strips, hell strips, curb lawn, parkways, and tree lawn.

34. Fredrick Law Olmsted, as quoted in Reps, *The Making of Urban America,* 344. Riverside and Llewellyn Park became important models for twentieth-century suburbs. In 1915, German city planner Werner Hegemann relied on Olmsted's plan for Riverside to support the use of curving roads through the Berkeley hills. Hegemann warned that Berkeley not be chopped into little pieces like nearby San Francisco and Oakland. "The new residential subdivisions, especially in the hill sections all over the East Bay region, very happily have broken away from the unfortunate old rectangular street system by which San Francisco and the lower parts of the East Bay have been chopped up," Heggeman wrote. Streets were best laid out to

follow the lay of the hills, with "bungalows rambling over the ground and following intimately and deliciously its nature and its moods" (see Hegemann, *Report*, 105).

35. As quoted in Hegemann, *Report*, 108.

36. Downing, *A Treatise.*

37. Downing was all the more influential because he was the first American to write a comprehensive garden design manual. See David Schuyler, *Apostle of Taste: Andrew Jackson Downing, 1815–1852* (Baltimore: The Johns Hopkins University Press, in association with the Center for American Places, 1996).

38. As quoted in Lynes, *Tastemakers*, 22.

39. As quoted in Michael Laurie and Grace Hall, editors, *Gardens Are For People*, 2nd ed. (1955; New York: McGraw Hill, 1983), 4. Church is California's—and possibly America's—most famous and influential garden designer.

40. "Humphry Repton's Landscape Plans For Hanslope Park," Hanslope & District Historical Society, http://www.mkheritage.co.uk//hdhs/Repton/repton.html (accessed December 6, 2007).

41. The picturesque combined the best attributes of nature and civilization into a romanticized place where, as Fred Schroeder puts it, "the wilds are attractively arranged around profound ruins, dancing nymphs, and unnatural satyrs" (from Fred Schroeder, "The Democratic Garden," *Outlaw Aesthetics: Arts and the Public Mind* (Bowling Green, Ohio: Bowling Green University Popular Press, 1977), 103). Sydney Robinson calls this combination of nature and civilization "a supremely human desire to have it both ways." See Sydney Robinson, "Picturesque Anticipations of the Avant-Garde and the Landscape," *Landscape Journal* (Spring 1991): 13.

42. Downing, *A Treatise*, 18.

43. Ibid., 23.

44. See Fred K. Buscher, "There is Nothing to Hide . . . But Foundation Planting Persists," *Landscape Architectural Yearbook 1977* (*Landscape Architecture* magazine, 1977): 59-62. This publication is a special edition of *Landscape Architecture* magazine.

45. As quoted in May Theilgaard Watts, "The Stylish House," *Reading the Landscape of America* (New York: Macmillan, 1957), 208. Watts's

essay—along with writings by J. B. Jackson, Fred Schroeder, and Paul Groth—is among the few I have found addressing the ordinary house and lot in their social and cultural dimensions.

46. Frank Jessup Scott, *The Art Of Beautifying Suburban Home Grounds* (New York: D. Appleton and Company, 1870), 153. In a manner characteristic of his time, Scott equated beautification—or the lack of it—with health and morality.

47. Ibid., 153.

48. Grace Tabor, "What Planting Does for a House," *House and Garden* (April 1911): 261.

49. Advertisement in *House and Garden* (May 1912): 58. Horticultural nursery ads appeared with greater frequency after the turn of the twentieth century, as middle-class Americans looked for ways to adorn their streetcar suburb lots.

50. As quoted in Carlton B. Lees, *Gardens, Plants and Man* (Englewood Cliffs, N.J.: Prentice-Hall, 1970), 214.

51. Thomas A. Brown, "A List of California Nurseries and Their Catalogs 1850-1900" (unpublished paper, Petaluma, California, 1982). See, also, H. M. Butterfield, "Early Nurseries in the Eastern United States," *California Horticultural Society Journal* (April 1966): 42–56.

52. Americans continued to stake homestead claims until the 1960s. Senator Chuck Hagel (R-NE) even proposed, in 2007, that a new homestead act be created for rural America to invigorate areas of the United States that are losing population, especially in the Great Plains.

53. For a brief but good history of the American nursery industry, see Harold Davidson, Roy Mecklenburg, and Curtis Peterson, *Nursery Management, Administration and Culture* (Englewood Cliffs, N.J.: Prentice Hall, 1988), 1–18.

54. Irene Virag, "An Evolving Eden," *Newsday.com,* http://www.newsday.com/community/guide/lihistory/ny-history-hs8fgar1,0,5488263.story?coll=ny-lihistory-navigation (accessed December 6, 2007).

55. Brown, "A List," vii.

56. As quoted in Victoria Padilla, *Southern California Gardens* (Berkeley: University of California Press, 1961), 107.

57. *Extension News* (University of Arkansas Division of Agriculture Cooperative Extension Service), February 2, 2001.

58. Scott, *The Art Of Beautifying.*

59. Handlin, *The American Home,* 173. Handlin's chapter on the home grounds is one of the most useful overviews of the subject I have found. Like most housing studies, it focuses more on affluent communities than ordinary ones, but the former were nonetheless important for the ways they influenced the latter.

60. Handlin, *The American Home,* 175.

61. Scott, *The Art Of Beautifying,* 61.

62. Fred E. H. Schroeder, *Front Yard America* (Bowling Green, Ohio: Bowling Green University Popular Press, 1993), 107.

63. Leonard Johnson, *Foundation Planting* (New York: A. T. De La Mare Company, Inc., 1927), xv.

64. Foundation plantings not only live on, but some communities have codified them into law. As of the mid-1990s, the general plan of Mill Valley, California, required "appropriate screening for architectural elements, such as building foundations and deck supports, that cannot be mitigated through architectural design."

65. Paul Shepard, *Man in the Landscape* (New York: Alfred A. Knopf, 1967), 74.

66. John Falk, of the Smithsonian Institution, traces the origins of the lawn further back still, to the shortgrass meadows and savanna of Africa. "Many anthropologists place the origins of Man in the shortgrass savannas of East Africa one to three million years ago," Falk writes. "In any case, the majority of Man's development as a species has occurred in this habitat. Man, like most of the smaller savanna animals, probably restricted his movements to the shortgrass and avoided the tallgrass where predators could lurk undetected." Falk suggests that lawns had still another attraction: legibility (ease of comprehension). He believes that the American love of the lawn may be rooted in a deep collective prehistoric memory: "Could we be striving to create neosavannas in our own parks and front yards?" (From Bayard Webster, "Man and the Lawn: A Long Love Story," *The New York Times,* April 12, 1983).

67. Jackson, "Ghosts," 6.

68. James B. Beard, "Turfgrass: Science and Culture" (Englewood Cliffs, N.J.: Prentice Hall, 1973): 8.

69. Frank Waugh, *Book of landscape gardening; treatise on the general principles governing outdoor art; with sundry suggestions for their application in the commoner problems of gardening* (New York: Orange Judd Publishing Company, 1926), 66.

70. "The History of Mowing," Outdoor Power Equipment Institute, Inc., http://opei./mow.org/consumer/history/asp (accessed January 3, 2006).

71. For a detailed history of the lawn and the lawn mower, see Virginia Scott Jenkins, *The Lawn: A History of and American Obsession* (Washington, D.C.: Smithsonian Institution Press, 1994).

72. Johnson, *Foundation Planting*, xvi.

73. Scott, *The Art Of Beautifying*, 241.

74. Fred Gabelman, "Roadway and Lawn Space Widths and Maintenance of Boulevards and Streets in Kansas City, Missouri," *American City* (October 1912): 352.

75. John Normile, "We Take A Sight-Seeing Jaunt," *Better Homes and Gardens* (February 1937): 48–53.

76. As quoted in Johnson, *Foundation Planting*, xvi.

Chapter Three

1. Michael Southworth and Erin Ben-Joseph, *Streets and the Shaping of Towns and Cities* (Washington, D.C.: Island Press, 2003), 48.

2. M. Roberts Conover, "Transforming the Unsightly," *House Beautiful* (April 1912): 136.

3. Content York, "The Back Dooryard," *House Beautiful* (September 1915): xxx.

4. Esther Johnson, "Back Yard Versus Front Porch," *House Beautiful* (June 1922): 603.

5. Tarkington Barker, *Yard and Garden: A Book of Practical Information for the Amateur Gardener in City, Town or Suburb* (Indianapolis: Bobbs-Merrill Company, 1908), 8.

6. Ida D.Bennett, "Garden Possibilities of a City Lot," *House Beautiful* (July 1908): 48.

7. Harry Martin Yeomans, "Sanctifying the Backyard," *House Beautiful* (March 1912): 109.

8. David Tucker, *Kitchen Gardening in America: A History* (Ames: Iowa State University Press, 1993), 105.

9. Martin V. Melosi, *The Sanitary City, Urban Infrastructure in America from Colonial Times to the Present* (Baltimore: The Johns Hopkins University Press, in association with the Center for American Places, 2000), 117–20.

10. Ibid., 152.

11. Ibid., 175 and 183.

12. Digger O'Dell, "Musings of a Privy Digger," *Antique Glass and Bottle Collector Magazine,* http://www.glswrk-auction.com/013.htm (accessed July 31, 2007).

13. Susan Strasser, *Waste and Want A Social History of Trash* (New York: Henry Holt and Company, 1999), 118–25.

14. Barbara Dane (homeowner from Oakland, California), interview with the author, 1994. Professional gardeners and landscape contractors often find similar things when they start projects in older neighborhoods.

15. Melosi, *The Sanitary City*, 201. For a case study of how Minneapolis handled trash collection, waterworks, and sewerage, see Sigrid Arnott, "Twin Cities Sanitation History" (From Site to Story), http://www.fromsitetostory.org/sources/papers/tcmsanitation/tcmsanitation.asp (accessed July 31, 2007).

16. Daniel Boorstin, *The Americans: The Democratic Experience* (New York: Vintage Books, 1973), 317–18 and 330–31.

17. Frank Jessup Scott, *The Art Of Beautifying Suburban Home Grounds* (New York: D. Appleton and Company, 1870), 23.

18. Daniel Boorstin, *The Americans,* 330.

19. Russell Fisher, "The Service End of the House," *House and Garden* (August 1910): 94.

20. John A. Jakle, *The American Small Town* (Hamden, Conn.: Archon Books, 1982), 138.

21. Gillian Darley, "Cottage and Suburban Gardens," in John Harris, editor, *The Garden: A Celebration of One Thousand Years of British Gardening* (London: New Perspectives Publishing Limited, 1979), 151.

22. One of the first landscape architects to design gardens in a uniquely American manner was Jens Jensen, who drew inspiration from the prairies of the Midwest. See Robert E. Grese, *Jens Jensen: Maker of Natural Parks and Gardens* (Baltimore: The Johns Hopkins University Press, in association with the Center for American Places, 1992).

23. Wilhelm Miller, Ph.D., *What England Can Teach Us About Gardening* (Garden City, New York: Doubleday, Page and Company, 1911), 3.

24. Peirce F. Lewis, "Common Houses, Cultural Spoor," *Landscape,* Vol. 9, No. 2 (1975): 3.

25. As quoted in Tom Carter, *The Victorian Garden* (Salem, Mass.: Salem House, 1984), 23. The *Sunset Low Maintenance Gardening* book gave out the same advice a century later.

26. As quoted in Gerald Clear, "Thoughts on the Cottage Gardens," *Pacific Horticulture* (Spring 1985): 1.

27. As quoted in an editorial, "Jekyll's Cottage Gardens," by the editor, *Pacific Horticulture* (Summer 1988): 1.

28. Penelope Hobhouse, editor, *Gertrude Jekyll on Gardening* (New York: Vintage Books, 1985), 260–61.

29. William Draper Brinckle, "Making a Garden of the City Backyard," *House and Garden* (November 1910): 294.

30. Edward T. Hartman, "Town and Village," *American City* (August 1910): 90.

31. "A City of Gardens," *American City* (January–June 1910): 42.

32. "A Home Garden Club," *American City* (July 1914): 55.

33. C. J. Kellan, "Cleaning Up Kewanee," *American City* (March 1915): 250.

34. All quotes regarding this contest are found in Miriam Adelaide Tighe, "Salem's Garden Contest," *American City* (January 1911): 109–11.

35. H. L. W., "The Evolution of the Porch," *House Beautiful* (August 1914): 85.

36. Advertisement in *House and Garden* (September 1930): 150.

37. Johnson, "Back Yard," 604–06.

38. Fletcher Steele, "Models For Suburban Lot Design And Planting," *House Beautiful* (June 1923): 626.

39. Fletcher Steele, *Design in the Little Garden* (Boston: The Atlantic Monthly Press, 1924).

40. Ibid., 88.

41. Leonidas W. Ramsey, *Landscaping the Home Grounds* (New York: The MacMillan Company, 1930), 64–66.

42. Leonidas W. Ramsey and Charles H. Lawrence, *The Outdoor Room* (New York: The MacMillan Company, 1930), 4.

43. Robert Franklin Ross, "Gardening in the American Manner," *Better Homes and Gardens* (September 1937): 29.

44. Frank Waugh, *Everybody's garden; the how, the why and especially the wherefore of the home garden, with emphasis upon the interests of the average American* (New York: Orange Judd Publishing Company, Inc., 1930), 18.

45. Christopher Tunnard and Boris Pushkarev, *Man Made America, Chaos or Control?* (New Haven: Yale University Press, 1963), 134.

Chapter Four

1. "The Recent Rise Of An Old Habit—Staying Home," *House and Garden* (January 1930): 66.

2. Home vegetable gardens have long been associated with economics rather than leisure or recreation. An integral part of the agrarian yard was the vegetable, or kitchen, garden, which resurged during World War I, the Great Depression, and World War II, times when consumer goods were scarce and personal incomes were down. Though post-World War II Americans continued to grow vegetables, it was usually to save money. A 1980 Gallup survey found that the number of home vegetable gardens closely paralleled the consumer price index. "As food prices have increased so have the number of households gardening. Conversely, as Real Gross National Product and Real Gross Weekly Earnings have decreased, the incidence of gardening has increased." The poll showed that suburbanites were ten times more likely to raise vegetables to save money than to relax, exercise, or simply be outdoors. See Bruce Butterfield, *1981–82 Gardens For All Fact Sheet.*

In 1984, Marcia McNally asked 200 Californians if they depended on their garden in any way. Affluent Danville residents used their gardens "to get away from it all." One man said: "I go out there to listen to music, sit in the Jacuzzi, relax . . . I have privacy, a feeling of being far away. No one can breathe down my neck." On the other hand, working-class residents of East Oakland and Emeryville rarely mentioned privacy, while almost a third grew food in their yards. See Marcia McNally, "Valued Places," in Mark Francis and Randy Hester, editors, *Meanings of Gardens* (Cambridge, Mass.: The MIT Press, 1990), 173.

David Tucker, after reviewing several national gardening surveys, found that frugality and thrift were the most common reasons people gave for vegetable gardening: "Almost 70% claim they grow to save money, while only half the gardeners point to health, recreation, or better tasting food as the major explanation for practicing their craft." See David Tucker, *Kitchen Gardening In America: A History* (Ames: Iowa State University Press, 1993), 176.

3. David Halberstam, *The Fifties* (New York: Villard Books, 1993), 134.

4. Kenneth Jackson, *Crabgrass Frontier: The Suburbanization of the United States* (New York: Oxford University Press, 1985), 326.

5. Halberstam, *The Fifties*, 142.

6. "Planning Profitable Neighborhoods," *Technical Bulletin No. 7* (Washington, D.C.: U.S. Federal Housing Administration, 1938).

7. Ibid.

8. "Minimum Property Requirements," *FHA Form No. 2257* (Washington, D.C.: U.S. Federal Housing Administration, May 1952), 201A.

9. "Principles of Planning Small Houses," *Technical Bulletin No. 4* (Washington, D.C.: Federal Housing Administration, 1940): 43–44.

10. "Planning Profitable Neighborhoods," 25.

11. John Archer, "Individualism, the Middle-Class, and the Genesis of the Anglo-American Suburb," *Journal of Urban History* (February 1988): 240–41.

12. Christopher Tunnard and Boris Pushkarev, *Man Made America, Chaos or Control?* (New Haven: Yale University Press, 1963), 104.

13. For more on the FHA's rationale for recommending curved streets, see "Principles of Planning Small Houses," 42–43.

14. Fence regulations have become widespread throughout the nation. In 1981, *Sunset* magazine called the planning departments of twenty-five California cities to inquire about front yard fence laws and reported that " . . . every community we contacted—a total of 25, throughout the West—has regulations governing the height of fences and walls within the setback area of the lot. Of these, eight limit fence height to 3 feet, four to 3 1/2 feet, seven to 4 feet, one to 4 1/2 feet, and five to 6 feet. In 15 cases, restrictions applied to fences (or walls) only, but four included hedges with fences, and four more set height limits for fences and all types of planting." See "Between You and the Street, What's Legal, Possible? Much," *Sunset* (April 1981): 110.

15. Peter G. Rowe, *Making a Middle Landscape* (Cambridge, Mass.: The MIT Press, 1991), 205.

16. Marc A. Weiss, *The Rise of the Community Builders* (New York: Columbia University Press, 1987).

17. Michael Southworth and Erin Ben-Joseph, *Streets and the Shaping of Towns and Cities* (Washington, D.C.: Island Press, 2003), 82.

18. For accounts of Levittown, see Herbert Gans, *The Levittowners* (New York: Vintage Books, 1969); Halberstam, *The Fifties*; and Jackson, *Crabgrass Frontier*. See, also, Greg Hise, *Magnetic Los Angeles: Planning the Twentieth-Century Metropolis* (Baltimore: The Johns Hopkins University Press, in association with the Center for American Places, 1997); Becky Nicolaides, *My Blue Heaven: Life and Politics in the Working-Class Suburbs of Los Angeles, 1920–1965* (Chicago: University of Chicago Press, 2002); and D. J. Waldie, *Holy Land: A Suburban Memoir* (New York: W. W. Norton, 1996).

19. Halberstam, *The Fifties*, 132.

20. Jackson, *Crabgrass Frontier*, 233.

21. For a fresh look at the emergence of the suburb, see Ann M. Wolfe, *Suburban Escape: The Art of California Sprawl* (Santa Fe and Staunton: The Center for American Places, in association with the San Jose Museum of Art, 2006).

Chapter Five

1. Gwendolyn Wright, *Building the Dream: A Social History of Housing in America* (New York: Pantheon Books, 1981), 255.

2. In places such as California, where land values were high, the incorporation of the garage into the house did not guarantee a larger lot.

3. "Who Wants To Dine Among Cans and Clotheslines?," *House Beautiful* (January 1950): 62–63.

4. "How Our Cars Have Changed Our Gardens," *House Beautiful* (November 1956): 254.

5. "Planning with the Automobile," *Sunset* (June 1956): 73.

6. "Let's Get Parked Cars Off the Street," *House Beautiful* (February 1953): 103.

7. Cities commonly enact parking regulations to control residential developments and densities. Oakland, California, requires property owners who want to build second units to provide off-street parking for the tenants. Berkeley, California, recently rejected a homeowner's application to rent a back yard studio on the grounds that an additional car would congest the street.

8. Rebecca Robeledo, "Pioneers in Leisure: Birth of an Industry," *Pool & Spa News,* (July 21, 1999): 17–18. This July issue, entitled "The History of Pools and Spas," provides numerous inside details on the evolution of the swimming pool industry, including the backgrounds of successful builders, the dates that specific types of equipment were introduced, detailed budget numbers, and the personalities that have helped to shape the industry.

9. Compact excavators became common in the building trade in the 1960s. For details, see Keith Gribbins and Nick Zubko, "Digging Up Your Options for Compact Excavators CE Uncovers 14 Manufacturers and their Product Lines in the Mini Excavator Market," *Compact Equipment,* http://www.compactequip.com/coverstory.php?Show=december2004 (accessed January 3, 2006).

10. See Rebecca Robeledo, "The People's Pool," *Pool & Spa News* (July 21, 1999): 27–29. Robeledo writes that the first naturalistic pool came about in the 1940s when a crew working for Los Angeles pool

builder Philip Ilsley, unhappy about the difficulties of installing gunite (a relatively new product at the time), attempted to sabotage the operation by distorting the shape of the pour. Ilsley quickly repaired the irregularities by adding large boulders and extra cement to the uneven edge. The result was superior to the original scheme, and purportedly it ushered in the era of the naturalistic pool.

11. See Rebecca Robeledo, "Package Pools: New Market in a Box," *Pool & Spa News* (July 21, 1999): 36–38, and Margi Millunzi, "Playing For Keeps, Aboveground pools, once a toy-store novelty item, helped a new generation get in the swim," *Pool & Spa News* (July 21, 1999): 120–22.

12. See Juliet B. Schor, *The Overworked American: The Unexpected Decline of Leisure* (New York: Basic Books, 1991): 34–38 and 86–87.

13. "Ten men in your life, They design appliances that help to take the work out of housework," *House and Garden* (September 1947): 122.

14. Susan Strasser postulates that, by raising standards of convenience and household care, modern appliances may have contributed to an increase in housework. See Strasser's book, *Never Done: A History of American Housework* (New York: Henry Holt and Company, 1982).

15. See F. Raymond Brush, "Inventing the Garden Center," sidebar in "NLA: The First Decade," *American Nurseryman* (August 15, 1989): 35.

16. By 1972, garden center sales in California totaled $117,000,000, almost three times that of Michigan, New York, Ohio, Pennsylvania, and Texas. Sales were about equally divided between hard goods and plants. See Harold Davidson, Roy Mecklenburg, and Curtis Peterson, *Nursery Management: Administration and Culture* (Englewood Cliffs, N.J.: Prentice Hall, 1981), 10–11; see, also, "Market Watch," *American Nurseryman* (March 1, 1989): 11. *American Nurseryman,* written from a businessperson's point of view, provides an "insider's" view of economic forces that drive the green industry.

17. F. Raymond Brush, "The Residential Competition Tradition," sidebar in "NLA: The First Decade," *American Nurseryman* (August 15, 1989): 37. The National Landscape Association did not limit its focus to private homes. It also published a booklet called *Industry Need Not Be Ugly,* featuring pictures of freshly planted grounds of the National Cash Register Company, Ford Motor Company, and Dayton Rubber Company, among other prominent businesses.

18. See Carl E. Whitcomb, *Plant Production in Containers* (Stillwater, Okla.: Lacebark Publications, Inc., 1988), i–iii.

19. Davidson, et al., *Nursery Management,* 10–11. Robert Perry, a chemist from Livermore, California, worked as a boy at his father's company, Perry's Nursery in Forest Hills, California. He remarks that the lighter weight of the artificial soil mixes used in canisters greatly reduced the nursery's shipping costs. Interview with the author, February 2005.

20. See the *United States Census of Retail Trade* for statistics in the period 1900–2000. Florida is a respectable but distant second to California in nursery sales, with houseplants representing a significant portion of inventories.

21. Tokuji Furuta, *Environmental Plant Productions and Marketing* (Arcadia, Calif.: Cox Publishing Company, 1974), 1–2.

22. See "Landscape Plants and Lawns in the South: Homeowner Expenditure and Use Patterns," *Bulletin 180* (Southern Cooperative Series, November 1973).

23. Strictly speaking, "hardiness" refers to a plant's ability to withstand low temperatures, as opposed to its "toughness." Victoria Padilla remarked that, in 1960, California produced sixty-five percent of flower seeds sold worldwide and ninety-eight percent of those sold in the United States. Padilla notes that many Californians returned from European vacations with packets of seeds originally grown a few miles from their own Southern California homes. See Victoria Padilla, *Southern California Gardens: An Illustrated History* (Berkeley: University of California Press, 1961): 276. See, also, Russell Beatty's article, "Is Horticulture Too Ornamental," *Pacific Horticulture* (Fall 1978): 15–23, in which Beatty questions the popular notion that plants are important mainly for their beauty.

24. Most of these watering devices, along with the hand-powered lawn mower, still look remarkably similar more than a century after their invention.

25. See Terry Howell, "Drops of Life in the History of Irrigation," *Irrigation Journal* (December 27, 1999): 8–10 and 13–15.

26. "The Naturalizing of a City Man," *House and Garden* (October 1912): 220.

27. Ibid., 220–21.

28. For a detailed look at the development of the sprinkler irrigation industry, see Robert M. Morgan, *Water and the Land: A History of American Irrigation* (Fairfax, Va.: The Irrigation Association, 1993).

29. Laurie Davidson Cox, "Park Sprinkling Without Hose," *American City* (July 1914): 199.

30. See "Underground Sprinklers Are Easy to Install," *House Beautiful* (August 1955): 116–17, and "Sprinkling, Irrigating, Misting, or Just Watering," *Sunset* (July 1956): 52–55. Articles such as these started to appear with increasing frequency in the mid-1950s.

31. See, also, Robert B. Gray, "The Development of Sprinkler Irrigation" (unpublished paper, Azusa/Glendora, Calif.: Rain Bird Corporation, 1977). Gray recounts numerous names and details associated with the sprinkler industry in this brief manuscript.

32. In 1969, I recall my mother's plumber muttering, "PVC is a dirty word," when I told him about a plastic sprinkler system I was helping a friend's father install during a summer job.

33. Sales representatives from the Rain Bird and Toro companies tell me that their residential markets are biggest in the South and arid Southwest, where residents rely on sprinklers to water their yards. In 1998, Bruce Shank of the Irrigation Association reported, "the percentage of new construction that includes irrigation has reached 65 percent in the Southwest, 40 percent in the Southeast, 5 percent in the Midwest and 2 percent in the Northeast. A recent industry survey revealed that 40 percent of landscape contractors perform some type of irrigation work on a regular basis." See Bruce Shank, "Irrigation retrofit improves responsible water use," Grounds Maintenance, http://groundsmag.com/mag/grounds_maintenance_irrigation_retrofit_ improves/ (accessed January 3, 2006).

34. The acreage is undoubtedly even higher today, despite a growing wave of anti-lawn sentiment. Paul D. Thacker, "American Lawns Impact Nutrient Cycles," *Environmental Science and Technology Online,* http://pubs.ocs.org/subscribe/Journals/esthaq-w/2005/Feb/science/pt_lawns.html (accessed January 3, 2006).

35. For a brief but revealing history of sod harvesting techniques, see *Turfgrass: Nature's Constant Benediction* (Rolling Meadows, Ill.: The

American Sod Producer's Association, 1992), 12–16. This trade publication supplies a detailed "nuts and bolts" look into the turfgrass industry.

36. For a critique of marketing practices conducted by the lawn industry, see Virginia Scott Jenkins, *The Lawn: A History of an American Obsession* (Washington, D.C.: Smithsonian Institution Press, 1994).

37. See Jenkins, *The Lawn*, 145, and the 2002 *United States Census of Agriculture.*

38. "The History of Mowing," Outdoor Power Equipment Institute, Inc., http://opei.mow.org/consumer/history.asp (accessed January 3, 2006).

39. According to Tammy Wynette, country singer George Jones (her husband) once drove a power mower eight miles to get a drink. The power mower was also featured prominently in the 1999 movie, *The Straight Story* (directed by David Lynch), in which Iowan Alvin Straight drove a John Deere lawn mower several hundred miles to visit his ailing brother.

40. Apparently the lawn mower is nowhere near the end of its evolution, as witnessed by the Robotic Solar Lawn Mower, the "Mow-Bot." Introduced in 1993, the Mow-Bot is a self-propelled mower controlled by a computer chip. An *Oakland Tribune* journalist wrote, "the gas-powered mower relies on three navigation systems. First, the computer map tells it where to cut and when to turn or slow down for a hill. Because mechanical problems, like wheel slippage, can still knock it off its route, it adjusts its position by using sensors to detect metal markers or guide paths buried at intervals in the lawn. . . . Ultrasonic sensors also tell the mower to shut down if there is an obstacle in its path. An alarm would alert the mower's owner to put down the iced tea and check out the problem. Noonan and his partners received patent #5,204,814." See "The Robo-Mower Could Simplify an Old Tradition," *Oakland Tribune,* March 12, 1994. As of this writing, robotic mowers were available at Costco for $1,699.00. See Costco's Website: http://www.costco.com/Browse/Product.aspx?Prodid=11042241&whse=&topnav=&browse=&s=1 (accessed July 27, 2007).

41. *Ortho Problem Solver* (San Ramon, Calif.: Chevron Chemical Company, 1989).

42. "Children in the Blueprint," *House and Garden* (January 1951): 48–49.

43. "36 Ideas Show You How To Use the Outdoors as Part of Your House," *House and Garden* (July 1951): 34–44.

44. "Let Power Do the Work in Your Garden," *House Beautiful* (January 1950): 98–99; "Why Make Gardening Such Hard Work," *House Beautiful* (June 1951): 131; "We Believe Gardening Should Be Painless," *House Beautiful* (April 1946): 92–93; "Now You Can Garden Without a Lick of Work," *House Beautiful* (April 1949): 160; "Landscapes Without Waiting," *House Beautiful* (May 1951): 154–55.

45. "Gardening" section (table of contents), *House Beautiful* (January 1949): 4.

46. Reasons one through five are taken from "Why Has America Invented Its Own Style in Gardens," *House Beautiful* (February 1951): 76–79.

Chapter Six

1. John Keats, *The Crack in the Picture Window* (Boston: Houghton Mifflin, 1957), xi.

2. Russell Lynes, *Tastemakers, Harper's Magazine* (June 1947): 236.

3. Keats, *The Crack in the Picture Window*, xii.

4. Scott Donaldson, *The Suburban Myth* (New York: Columbia University Press, 1969), 72.

5. James Rose, "The Sensible Landscape," *Landscape* (Spring 1961): 25. Rose was an outspoken critic of traditional landscape design, which he felt produced too many old and tired gardens that failed to spark anyone's imagination.

6. Bernard Rudolphsky, *Behind the Picture Window* (New York: Oxford University Press, 1955), 157.

7. As quoted in Michael Cader and Lisa Cader, *But I Wouldn't Want To Live There* (Philadelphia: Running Press, 1993), 26.

8. Lynes, *Tastemakers*, 254.

9. Sam Bass Warner, Jr., *The Urban Wilderness: A History of the American City* (New York: Harper & Row Publishers, 1972), 206–07.

10. Estelle Reise, "Gracious Little Gardens," *Better Homes and Gardens* (May 1937): 25.

11. Elizabeth Gordon, "Does Your Front Yard Belong to You or the Whole Neighborhood?," *House Beautiful* (May 1960): 152.

12. Herbert Gans, *The Levittowners* (New York: Random House, 1967), 176–77. I interviewed around fifty residents in Albany, Berkeley, and Oakland, California, in 1981 and found similar sentiment regarding care of the front yard. Conflicts regarding yard care extend beyond neighborly disputes. In his book, *The American Lawn,* George Teyssot describes lawsuits that cities filed against citizens who failed to keep their lawns mowed and weeds down, placed signs and nativity scenes in their front yards, and engaged in other activities that questioned front yard etiquette. In one case, the United States Postal Service sued the city of Pittsburg, California, for prohibiting mail carriers from crossing front lawns while walking their routes. These lawsuits underscore the tension that has existed for decades between the public and private dimensions of the front yard. See George Teyssot, *The American Lawn* (Princeton, N.J.: Princeton Architectural Press, 1999).

13. Rolf Meyersohn and Robin Jackson, "Gardening In Suburbia," in William M. Dobriner, *The Suburban Community: A Sourcebook Of The Sociological Patterns That Shape The Lives Of 40 Million Americans* (New York: G. P. Putnam and Sons, 1958), 275.

14. Rachel Kaplan, "The Psychological Benefits of Gardening," *Environment and Behavior* (June 1973): 158.

15. "Landscape Plants and Lawns in the South: Homeowner Expenditure and Use Patterns," Bulletin 180, 3.

16. Criticisms of the suburban lifestyle have by no means disappeared, but the focus has shifted to questions about the long-term effects of disappearing farmlands, the infrastructure costs of sprawl, traffic jams, and the loss of "community" in low-density developments. As an alternative, many planners and architects are now embracing a so-called "new urbanism" movement in which townhouses replace single-family dwellings, shops, schools, and parks sit closer to residences, and mass transit offers an effective alternative to driving—all of which ideally takes place in a small-scale green environment that blends the best aspects of urban and suburban living. For some preliminary details, see the Website for The Congress for the New Urbanism, http://www.cnu.org/index.cfm (accessed January 3, 2006).

Chapter Seven

1. See Victor and Aladar Olgyay, *Design with Climate: Bioclimatic Approach to Architectural Regionalism* (Princeton, N.J.: Princeton University Press, 1963).

2. "How to Build When Your Climate Has the Best and the Worst Weather," *House Beautiful* (April 1954): 140.

3. Bernard Rudolphsky, *Behind the Picture Window* (Oxford: Oxford University Press, 1955): 157. His chapter, "The Air-Conditioned Room," is a provocative commentary on how human beings have (or have not) adapted their dwellings to climate.

4. George H. Manaker, *Interior Plantscapes: Installation, Maintenance, and Management* (Englewood Cliffs, N.J.: Prentice-Hall, 1981), 2.

5. Madge Garland, *The Small Garden in the City* (New York: George Braziller, 1973), 38.

6. Harold Kirker, *California's Architectural Frontier* (Salt Lake City: Gibbs E. Smith, Inc., Peregrine Smith Books, 1986), 1–22. See, also, David Streatfield, *California Gardens: Creating a New Eden* (New York: Abbeville Press, 1994), 31.

7. David Streatfield, "The Evolution of the California Landscape: 1. Settling Into Arcadia," *Landscape Architecture* (January 1976): 42. There are four parts to this essay (all published in *Landscape Architecture*), the sum of which constitute an informative overview of the evolution of the state's cultural landscape.

8. Charles Adams, "The Spanish Influence in California Gardening," in Elevinia Slossen, editor, *Pioneer American Gardening*, (New York: Coward-McCann, Inc., 1951), 274. In horticultural terms, "exotic" means "non-native," rather than the popular definition of "strikingly unusual or special." See, also, Tom Brown, "Gardens of the California Missions," *Pacific Horticulture* (Spring 1988).

9. Edgar Anderson, *Plants, Man and Life* (Berkeley: University of California Press, 1969), 13.

10. See Maureen Gilmer, *Redwoods and Roses* (Dallas: Taylor Publishing Company, 1995), Chapter Three.

11. As quoted in Gilmer, 63.

12. See "The Spanish Influence in California Gardening," in Elvenia Slosson, editor, *Pioneer American Gardening* (New York: Coward-

McCann, 1951), 274. I occasionally find homeowners today who still believe in the mysterious and paranormal qualities of plants and who guard these species jealously against pruning, replacement, or any other interventions.

13. The name "California" comes from a Spanish word meaning "paradise," according to Erwin G. Gudde. "California, like El Dorado, Quivira, and The Seven Cities of Cibola, was the name of one of the utopias which originated in the imagination of the people after the discovery of "America" had revived the age-old dream of a paradise on earth," Gudde wrote. "The mythical realm was apparently created by the Spanish writer Montalvo in the romance *Las Sergas de Esplandian* (the exploits of Esplandian) and endowed with beautiful black Amazons, gold, and pearls. The name is a fanciful creation; none of the many explanations of the meaning of California can be substantiated. *Golfo de la California* and a *Cabo California* appear on maps of 1562. In 1569 the name was applied to the peninsula of what is now Lower California; on later maps it was often extended to include the entire Pacific coast. From 1769 to 1846 the area which is approximately included in the present state was termed *Alta* (upper), or *Nueva* (new), California." From Erwin Gudde, *1000 California Place Names,* 3rd ed. (1949; Berkeley: University of California Press, 1959), 11–12.

14. Daniel Boorstin, *The Americans: The Democratic Experience* (Random House, 1973): 275.

15. Ibid., 274.

16. "Beautiful Berkeley and Some of its Progressive Features," *San Francisco Call* (July 6, 1896), as quoted in William Derrenbacher's Masters thesis, "Plants and landscape: An Analysis of Ornamental Plantings in Four Berkeley Neighborhoods" (University of California, Berkeley, 1969), 56.

17. *Oakland and Surroundings: Illustrated and Described, Showing Its Advantages for Residence or Business* (Oakland, Calif.: W. W. Elliot, 1885).

18. "Beautiful Berkeley," 56.

19. Streatfield, "The Evolution of the California Landscape," 42. See, also, note #20.

20. Marcus Whiffen, *American Architecture since 1780* (Cambridge, Mass.: The MIT Press 1969), 217.

21. The word "bungalow" originated in India and meant "a temporary or seasonal dwelling with a low roof and a wide porch." For a brief definition of the style, see Whiffen, *American Architecture since 1780,* 218.

22. Kenneth Trapp, "The Bungalow," *The San Francisco Arts & Crafts Movement,* http://www.geocities.com/SiliconValley/Orchard/8642/bungalow.html (accessed July 31, 2007).

23. As quoted in Robert Winter, *The California Bungalow* (Los Angeles: Hennessey & Ingalls, Inc., 1980), 44.

24. See Gustav Stickley, *Craftsman Bungalows: 59 Homes from "The Craftsman"* (New York: Dover Publications, Inc., 1988).

25. Winter, *The California Bungalow,* 42.

26. As quoted in Trapp, "The Bungalow."

27. See David Streatfield, "The Arts and Crafts Garden in California," in Kenneth Trapp, *The Arts and Crafts Movement in California: Living the Good Life* (Oakland, Calif.: The Oakland Museum, 1993), 35–53.

28. Eugene O. Murmann, *California Gardens: How to Plan and Beautify the City Lot, Suburban Grounds and Country Estate, Including 50 Garden Plans and 103 Illustrations of Actual Gardens from Photographs by the Author* (Los Angeles: Eugene O. Murmann, 1914), 61.

29. John McLaren, *Gardening in California: Landscape and Flower* (San Francisco: A. M. Robertson, 1909, 1914, 1924).

30. Ernest Braunton, *The Garden Beautiful in California* (Los Angeles: Cultivation Publishing Company, 1915), 21.

31. Charles E. White, *The Bungalow Book* (New York: The MacMillan Company, 1923): 207–08. Reprinted by Gustav's Library, Davenport, Iowa, 2003.

32. Bruce Kamerling, *Irving J. Gill, Architect* (San Diego: San Diego Historical Society, 1993), 128. See, also, *Irving Gill 1870–1936* (Los Angeles: Los Angeles County Museum, 1958).

33. Eloise Roorbach, "The Garden Apartments of California," *The Architectural Record* (December 1913), Irving Gill Central, http://www.irvinggill.com/roorbach-gill.html#anchorgardenapts (accessed December 6, 2007).

34. As quoted in Dan Gregory, "The Ranch House Style Rides Again," *Sunset* (March 1992): 89.

35. Ibid., 89.

36. Garrett Eckbo, *The Art of Home Landscaping* (New York: F. W. Dodge Corporation, 1956), 175. Eckbo believed that the primary purpose of residential garden design is to make a property functional and livable, a goal that requires expertise far beyond horticultural skills.

37. Clifford Edward Clark, Jr., *The American Family Home, 1800–1960,* (Chapel Hill: University of North Carolina Press, 1986), 212.

38. Dan Gregory, "Living with Lariats: Cliff May and *Sunset* Magazine," symposium paper on the life and work of Cliff May (Los Angeles, Dickson Art Center Auditorium, March 5, 1988). Gregory adapted his talk for publication as "Visions and Subdivisions: *Sunset* and the California Ranch House," *Architecture California* (February 1991): 32–35.

39. Real Estate section, *Oakland Tribune,* October 3, 1993.

40. Real Estate section, *Oakland Tribune,* May 28, 2005.

41. Staff of *Sunset* magazine, *California Ranch Houses by Cliff May* (Menlo Park, Calif.: Lane Publishing Company, 1946).

42. John A. Jakle, Robert Bastain, and Douglas K. Meyer, *Common Houses In America's Small Towns* (Athens: University of Georgia Press, 1989), 69 and 182–95.

43. See, for example, "Use the Outdoors as Part of Your House," *House and Garden* (July, 1951): 34. With more and more Americans using their yards for outdoor living, house and garden magazines ran frequent stories on climate control.

44. "The Perfect House that Wasn't Good Enough," *House Beautiful* (June 1951): 84.

45. The popularity of the ranch house is diminishing. In October 1991, nearly 3,500 homes—many in the ranch style—burned in the Oakland Hills fire in California. Of the thousands of homes that have since been rebuilt, few are in the ranch style. *Sunset* editor Dan Gregory, an authority on the ranch house, cites problems that recent generations have found with the style—too much space devoted to the automobile, hidden or abrupt entries, dead-end living rooms, lack of solar orientation, and gloomy hallways—and proposes schemes for remodeling. (See note #34.)

Chapter Eight

1. Tom Wolfe, *From Bauhaus to Our House* (New York: Washington Square Press, 1981).

2. See Thomas Church, *Gardens Are For People,* Michael Laurie and Grace Hall, editors, 2nd ed. (New York: McGraw Hill, 1983), and Garrett Eckbo, *The Art of Home Landscaping* (New York: F. W. Dodge Corporation, 1956).

3. Garrett Eckbo, *Landscape For Living* (New York: F. W. Dodge Corporation, 1950), 135.

4. Ibid., 137–43.

5. As quoted in Carlton B. Lees, *Gardens, Plants and Man* (Englewood Cliffs, N.J.: Prentice-Hall, 1970), 131. Rose is credited, along with Dan Kiley and Garrett Eckbo, for starting the modern movement in landscape architecture while the three were students at Harvard University during the 1930s. The Beaux Arts style was thoroughly entrenched at Harvard at the time, and the department suspended Kiley, Eckbo, and Rose for refusing to prepare designs in that style. Eckbo and Kiley returned to school, but Rose did not. He went on to a successful private practice and wrote the insightful and humorous book, *Gardens Make Me Laugh* (Norwalk, Conn.: Silvermine Publishers, Inc., 1965; revised edition, Baltimore: The Johns Hopkins University Press, 1988).

6. Elizabeth Gordon, "A Garden Is American Style," *House Beautiful* (February 1951): 58.

7. Ibid., 154.

8. For a detailed history of *Sunset* magazine, see "*Sunset* Magazine: A Century of Western Living, 1898–1998," Stanford University Library, http://sunset-magazine.stanford.edu/index.html (accessed July 31, 2007).

9. *Sunset* (April 1954), 26.

10. *Sunset* (March 1954), 16.

11. *Sunset* (April 1954), 26.

12. *Sunset* (March 1954), 16.

13. Dwana Bain, "100 Years of *Sunset,*" *Palo Alto Weekly,* http://www.paloaltoonline.com/weekly/morgue/monthly/1998_Apr_22.SUNSET.html (accessed July 31, 2007).

14. *Sunset Flower Garden Book* (Menlo Park, Calif.: Lane Publications, 1948), foreword.

15. *Sunset Western Garden Book* (Menlo Park, Calif.: Lane Publications, 1937), 2.

16. "Landscaping the New Subdivision House," *Sunset* (May 1955): 64–65.

17. *Landscaping For Western Living,* (Menlo Park, Calif.: Lane Publications, 1968), 6.

18. Ibid.

19. Ibid., 5.

20. *Sunset Low Maintenance Gardening* (Menlo Park, Calif.: Lane Publications, 1974), 4.

21. "Whatever Your Needs, Consider Xylosma," *Sunset* (April 1980), 230.

22. Bud Stuckey (*Sunset* magazine employee), interview with the author, May 2003. Stuckey has worked at *Sunset* for several years, testing plants and building projects before articles on these topics go to press. For an account of American mobility, see James M. Jasper, *Restless Nation: Starting Over in America* (Chicago: University of Chicago Press, 2000).

23. As quoted in R. Burton Litton, *Landscape Architecture 1958* (San Francisco: San Francisco Museum of Modern Art, 1958): 35.

24. For an engaging account of the relationship between Church and *Sunset* magazine, see Dan Gregory's essay, "Just Add Water: The Productive Partnership Between Thomas Church and *Sunset* Magazine," in Marc Treib, editor, *Thomas Church Landscape Architect, Designing a Modern California Landscape* (San Francisco: William Stout Publishers, 2003).

25. Dan Gregory (Home Editor, *Sunset* magazine), interview with the author, 1993.

26. *Sunset Complete Garden Book* (Menlo Park, Calif.: Lane Publications, 1939).

27. "Landscaping the New Subdivision House," *Sunset* (May 1955). This article is essential for any student of the post-World War II house and garden. This comprehensive feature article explained the steps suburban homeowners should take to develop the bare

grounds surrounding their homes, and it set the stage for numerous *Sunset* garden design books and articles (as well as similar books from Ortho and other publishers) to follow.

28. All quotes are taken from "Landscaping the New Subdivision House."

29. "Between You and the Street, What's Legal, Possible? Much," *Sunset* (April 1981): 107. In my design experience, fence restrictions have eased little if any in the San Francisco Bay Area in the years since this article was written.

30. Jackie Krentzman, "How the West Was Done," *Stanford Magazine*, http://www.stanfordalumni.org/news/magazine/1998/mayjun/articles/how_west_was_done/how_west_was_done.html, 1998, accessed November 1, 2006. See, also, Melvin B. Lane, "A Commentary on *Sunset* Books," in "*Sunset* Magazine: A Century of Western Living, 1898–1998," the Stanford University Library, http://sunset-magazine.stanford.edu/index.html (accessed July 31, 2006).

31. California Digital Library http://www.oac.cdlib.org/view/mets/jk/kt2k4004jk.mets.xml (accessed November 1, 2006). I also received information on this topic in correspondence with David Streatfield, September 2006.

32. *Sunset* tour guide, interview with the author, 1981. Since being bought out by Time-Warner, *Sunset* no longer provides public tours, but it allows visitors to wander on their own through the magazine's garden during business hours.

In numerous ways—nursery expenditure patterns, landscape architect offices, enrollments in horticulture programs, sociological studies, and garden club memberships—women have outnumbered men when it comes to interest in gardens. Since their inception in the mid-1800s, garden club memberships have been almost exclusively female. In 1953, the National Council of State Garden Clubs embraced more than 310,000 members more than 10,000 clubs across the nation. Just three percent (10,000 members) were men. According to Helen S. Hull, men felt so outnumbered that they started their own clubs—in much smaller numbers—focusing on "no-nonsense" activities such as hybridizing and grafting. The Men's Garden Club of America established itself in 1932 partly through "insurrection," writes Hull. " . . . The men claim, and the women concede, that there is a higher percentage of expert gardeners among the members of the Men's Garden Clubs. Although there are exceptions, in the main they refuse to be diverted by other activities that command the attention of the women, such as conservation and civic beautification." See Helen S. Hull, "The Garden Club Story," in John R. Whiting, *A Treasury of American Gardening* (Garden City, N.Y.: Flower Grower—*The Home Garden* Magazine and Doubleday and Company, 1954–55), 242–68.

Garrett Eckbo practiced landscape architecture in California for sixty years and found that many offices typically divided the work between men and women. ". . . Somehow planting is persistently relegated to a decorative auxiliary role. In the well-run larger office there will be a planting department, probably run by lady landscape architects, who take over the designs prepared by the gentlemen landscape architects and fill in the plant names." See Garrett Eckbo, *The Landscape We See* (New York: McGraw Hill, 1969), 152. In 1986, Bonnie Loyd, who was the managing editor of *Landscape* magazine for many years after J. B. Jackson sold it to Blair Boyd, of Berkeley, investigated the appeal of flower and seed catalogs, and she found that "as many as 60–80% of the people who order seeds and plants are women." From Bonnie Loyd, "Armchair Gardening: The Pleasure of Garden Catalogs," as presented at the annual meeting of the Association of American Geographers, Phoenix, Arizona, April 7, 1988.

Chapter Nine

1. *Landscaping For Western Living* (Menlo Park, Calif.: Lane Book Company, 1961): 129.

2. Constance Perin, *Belonging In America* (Madison: University of Wisconsin Press, 1988): 29–30.

3. These articles, all of which appeared in *House Beautiful* (January 1950), put forth a sociological perspective unusual for house and garden magazines.

4. "How to Achieve Privacy," *House Beautiful* (January 1950): 29.

5. Dr. Joseph E. Howland, "Good Living Is NOT Public Living," *House Beautiful* (January 1950): 30.

6. Ibid.

7. Robert M. Jones, "Privacy Is Worth All That It Costs," *Better Homes and Gardens* (March 1952): 57.

8. Gerald D. Patten, "Cultural Landscapes: The Intent and the Tenor of the Times," *Cultural Resource Management,* Vol. 14, No. 6 (1991): 3–4.

9. Tom (Berkeley, California, homeowner), interview with the author, 1981.

10. Brian (Danville, California, homeowner), interview with the author, 1993.

11. Tim (Oakland, California, renter), interview with the author, 1995. Such sentiment is still prevalent today, as witnessed by this 2002 exchange on the Internet between two people discussing life in California:

> Message: "What we noticed was that many of the homes had fences around their yards. Not just decorative fences but Serious Fences. Yeah we have fences in NY but they're either to keep in livestock in the country, or to divide properties in the suburbs. Many places don't have fences at all. Nothing like CA—we'd be driving along and there'd be a house along the road, substantially fenced. No animals or neighbors to be seen! Is it to keep something out? Keep something in? Maybe you don't know but I thought I'd ask!"
>
> Response: "Your observation was the first impression I got also when we moved to LA from the east coast. Less land per house than what I was used to. I figured out that people seem to feel that because there is less land per person in the towns along the way so they usually put up fences for privacy purposes. Although people are friendly here, it's not like the east coast where you know your neighbors really well."
>
> See "Re: California Question?" http://www.getty.edu/education/teacherartexchange /archive/Aug02/0260.html.

12. "America By the Numbers," *Oakland Tribune,* April 28, 2000.

13. Helena Worthen, "How Does A Garden Grow?," *Landscape,* Vol. 19, No. 3 (1975): 19.

14. If anything, lot sizes have gotten even smaller, probably as a result of high housing costs that have pushed buyers into smaller

homes and condominiums. Home prices in the San Francisco Bay Area have long been at the top of house prices nationally. In 2001, the *Los Angeles Almanac* reported that four California markets—the Bay Area (ranked first), Orange County (third), San Diego (fourth), and Los Angeles (eighth)—ranked in the top eight highest home price areas in the United States. See "Highest Priced Housing Markets in United States, Second Quarter, 2001," *Los Angeles Almanac*, http://www.losangelesalmanac.com/topics/Economy/ec37h.htm (accessed July 31, 2007). An American Community Survey done in 2003 revealed that half of the top ten highest price counties in the nation are in the San Francisco Bay Area. See Michele R. Marcucci, "Bay Area Housing Costs Top U.S. List," *Oakland Tribune*, May 30, 2005.

15. "Land Use and Land Loss in the United States," The National Association Of Realtors, http://www.realtor.org/SG3.nsf/files/Land-use.pdf/$FILE/landuse.pdf (accessed July 31, 2007). Christopher Tunnard and Boris Pushkarev found that, between 1954 and 1959, eighty-four percent of residential lots in Santa Barbara County, California, and Pima County, Arizona, contained less than 10,000 square feet. In comparison, less than twenty percent of the lots in representative New England communities were smaller than 10,000 square feet. Tunnard and Puskarev remarked, "the proportions of . . . small lots ranges from about 90% in California to less than 10% in some Connecticut towns." See Christopher Tunnard and Boris Pushkarev, *Man Made America, Chaos or Control?* (New Haven: Yale University Press, 1963), 93–94.

16. Marc Reisner, *Cadillac Desert: The American West and Its Disappearing Water* (New York: Penguin Books, 1987), 2–3.

17. Courtenay M. Slater and George E. Hall, *Places, Towns and Townships* (Lanham, Md.: Bernan Press, 1993), xvi–xxi.

18. *National Housing Survey* (Washington, D.C.: Federal National Mortgage Association, 1997), 130.

19. In June 1994, I surveyed 500 front yards in Berkeley and Oakland, California—cities that allow six-foot-high fences or walls right up to the sidewalk. Ninety-three percent of the yards were without enclosure, save a few low, open fences or hedges. In neighborhoods close to commercial districts, the lots became smaller and the

numbers of fences increased to twenty percent of the total. Residents in these neighborhoods built fences to keep transients out of their yards, to block out traffic noise, and to provide screening from closely spaced homes. There was little evidence of residents using the enclosed space for outdoor living (in the way of patios, decks, or outdoor furniture). In the Berkeley and Oakland hills, the number of front yard fences was again higher (also about twenty percent of the total) than in the flats. These fences, though, mainly served as guardrails along steep slopes or to keep out deer, rather than provide privacy for family activities.

20. See "How Much Is a Landscape Worth," *Landscape & Irrigation* (September 1989): 12–13. See, also, Dennis Tostelian's report, *The Economic Impact of California's Landscaping Industry* (School of Business Administration, California State University, Sacramento, 1993): 16; Dennis Tostelian, "The Value of Landscaping: A Qualitative Appraisal," *Landscape & Irrigation* (September 1989): 22–25; and William Banks, "Buy a House That Needs Paint," *Money Magazine* (April 1986): 66–72. Banks compared the value of bathroom, bedroom, kitchen, deck, and garden improvements, and he found that the latter (excluding swimming pools) returned 100 to 200 percent of their original cost when a house was sold, a figure nearly twice that of interior remodels.

After the Oakland Hills fire in October 1991, I prepared several replacement value estimates for landscapes that had burned to the ground and learned many details from the insurance agents regarding scopes of coverage. Most of the policies limited the coverage to about two-and-one-half percent of the worth of the house, and in each case the agents told me that these figures were based on standard national rates. The policies all defined "garden" or "landscape" as "plants, irrigation, and minor garden structures." More expensive items that one might find in a nicely furnished outdoor room were either excluded or covered under other parts of the homeowners' policies.

21. These percentages are based on my professional experience as a landscape architect and designer since 1974 and on discussions with other designers in the profession. They appear to be consistent throughout the San Francisco Bay Area and the state.

Chapter Ten

1. "Landscaping the New Subdivision House," *Sunset* (May 1955), 63.

2. For an interesting overview of iceberg towing, see Joe A. Holmes, "Antarctic Icebergs: A Source of Fresh Water?" *Peace and Environment News,* http://perc.ca/PEN/1993-06/holmes.html (accessed December 6, 2007).

3. Statistics and figures courtesy of Nora Harlow, Erica Aschmann, and Scott Sommerfield, Water Conservation Department, East Bay Municipal Utility District (EBMUD), Oakland, California. Aschmann visited numerous homes to counsel the owners on water-saving strategies as part of EBMUD's water conservation program, and she found most homeowners grateful for her help and willing to conserve if only they knew how.

4. Russell Beatty, "Browning of the Greensward," *Pacific Horticulture* (Fall 1977): 5. Beatty's article was one of the first to put the drought of 1976–1977 into a broad historical context, in which people's values and tastes contributed, along with population growth and rainfall levels, to residential water use.

5. As quoted in Gayle M. Groenendal, "Eucalyptus Helped Solve a Timber Problem," *Eucalyptus In California,* General Technical Report PSW-69 (Berkeley, Calif: United States Department of Agriculture, U.S. Forest Service, Pacific Southwest Forest and Range Experiment Station, October 1983), 5–6.

6. Ibid. 1–8.

7. For a detailed overview of the introduction of eucalyptus into California estates and gardens, see Victoria Padilla, *Southern California Gardens* (Berkeley: University of California Press, 1961) 58–90. See, also, Robin Doughty, *The Eucalyptus: A Natural and Commercial History of the Gum Tree* (Baltimore: The Johns Hopkins University Press, in association with the Center for American Places, 2000). Ironically, California plants would eventually become so widespread in Australia and New Zealand that, like eucalyptus in California, locals began to regard them as natives. In 1978, San Diego botanist Helen Chamlee visited Australia and New Zealand and found "California in reverse—all the wild forest trees are eucalyptus and all the planted forests are of pines, California pines at that . . . I kept meeting old friends. There

were sequoias, California fan palms, Monterey cypresses, our very own torrey pines, and California big trees, all of great size." She also found liquidambars, magnolias, bald cypress, coral trees, and "Yup, California poppies." Helen Chamlee, "California Natives In Australia," *Fremontia* (July 1979): 25.

8. Groenendal, "Eucalyptus," 4.

9. Barbara Trowbridge, "Eucalyptus On Albany Hill," *California Horticultural Journal* (April 1962): 36.

10. As quoted in Werner Hegemann, Ph. D., *Report on a City Plan for the Municipalities of Berkeley and Oakland* (Oakland: Kelley-Davis Company, 1915):112.

11. As quoted in Padilla, *Southern California Gardens,* 59.

12. John Mitchell, "Los Angeles In the Making," *American City* (April 1910): 149–50.

13. Charles Keeler, *The Simple Home* (San Francisco: P. Elder and Company, 1904), 13 and 14.

14. Hegemann, *Report on a City Plan,* 107.

15. Ibid., 114.

16. John McLaren, *Gardening In California: Landscape and Flower* (San Francisco: A. M. Robertson, 1909, 1914, 1924), 2.

17. D. W. Cozad, "Municipal Enterprise Supplies Water Free for Citizens," *American City,* Volume XVIII, No. 3 (March 1918): 229.

18. As quoted in Padilla, *Southern California Gardens,* 170.

19. Ibid.

20. Lockwood de Forest, "Do Lawns Belong in Southern California?" *Garden Magazine* (December 1924): 232.

21. James Schmid, *Urban Vegetation,* Research Paper No. 161 (Chicago: The University of Chicago Department of Geography, 1975), 134–48.

22. William Derrenbacher, Master's thesis, "Plants and Landscape: An Analysis of Ornamental Plantings in Four Berkeley Neighborhoods" (University of California, Berkeley, 1969), 202–23.

23. The costs of ornamental vegetation are not just measured in water use; they are also manifest in California's tremendous "green industry." During the drought of 1987–1991, green industry officials

commissioned a study to document the size of the landscape market and potential job losses resulting from water conservation legislation. The study found that, in 1987, the landscape service industry in California alone exceeded 5.4 billion dollars, which was more than wholesale nursery and landscape equipment revenues combined and which equaled national revenues for lawn care—the typical source of garden expenditures in places other than California. See Dennis H. Tootelian's report, "Economic Impact of California's Landscaping Industry" (School of Business Administration, California State University, Sacramento, 1993).

24. Beatty, "Browning of the Greensward," 6.

25. Jerry Allison, "Native Plants," *California Landscaping* (January 1995): 22.

26. Tom (Berkeley, California, homeowner), interview with the author, 1981.

27. Nora (Kensington, California, homeowner), interview with the author, 1981.

28. Jerod (Berkeley, California, homeowner), interview with the author, 1981.

29. Jim Broadstreet (Oakland, California, homeowner), interview with the author, 1994.

30. Virginia (Albany, California, homeowner), interview with the owner, 1981

31. Harry Delmer (Berkeley, California, homeowner), interview with the author, 1981.

32. Henry (Albany, California, homeowner), interview with the author, 1981.

33. Romana Downey (Berkeley, California, homeowner), interview with the author, 1981.

34. Stephen (San Francisco, California, landscape designer), interview with the author, 1990.

35. Nina Feldman (Berkeley, California, renter), interview with the author, 1994.

36. Susan Saperstein (San Francisco, California, homeowner), interview with the author, 1994.

37. Rachel Sebba, "The Landscapes of Childhood: The Reflection of Childhood's Environment in Adult Memories and in Children's Attitudes," *Environment and Behavior* (July 1991): 395–422. See, also, Rachel S. Sebba, "Remembrance of Landscapes Past," *Landscape,* Vol. 22, No. 3 (1975): 34–43, and John R. Stilgoe, "Boyhood Landscape and Repetition," in George F. Thompson, editor, *Landscape in America* (Austin: University of Texas Press, 1995), 183–202.

38. Clare Cooper Marcus, *House as A Mirror of Self: Exploring the Deeper Meaning of Home* (Berkeley, Calif.: Conari Press, 1995), Marcus's in-depth investigation shows how peoples' attitudes and feelings towards their dwellings can reveal aspects of their personalities. I have had my landscape design students at Merritt College prepare ideal environment drawings since 1986, and I found a strong correlation between people's birthplaces (or places where they were raised) and their landscape tastes and plant preferences.

39. David Streatfield, "The Evolution of the California Landscape: 1. Settling Into Arcadia," *Landscape Architecture* (January 1976): 42.

40. Peirce F. Lewis, "Axioms for Reading the Landscape," in D. W. Meinig, editor, *The Interpretation of Ordinary Landscapes* (New York: Oxford University Press, 1979), 15.

41. Russell Beatty, "Greening of the Brownsward," *Pacific Horticulture* (Fall 1977): 30.

42. Suki Dewey-White (Merritt College student and Oakland, California, homeowner), interview with the author, 1996.

Chapter Eleven

1. See Eric Schmitt, "For First Time, Nuclear Families Drop Below 25% of Households," *The New York Times On The Web,* http://www.uscsumter.edu/~tpowers/hist112/nucfams.htm (accessed July 31, 2007), and Amy Benfer, "The Nuclear Family Takes A Hit," *Salon* http://archive.salon.com/must/feature/2001/06/07/family_values/ (accessed January 3, 2006).

2. According to the Family and Home Network, U.S. Department of Labor (DOL) statistics indicate that "the percentage of married women who hold a job and whose youngest child is between ages six and eighteen rose from 49.2% in 1970 to 74.7% in 1990. For moth-

ers of younger children (under six years old), the increase was even more dramatic, rising from 30.3% in 1970 to 58.4% in 1990. . . . The DOL statistics reported here are for 1990. However, media reports today show no substantive change." See "Understanding Employment Statistics: What Do They Really Mean?," Family and Home Network, http://www.familyandhome.org/policy/pub_stats.htm, 2002 (accessed July 31, 2007). By 2005, the number of married mothers (with children under 18) in the labor force had slipped to just under 70%, Still, this percentage represented an enormous increase from the 20% figure in 1950. Source: Sharon R. Cohany and Emy Sok, "Trends in Labor Force Participation of Married Mothers of Infants," *Monthly Labor Review*, Bureau of Labor Statistics, February 2007, p10, http://www.bls.gov/opub/mlr/2007/02/art2full.pdf (accessed July 27, 2007).

3. Juliet B. Schor, *The Overworked American: The Unexpected Decline of Leisure* (New York: Basic Books, 1991), 35–36.

4. See "Data on U.S. Community Associations," Community Associations Institute, http://www.caionline.org/about/facts.cfm (accessed July 31, 2007), and Reed Smith Online, "Real Estate: Condo PUD Development," http://www.reedsmith.com/practice_areas.cfm?widCall1=CustomWidgets.content_view_1&cit_id=6856&cta_tax_id=262&CFID=641732&CFTOKEN=20653846 (accessed July 31, 2007).

5. *Sunset*, Oxmoor House, Hazel White, *Landscaping Small Spaces* (Menlo Park, Calif.: *Sunset* Publishing Company, 2001), 5.

6. Real Estate section, *Oakland Tribune*, October 3, 1993.

7. *Owner's Manual* (Harbor Bay Villages, Alameda, California, 1999).

8. Homeowner associations are not alone in passing strict planting guidelines. In 1991, the City of Vallejo, California (population 100,000), passed an ordinance (since revised) restricting forty common plants (including tulip trees, willows, horse chestnuts, and native oaks, which many communities protect as heritage trees) and placed an outright ban on seventy-eight more. The criteria for banishment included fire hazard, insect problems, and high maintenance, but the city outlawed mulberries, African daisies, pines, cherries, eucalyptus, camphors, ivy, and cypress on the grounds that there were simply *too many* of them already in the city.

9. Anonymous (Woodbridge, California, resident), interview with the author, 1995.

10. Edward J. Blakely and Mary Gail Snyder, *Fortress America: Gated Communities in the United States* (Washington, D.C.: Brookings Institute Press, 1999), 62. A colleague of mine described a (perhaps) apocryphal tale of a suburban homeowner who used his garage to work on household projects and kept the door open. One day, he got a letter from his homeowner's association informing him that the open garage was an eyesore and the door could only stay up for two hours a day. He refused to comply, so the association sued and won. The day after the verdict, he bought several buckets of paint and drew pictures of jalopies, bikes, trashcans, rags, and piles of lumber on his now-closed garage door.

11. Blakely's and Snyder's theory paralleled Helena Worthen's findings in Springtown, California, where residents struggled to set standards of neighborliness in a community too new to have an established base of mutually agreed-upon rules. See Helena Worthen, "How Does A Garden Grow?" *Landscape*, Vol. 19, No. 3 (1977): 19.

12. Bruce M. Pavlik, Pamela Muick, Sharon Johnson, and Marjoire Popper, *Oaks of California* (Los Olivos, Calif.: Cachuma Press, 1991), 111.

13. Golden Eagle Farm, *Landscape Design and Irrigation Guidelines* (Pleasanton, Calif.: ca. 1993), 1.

14. See *Oak Woodland Preservation and Land Planning*, 3rd ed. (Palo Alto, Calif.: Hardesty Associates, 1991). This development is worth a visit for anyone interested in designing with regional plants. The head of the ranch's landscape committee reports that the current generation of homeowners still follow Hardesty's plans, if not strictly, then according to their original intent, and nearly every plant in the development is a regional native.

15. Ted Williams, "The Joe Pye Weed Is Always Taller in the Other Person's Yard," *Audubon* (July 1981): 108. For an overview of weed legislation and the premises behind it, see "Green Landscaping with Native Plants," *The John Marshall Law Review*, Vol. 26, No. 4 (Summer 1993), U.S. Environmental Protection Agency, http://www.epa.gov/greenacres/weedlaws/JMLR.html#INTRODUCTION (accessed July 31, 2007).

16. See "Clean Air Lawn Care," South Coast Air Quality Management District, http://www.aqmd.gov/monthly/garden.html (accessed January 3, 2006) for details regarding power mowers and pollution.

17. Virginia Jenkins, *The Lawn: A History of an American Obsession* (Washington, D.C.: Smithsonian Institution Press, 1994), 134.

18. Ibid., 115.

19. See "Overview of the Turfgrass Sod and Green Industry," Turfgrass Producers International, http://www.turfgrasssod.org/pressroom/turf_overview.pdf (accessed July 31, 2007).

20. Jerry Adler, "Bye-Bye, Suburban Dream," *Newsweek* (May 15, 1995): 43.

21. The quotes in parentheses are from Michael Pollan, *Second Nature: A Gardener's Education* (New York: Dell Publishing, 1991). Pollan's quote about lawn mowing is from "Why Mow? The Case Against Lawns," *The New York Times Magazine* (May 28, 1989): 44.

22. F. Herbert Bormann, Diana Balmori, and Gordon T. Geballe, *Redesigning the American Lawn* (New Haven: Yale University Press, 1993), 119.

23. One can get an especially good view of such yards from the Bay Area Rapid Transit train along the stretch between the Oakland 12th Street and West Oakland stations. Many of the homes and home grounds visible from the train were built around the turn of the twentieth century and, but for the automobiles and other elements of modernity, bear a strong resemblance to photographs of city properties taken at the time of their making.

Acknowledgments

A number of people have figured prominently in the development of the ideas in this book. I wish to thank Clare Cooper Marcus and the late Michael Laurie at the University of California, Berkeley, for encouraging me to write about the social meanings of gardens for my master's thesis in landscape architecture, and Bonnie Loyd at *Landscape* magazine, for working with me on the publication of two articles based on my thesis that later became the basis for this book. I also wish to thank Paul Groth, for introducing me to the field of cultural landscape studies while I was a graduate student at Berkeley, from 1978–1981 and for his continued advice and encouragement ever since. Not only was Paul my "unofficial" thesis advisor, but he also helped me immeasurably in the preparation of this manuscript as a reader, advisor, and overall fountain of support and inspiration. Had Paul's path and mine not crossed, I may never have been stirred to create this project.

My thanks go out to my design students in the Department of Landscape Horticulture at Merritt College in Oakland, California, for provoking me to scrutinize many of the ideas in this manuscript. I also extend thanks to Dan Gregory at *Sunset* magazine, for steering me towards several significant articles in the *Sunset* archives, and to Fred Schroeder, whose writings on front yards and cultural landscape have been invaluable in helping me to establish a foundation for my own ideas.

More thanks are extended to the Library of Congress, for developing the "American Memory" Web page. The photographs I found on this site proved to be enormously useful in helping me to develop and substantiate the first section of this book, and I urge anyone researching American history since 1850, if they have not done so already, to look at this site. The site led me to valuable images from the Chicago, Colorado, and Nebraska historical societies and from the Francis Loeb Library at Harvard University, and I thank these institutions for granting permissions to use materials and for acting on my requests so quickly. Similar thanks go out to all of the other copyright holders who granted me permission to use photographs and other illustrations. Thanks, also, to Mary Praetzellis, of the Anthropological Studies Center at Sonoma State University, California, for sending valuable material on the history of Oakland, California, and special thanks to Adam Cavan, of San Francisco, for providing hours of expert help formatting the illustrations.

I am grateful to George F. Thompson, founder and director of the Center for American Places at Columbia College Chicago, for expressing interest in my research nearly two decades ago, for inviting me to prepare a manuscript, and for encouraging me while I developed this project into the current book form. I am also grateful to David Streatfield, for his careful reading of the manuscript and his valuable suggestions regarding Arts and Crafts gardens, *Sunset* magazine, and early twentieth-century garden design literature. I also thank Kristine Harmon of Charlottesville, Virginia, for her careful copyediting, suggestions, and guidance. Thanks, also, go to Marcie McKinley and David Skolkin, of Santa Fe, for their book design.

Most of all, I thank my wife, Nina Feldman, for encouraging me to finish what turned out to be a much more difficult and elaborate project than I first imagined. Without her support, advice, encouragement, patience, and readings of the manuscript, I cannot imagine finishing this project. This book is dedicated to her.

Index

Note to the Reader: Page numbers refer to items within the main body of text *and to* the figures. Indexed items appearing in the *Notes* section are followed by the letter "n."

About the Author

Christopher Grampp was born in Chicago, Illinois, and he moved to Berkeley, California, with his family in 1959. He received his B.A. in politics from the University of California, Santa Cruz, and his M.L.A. in landscape architecture from the University of California, Berkeley. Grampp is a registered landscape architect in California, where he has practiced since 1984. He has taught landscape architectural design at Diablo Valley College, the University of California, Berkeley, and since 1986 in the Department of Landscape Horticulture at Merritt College in Oakland, California. His writings about the social and cultural meanings of residential gardens have appeared in *Landscape* magazine and in *The Meanings of Gardens,* edited by Mark Francis and Randolf T. Hester (The MIT Press, 1990). This is his first book. He resides in Oakland, California.

The Center for American Places at Columbia College Chicago is a nonprofit organization, founded in 1990 by George F. Thompson, whose educational mission is to enhance the public's understanding of, appreciation for, and affection for the places of the Americas and the world—whether urban, suburban, rural, or wild. Underpinning this mission is the belief that books provide an indispensable foundation for comprehending and caring for the places where we live, work, and commune. Books live. Books endure. Books make a difference. Books are gifts to civilization.

Since 1990 the Center for American Places at Columbia College Chicago has brought to publication more than 320 books under its own imprint and in association with numerous publishing partners. Center books have won or shared more than 100 editorial awards and citations, including multiple best-books honors in more than thirty fields of study.

For more information, please send inquiries to the Center for American Places at Columbia College Chicago, 600 South Michigan Avenue, Chicago, Illinois, 60605-1996, U.S.A., or visit the Center's Website (www.americanplaces.org).

About the Book:

From Yard to Garden: The Domestication of America's Home Grounds is the thirteenth volume in the *Center Books on American Places* series, George F. Thompson, series founder and director. The book was brought to publication in an edition of 3,000 hardcover copies with the generous financial support of the Friends of the Center for American Places, for which the publisher is most grateful. The text was set in New Baskerville. The paper is Grycksbo matt, 150 gsm weight. The book was printed and bound in Singapore.

For The Center For Amercian Places at Columbia College Chicago:

George F. Thompson, Founder and Director
Bonnie Loyd, Consulting Editor
Amber K. Lautigar, Operations Manager and Marketing Coordinator
A. Lenore Lautigar, Publishing Liaison and Associate Editor
Ashleigh A. Frank, Brian M. Venne, Catherine R. Babbie,
and Elizabeth S. Dattilio, Editorial and Production Assistants
Kristine Harmon and Purna Makaram, Manuscript Editors
Marcie McKinley, Book Designer
David Skolkin, Art and Production Director